Patricia Morgan was born during the 1950s and brought up in the North Midlands. She left school early to work in a factory to help support her fairly large family. In her mid-20s, whilst working full time, she studied part time to become a general practice surveyor and qualified some eight years later. Patricia has lived in Somerset with her husband Arthur and various cats for the past 30 years. She enjoys golf, yoga, reading, gardening, researching her family history and collecting stamps. This is her first attempt at writing a book. She has found the whole experience extremely cathartic.

For Arthur; my love and admiration always.

For my incredible ancestors, in particular Gramps, and Great Uncle Fred who made the ultimate sacrifice.

For Mum and Dad who always did their best and helped shape me into the person I've become.

For my siblings with whom I've shared many of life's experiences, both good and bad.

For my adorable descendants; may life be kind to you all.

For Heather and Timmy; thank you for your forgiveness and love.

For Jonathan, Simon, Judy, Nita, Rachel, Ros, Colin and Daniel who all died too young.

For all of my dear friends including golf and yoga buddies and work mates too, with whom I've shared many happy times and some sad and difficult times too: I dare not try and list you all by name for fear of missing someone out! Thank you for your friendship and caring over the years.

For Frank, Colin and Hazel for your inspiration and support during my working career.

For Trish, Beccy, Nicky and Veronica, thank you for helping to keep me fit and well.

For everyone who has suffered with, or been affected by mental health issues: may you stay strong, find peace and most importantly receive the help you need.

Patricia Morgan

SOLACE IN STAMPS

AUSTIN MACAULEY PUBLISHERS™

LONDON * CAMBRIDGE * NEW YORK * SHARJAH

A CIP catalogue record for this title is available from the British Library.

ISBN 9781528980166 (Paperback)
ISBN 9781528980180 (ePub e-book)

www.austinmacauley.com

First Published 2022
Austin Macauley Publishers Ltd®
1 Canada Square
Canary Wharf
London
E14 5AA

My huge thanks and appreciation goes to Wendy who has helped both Arthur and I through thick and thin, and who encouraged me to write my story in the first place.

Janet who has supported me enormously over the years, and offered great advice with my writing too; it was her brilliant idea to include a picture of a stamp at the beginning of each chapter, and I had great fun in choosing the most appropriate ones from my collection.

Paul and Ursula who recorded Gramps' wartime stories so well.

Alice and the editorial team at Austin Macauley who felt my memoir was worthy of being published, and for the marvellous assistance of the proof readers, also the graphics team who designed such a superb cover, and Vinh with his hugely helpful staff in the production team, including Adam, Stuart and Nathan.

Lucie at Royal Mail Stamps who organised the permission to print the British Stamps, Emily at Trerice Manor who put me in touch with Jo Wood, Diane, local Holsworthy Historian who helped track down many of my ancestors, the staff at the Exeter Records office, Megan at The National Trust and Paul at the County Gazette – all have provided wonderful help and guidance.

Everyone who has given permission for their photographs to be printed, which has made my memoir spring to life.

Table of Contents

Author's Note

I appreciate that I have covered some really sensitive issues in my Memoir and because of this I have, in some instances, given folks a different name to protect their identity.

It has not been my intention to deliberately upset anyone, although I have been honest and at times (you may feel) rather outspoken in my recollection of any episodes or incidents quoted. I fully understand that someone else within the same circumstance may have remembered things in a slightly, or indeed, altogether different way.

It has been one of my aims to hopefully try and end the feelings of shame and failure if at any time anyone thinks they are developing some kind of mental health issue. Whether it be suffering from anxiety, depression, bi-polar, paranoia, anorexia, self-harming, post-natal depression or anything else remotely connected with problems of the mind, the stigma attached to these types of illnesses has to end soon. Folks should no longer feel ashamed to seek the help they need because we nearly all have moments in our lives when we may feel inadequate and we can no longer cope. Desperation must not be allowed to set in.

In addition, it must be recognised that the lives of family and friends surrounding someone experiencing any sort of break down are often adversely affected too. And they are certainly in need of some help and support during such difficult times.

Prologue

I've only recently revealed all. Until then, others saw me as a 'fun loving woman' and the inevitable life and soul of any party. My main interests were playing golf, practising yoga, gardening, unearthing fascinating stories of my ancestors, anything historical including my husband, and having folks over for dinner.

But since child hood I've kept a dark secret—I am also a closet Philatelist, otherwise known as a stamp collector. When wishing to escape from the trauma of real life, I've spent hours, days, even months come to that, pouring over little scraps of postage paper wondering perhaps where they came from, what stories they might tell, were they flawed or even better quite rare? Would I be the next school child to discover an early British Guiana stamp worth hundreds of thousands of pounds as featured in the Stanley Gibbons monthly?

It wasn't a conscious decision to 'come out'. Late last year I'd discovered the most peculiar set of circumstances and coincidences involving stamps and another family from a bygone age. These events and findings had occurred over previous years during my life and theirs, and I needed to share this tale with someone. So, one afternoon when at tea with ladies from my local Golf Club, I blurted it out; I had a secret passion for collecting stamps. Reactions were mixed; surprise, slight shock, embarrassed laughter and quizzical looks said it all. And this was before I got to tell the full story! I was now being mentally registered as a geek or possibly an anorak or any other expression along those lines. Fun loving outgoing Patsy was disappearing before their very eyes and someone else was taking her place.

And then I got to thinking. After undertaking several years of research on my family history I have been surprised time and time again at the number of inherited character traits and the quirky twists of fate. And also wonder at the most amazing coincidences forming connections through the years between my generation and theirs.

Hence, I've included some of those wonderful stories so you can judge for yourselves.

Chapter One
Early Years

1955

British stamp – Queen Elizabeth 10/-

Aside from escapism, what had brought me to such a hobby? Well I was born in 1955, in Nottingham City hospital, the second child of a large family containing four brothers and years later one little sister. And yes, just like Jo in 'Little Women', I was a Tom boy. Mum tried her best to get me interested in the dolls she never possessed due to rationing and the war; yet, I gamely threw them out of the little pram I was pushing, in order to load it up with stones and rubble and anything else it would carry. I had a strange fascination for watching my dad mix concrete for his latest 'Do It Yourself' project. This possibly instilled in me an interest in buildings and all that that entailed in later life.

But my childhood was a mixture of extremes, super happy memories and at times, very sad and frightening ones.

When my eldest brother, Tony and I arrived on the scene, Dad was an engineer and design drafts man working at Rolls Royce in Nottingham and Mum was a stay at home mother because that's what they sometimes did in those days. With two little ones to look after and miles away from her home and family, Mum often had what is now termed as post-natal depression. So, becoming pregnant seven times in all may not, in hindsight, have been the best of things to do. This depression led to bouts of obsessive jealousy on her part and the rows,

14

accusations and fights that followed were to punctuate our upbringing on many an occasion.

My two earliest memories were firstly, standing at the doorway of our terraced house, number 10 High Church Street, Basford, Nottingham watching dad take our collie dog Blackie away to be put down. Unfortunately, he had developed canker of the ear—the dog that is, not my dad. Mum was adamant that our well-being be put first and so he was a goner. She stood there holding my hand crying. Of course as a toddler all I knew was that something really sad and upsetting was happening.

The other fleeting memory around this same time was of Mum and Dad shouting at one another and me watching the scene from the corner of the front room. Dad could see I was frightened and held his arms out to me but I wasn't sure who to go to and so ran to Mum instead. I'll never forget Dad's hurt expression and him turning away from me as though I'd betrayed him. It wasn't until some years later that we siblings understood what all the arguing and upsets were about. As time went by, we lived in fear that Mum and Dad would split up or that Dad, not able to take the strain any more would end up really hurting Mum. He often had to try to restrain her as she got quite physical herself.

Mum with Anthony and I as toddlers

By contrast, when Mum was well things were great! Our tea parties were legendary and when we moved to a three-bedroom semi, number 76 Austin Street in Bulwell all the children in the street would be invited. Mum would get the hose from the twin tub, attach it to the cold-water tap and squirt water at us through the open window. We had tremendous water fights where only the towel was a sanctuary until Mum gave you the nod and the sheltering kid got soaked! Then we'd turn the large tin bath (brought from our old house where we didn't have a bathroom) upside down and Mum would serve homemade cakes and jellies, jam tarts and Tizer or Dandelion & Burdock pop. Quite frankly Enid Blyton's 'Famous Five' didn't have it any better.

Lunchtimes were given up to us kids viewing '*Watch with Mother*' on an old black and white telly. Stories included Tales of the Riverbank with real live animals, Andy Pandy '*coming out to play*', and the Flower Pot Men, who didn't speak a word of English but muttered sounds like Flob a Dop and Weed.

Bonfire night was another treat and we'd roll out our home-made Guy and ask for 'a penny for the Guy' from passers-by with which to buy fireworks. We always had a bonfire, sparklers, a box of fireworks with rockets, Catherine wheels and jumping jacks, along with roasted chestnuts and jacket potatoes to eat. Great fun was had by all!

The annual Rolls Royce Christmas party was yet another good memory as I always got to have a new dress, rather than the usual hand me downs from my cousins in Stourbridge. We each came home with a present from Santa. And yes, we did all believe in Santa Claus until one year we discovered a secret cache of parcels at the back of our parents' wardrobe and then we had to pretend from there on in. Strangely enough we got to choose our main present, a pound each was allocated and that usually went on Lego or some equally educational toy. Then we'd all have a stocking with a small orange, an apple, some nuts and gold foil wrapped chocolate pennies in, plus a present from our Auntie Rosemary that usually consisted of something useful but boring like new pants or socks. Other than tinned peaches I don't remember eating fruit at any other time of the year – it's a small wonder we didn't get scurvy. Over the years I received a Spirograph set, from which millions of drawings could be made; a Post Office Set that had more ink in the pad than a giant squid; a Potato Men set, which required real potatoes to stick ears, eyes, lips and noses in, and all manner of other imaginative games. One year two of my brothers were even given life size toy gas masks, based on those given to children during the Second World War in the event of a possible gas attack. The look of one adorning my brother was enough to scare you to death, no gas was required.

I also recall having an unhealthy attachment to a Minnie Mouse, whose nose I used to suck for comfort I'm guessing, and a large monkey that I just adored. I have a sad feeling thinking about this monkey because I'm pretty sure my mum threw it away as she probably decided it was unhealthy to keep it any longer. I was so upset when I found out he had gone.

So, going back to Christmas, whilst Mum and Dad went off to get the turkey and all the trimmings on Christmas Eve, we'd watch a Bob Hope and Bing Crosby film, usually the 'Road To' series that featured talking camels and all sorts of hilarious things. If we were lucky, we would get to see a Norman Wisdom film too. He was so comical we got the stitch with laughing so much.

I also have vivid memories of being at Nottingham Goose Fair; the sweet melting sensation of Candy Floss on your lips (I'm not sure we ever swallowed any), the taste of sticky toffee apples (that could glue your teeth together), the smells of engine oil (fumes of any description we were fairly used to) and the shrieks and shouts of folks being half scared to death on any number of the rides. Oddly enough I can't recall going on any of the rides myself, only looking up at the enormous brightly lit Ferris wheel wondering what it would be like to be suspended so high up in the night sky, along with the stars.

Mum often took us four kids out on the trolley buses into Nottingham, all dressed up and looking pucker. We visited the ruins of the castle and the dungeons, which held a morbid fascination for us all. Sometimes she would buy a platform ticket and a shilling bag of sweets to share so we could watch the steam trains come and go at Victoria Station. We lived close to Charringtons the Brewery and would often see the large Dray horses pulling wagons containing beer barrels along the busy roads into town.

Mum holding Peter, with Paul, Anthony and I all looking pucker!

Dad often worked Saturday mornings doing overtime, but Sundays we had a day out and he took us all to either Trent Bridge to play games or paddle in the local pool, Sherwood Forest, where Robin Hood and his merry men hung out, Wollaton Hall, full of stuffed animals, in particular a huge gorilla or the grounds of Nottingham University where we could all let off steam. We had a car with a bench seat in the back. We kids fitted in like sardines in a can, which is just as well because seat belts weren't in use back then! We even got to see the chimps that featured in the Ads for Brooke Bond PG Tips at Twycross Zoo.

Saturday afternoons were spent watching the wrestling and oddly enough we all seemed to enjoy it. With such figures as Giant Haystacks and Big Daddy getting in the ring, we would shout and cajole them along with the TV audience. Things got even more exciting when the tag wrestling began. These bouts would feature the Royale brothers and Mick McManus and his partner; the latter pair would always play dirty. And then Dad would take on my brothers' one or two at a time in their own wrestling bout, which would get a bit hectic to say the least.

Mablethorpe and Skegness were the holiday destinations of choice. We could never get over how far out the tide went at Skegness so much so that you were hard pushed to witness the sea at all. At the end of each trip, Dad who was promoted to corporal in the Royal Air Force (during his National Service) used to shout 'fall in' to round us all up, much to our collective embarrassment.

During the school holidays we would be given either some bread and dripping (I am not making this up, you could buy it by the quarter pound and with added salt it tasted delicious) fish paste or luncheon meat sandwiches and off we would go for the day. Sometimes as a treat we were allowed to take a bag of broken biscuits too, purchased from the local Co-op for a tanner. Purchasing anything from the Co-op was always a strange affair in terms of paying that is. Any monies handed over were transported in a tube to a place in the ceiling. Then magically it would return with your change; I never did work that one out.

We often ended up on the edge of what was and still is I believe Bulwell Golf Club. There was a deep cutting through the land to one perimeter, through which the trains ran and it had big boulders, a large area of sand dunes and loads of gorse bushes. It was here we lived out our John Wayne fantasies and played cowboys and Indians for much of the time. I don't recall any danger from stray golf balls when crossing the course, possibly a few shaken fists but that was about it. Mum didn't see us all day long. In fact, until the horrendous Moors Murders by Myra Hindley and Ian Brady, and the Aberfan disaster in which a school was flattened by a nearby coal tip and hundreds of children died, no one actually thought that any harm could come your way. Mum cried for two days solid over the loss of so many little ones in Wales.

When not charging around John Wayne country, we would either chalk and mark out squares to play hop-scotch in the streets, play snobs or jacks, or do hand stands up against someone's front wall. Us girls would tuck our skirts into our knickers and I think quite bravely throw ourselves upside down into mid-air, not displaying any fear at all. I also had a pair of roller skates that were responsible for at least one broken wrist. Skipping was another joy although we had to sometimes persuade reluctant brothers to hold the ends of the rope depending on numbers taking part.

We were occasionally allowed to go to the pictures on a Saturday morning. God knows whether we ever successfully watched anything all the way through as my main recollection is of us all stamping our feet like mad and throwing Kia Ora orange cartons at one another, with the manager threatening to cut the film if we didn't quieten down.

It was around this time that I nearly didn't live to tell this tale. As a child we attended the local Lido at Long Eaton with the idea we should learn to swim. Strangely enough the idea of teaching us kids to swim in the summer didn't seem to enter the teacher's head. Our lessons commenced during the autumn months when it was truly freezing cold outside. Our teeth were chattering that much and we had the largest goose pimples I've ever seen. We were expected to get into this unheated pool to learn to swim when actually just moving your limbs required extreme effort. Once you were in, oddly enough it seemed colder outside the water but I think this may have been something to do with the fact your body was slowly going numb.

As far as Mum was concerned I was being taught to swim, so when an older girl who allegedly could swim and who lived nearby, asked if she could take me to the indoor baths, Mum thought this was a good idea. So, I recall standing at the side of the pool, little realising this was at the deep end, and got to stand at the top of the steps that led into the water. Then without a further thought I stepped off to the side. I now know how it must feel to drown because down to the bottom I went in slow motion where everyone seemed out of focus and everything sounded quietly muffled. Up I came to the surface and then down I went again. I have no memory of fighting for my breath at all, which is surprising I admit, but as I came back up again, I had the presence of mind to grab hold of the side of the steps and that was it, my early brush with death averted.

As the family grew larger, we moved again to Sawley near Long Eaton to a newly built, three-bedroom chalet style house with heating no less. At our last house during the winter we only had a coal fire in the living room so when Jack Frost visited, we had patterns of ice on the inside of the windows, let alone the outside.

We lived perpetually with chilblains thanks largely to the numerous hot water bottles we cuddled in order to get warm in bed. Fogs during the winter months were called 'pea soupers' (heaven knows why) and you really could not see your hand in front of your face.

It was whilst living at Sawley that Ian and Kim were born. Ian was a surprise so to speak and Kim was planned as Mum and Dad didn't want a young child on its own who may become spoilt. The property had fields to the rear and a building site to the front. Gosh, did that farmer and those builders put up with a lot. During school holidays, we'd make dens with the bales of hay and run amok in the fields and half-finished houses risking life and limb. In fact, that was the beginning of a number of sprains and broken bones that I experienced, often after showing off my latest dare devil stunt that ended in yet another visit to the Emergency department at the local hospital. I seem to have been accident prone ever since.

We put on plays for our long-suffering mothers chiefly based on the adventures of Batman & Robin. Although my brother Anthony played Robin (because he was tall and lanky) he took charge because Batman (who was played by our tubby little friend Stephen) often became tongue tied and struck with stage fright. My friend Vicki and I were the damsels in distress dressing up in her Mum's old lacy full petticoats and high heels formerly used in her 'ballroom dancing' days.

With all of this moving around, you can imagine our schooling was much interrupted. No sooner had we gotten used to one school then it was all change and we'd have the horrid experience of standing at the front of a new class and being the newbies. Yet I really enjoyed learning about almost anything, my mind being like that of a sponge. I always spent hours at home perusing the latest Encyclopaedia that Dad had purchased in instalments from a very persuasive door salesman. Dissecting creatures with the awful smell of chloroform that lingered forever was an exception to this rule. I realised early on that I did, and still have, rather squeamish tendencies.

My older brother Tony did not enjoy school at all and it wasn't until he was in his fifties that he was eventually diagnosed as dyslexic. As this was not known about in the 1950s and '60s he was thought slow, lazy and not able to work things out, much to the chagrin of our dad who was super intelligent and did not suffer fools gladly. Mum could never understand why I, being the 'brighter' of the two always got the homework, whereas Tony, whom she felt needed extra tuition, never got any!

I think my earliest schooling had the most profound influence in shaping my character. At the tender age of 4, I was enrolled at a Roman Catholic school where Nuns were involved in teaching us. For talking in class, I was forever being hit on the hand with a ruler and religion was taught in a most fearful way. In one lesson we had to say what we would do if a giant dog was chasing us (with eyes as big as saucers and sharp teeth to match), where would we go to pray for God to save us? Well of course, as we went to Church Sundays, Tuesdays and every other Saint Day in between, we all felt we'd have to find the nearest Church in order to get the message across. Oh no, said the Nun, **God is everywhere!** And that was the beginning of my life with a Catholic conscience that remains with me to this day. I would find it really difficult to tell a fib to someone's face, such is the knowledge that God will know about it—and any other bad thing I happen to consider doing. I shall be spending years in purgatory as a consequence but according to my night school Literature tutor, I may well have something in common with the talented writer Graham Greene; no, not an ability to write well but a Catholic conscience.

My First Holy Communion 16th June, 1963

My brothers Peter and Paul were both born at home at Bulwell, with their respective arrivals being heralded by copious amounts of boiling hot water accompanied by a mid-wife with a flushed face. As Mum was busy caring for them, Anthony and I would be sent off to church on our own on a Sunday morning and we would always get the giggles, especially when folks went up for communion. One-time Anthony returned from taking communion clambering over adult kneeling legs to where he thought we were sat. Yet I was kneeling reverently in the row ahead. Much to our joint amusement and the annoyance of all-around, he then had to clamber back out of the wrong row and clamber back in to the right one to where I was smugly sat. One time the incense the priest took to shaking about reminded Anthony of The Holy Ghost and this sent us into even more fits of giggles. Taking God's name in vain hadn't transcended into our psyche by then.

My brothers Paul and Peter looking like butter wouldn't melt in their mouths!

It was around this time that we took in the first of a procession of stray cats who always seemed to follow me home. The first two, namely Sooty and Sweep were kittens from the Rescue Centre and much loved by us all but particularly me. With the strays that followed, I knew once Mum had let me purchase the initial tin of cat food they were in! I adored stroking them and feeling their little soft furry bodies next to mine. But I was only allowed to have boys, no girls due to the cost of sorting out their reproductive systems. Stray cats were grateful but as I found out much later adopted ones were definitely not.

So, what inspired me to begin collecting stamps, I hear you asking? Well, my dad encouraged me to take up the hobby from when I was about 7 or 8 years of age. I would receive a monthly book of 'Approvals' from a company in Bridgnorth and choose a set to spend my pocket money on. This book I would agonise over as I could only ever afford one set at most and I was often torn between several sets at once. I had my first stamp album which I would diligently fill in with my latest additions and Dad would show me in the Atlas or on the Globe the country where the stamps had originated from.

When times were sad and Mum was being depressed, stamp collecting was one form of escape. I could go to my bedroom during the day, a room always shared as we never got one each, and mull over my latest finds and acquisitions. My other reason for seeking solitude was that my brother Paul, one down from me, used to irritate and tease me to death. He could not leave me alone for some reason and often I would retaliate by thumping him one. One time I actually bit him in the arm, such was his persistent aggravation. And I, as next to eldest, was always the one in the wrong because I should know better. Even when, horror of horrors, my youngest brother, Ian (Mum's favourite child) found my stamp album and proceeded to scribble all over it and tear some of the pages up, I was still to blame and should have known better than to leave it out for him to find. These injustices stayed with me for many a year. Funnily enough when I left the fold, my brother Paul transferred his 'attentions' to our mum who couldn't believe what an aggravating devil he was!

My two other main forms of escapism at this time were listening to *Radio Luxembourg* on my very own transistor radio and *Pick of the Pops* during early Sunday evenings, and reading. I could get through four books in a week from the local library and my vivid imagination grew from there. I so wanted to have red hair like 'Anne of Green Gables' and adventures like 'What Katie did' and 'What Katie did next'. I was 'marbles champion' too and as a result possessed the largest bag of multi- coloured glass balls you've ever seen.

I still remember our family being the first ones in the street to own a radiogram, in addition to the aforementioned black and white telly, the latter with rather grainy reception. It was through this screen that we witnessed the assassination of Jack Kennedy in 1963 and the landing of the first Americans on the Moon. Neil Armstrong was broadcast walking on the moon's surface in 1969, although in reality it was more like him jumping about in slow motion. Dad was working long hours and for a large family, we were relatively well off then but it wasn't always so. Tony and I were allowed to buy one new 45-rpm single record each. I chose '*Down Town*' by Petula Clark and Tony chose '*The House of the Rising Sun*' by the Animals. That said quite a lot about the pair of us, I think.

When I was 12 years of age the local newsagent asked me to help out a couple of times a day serving the kids at one end of the sweet counter both before and after school. Being under age he paid me in sweets. It's a small wonder I have any teeth left at all with the amount I consumed. Sherbet dab dabs, liquorice laces, pink candy prawns, fruit salads and black jacks (that left you with black teeth to match) were some of my favourites. In the summer I would choose a Jubbly in lieu of payment. This consisted of a triangular shape of frozen orange flavoured ice and you could make one last for hours. I sometimes went to help out on a Sunday morning and then before he closed up shop, we would go through the tills looking for rare Houghton or Kings Norton 1897 or thereabouts Victorian pennies, or threepenny bits from the 1940s, I'm guessing made during the war. Well, one Sunday I found one of the aforementioned threepenny bits and needless to say the owner was extremely excited about this. I was given a whole bag of sweets in gratitude.

School nights were punctuated by editions of Cracker Jack with Leslie Crowther on a Friday and Blue Peter with Valerie Singleton and John Noakes plus dogs on Tuesdays and Thursdays. What those two couldn't make out of cardboard loo roll centres and sticky back plastic was nobody's business.

In the mid-60s, around the time England won the World Cup and we had to peel Dad off the ceiling following their winning goal, we moved again, this time to Shelton Lock a suburb located midway between Derby and Nottingham. This was a big disappointment for me because I had recently passed my 11 plus and as a result was eligible to attend the Roper Grammar School in Long Eaton. But with moving out of the area this was no longer possible and so I continued my studies at the local Comprehensive Secondary school. I was in the A stream and went on to do quite well academically, although at sport I was only mediocre, filling in when needed in either the Hockey or Netball teams.

Yet it was here that I was to experience yet another bout of bullying. When I was little my two front teeth stuck out and so I was fairly used to being called Bugs Bunny or Goofy for this very reason. It was hurtful and didn't do a lot for my self-esteem but it did mean having to wear braces was, as they would say nowadays, a 'no-brainer'. I so wanted straight teeth I endured wearing an extra contraption at night because the dentist thought my bite needed adjusting. This other device consisted of extra wires that were fixed to my existing brace with elastic that went around my neck; strange but true.

The other form of continual teasing came in the shape of my rather unusual maiden name, that being Barrable. Quite a mouthful I am sure you will agree. Well, I was called all sorts at this latest school; Barrowboy, Barrabell, Barrabull, Barrabum and so on and so forth. But the worst form of bullying came from a girl who actually seemed to want to befriend me but who had to act tough all of the time. Her name was Lorraine and, thankfully, once she got over whatever insecurities it was she had, we finally become friends. But initially at every break time she would seek me out on the pretence of a chat and then proceed to thump me hard on the top of my arms—and it really hurt. Was this payback for my treatment of my brother Paul I ask myself? I was too frightened to give as good as I got and put up with this for quite some time, until eventually she got bored and decided I wasn't such a bad kid after all.

It was around this time I got a crush on my English teacher, a chap called Mr Billingham. I'm sure he wondered why I would stare at him for ages at a time not realising I was fantasising about the possibility that he fancied me too! Of course due to the aforementioned braces I wore, I was so self-conscious and I hated the idea of standing out at the front of class being made to read my latest made up poem. Sometimes I would fake being sick so scared was I of being the chosen one. In the end this crush turned out to be a bit of a double-edged sword, as he tended to pick on me to do the deed. I've remained nervous of public speaking ever since.

One of my most embarrassing moments also occurred when attending this school. It was the swinging 60s and the mini-skirt and see-through lacy blouses were the latest fashion. I was so thin I could have given Twiggy a run for her money and bean pole was another taunt I had to get used to. Naturally all the girls were taking up the hems of their grey skirts, which were a usual part of the school uniform. Yours truly was no exception but then the headmistress got strict. A new ruling came out to say our skirts were getting too short and the hem now had to touch the floor when we were kneeling down. Well, my two skirts were shorter than this but would Mum replace them, not likely. As punishment, I had to sew back on the off-cut bottoms (retrieved from the bin) of the two pleated skirts and wear them both like that. To say they looked peculiar was an understatement. I think I have blotted out the reaction from the other pupils in class because I can't recall what it was I felt, other than sheer humiliation.

Another not great moment I can think of was when I wasn't allowed to go on a school trip due to a lack of funds. This was in my last year of schooling and when you read about our darker times in Chapter 3 you will understand why. Don't get me wrong, I had been fortunate to enjoy lots of great school trips in my earlier childhood. I loved sitting on the back seat of the coach usually with the boys because I much preferred their company to the girls. These trips included going to the Peak District, an area of outstanding natural beauty that I really enjoyed with its lime stone walls, small hilly fields and steep rocky outcrops; being rowed in a boat beneath Speedwell Cavern; exploring the stalagmite and stalactite caves and Blue John mines at Castleton; watching the play called '*The Taming of the Shrew*' and also visiting the theatre to see the ballet, '*Copellia*'. But it was when we were on a visit to Hardwick Hall in

Chesterfield that I had my first feeling of deja vu. As I gazed out of one of the large leaded light Elizabethan windows at first floor level, my attention was caught by a scene on the front lawn consisting of historical figures all dressed in mid-16th century clothes. I strongly felt as though I was a part of this tableau. And then this vision disappeared! Gosh, it was strange. Now I did really enjoy reading historical novels and read any book I could find by Jean Plaidy or Antonia Fraser so it may have been my young vivid imagination getting the better of me. But when you see later from whom I am descended then you may wish to keep an open mind.

So, back to the school trip in question, well, to not go on this latest trip meant that one of the teachers had to stay behind to keep an eye on me, and it was if I was sent to Coventry, as the saying goes. No one could understand why my parents could not afford to include me with in the numbers. I do still squirm with embarrassment when thinking about that occasion.

Thankfully, Mum was well and Dad was still working when we first moved to Shelton Lock and she and I would take trips into Derby to go shopping together. In the main, we enjoyed a good relationship. At times like this she was more like my sister than my mum. She was a real stunner to look at and to my chagrin, she would receive the wolf whistles from passing men, not me. I was also allowed to go to the local Lacarno dancing hall on a Saturday morning and thus my love affair with disco dancing began. Motown music was my favourite, with Al Green, Smokey Robinson, the Four Tops, the Jackson Five and Diana Ross fighting for pole position.

Me and Mum
(for the avoidance of doubt, I am on the left)

27

At 14 years of age I began working on a Saturday in Derby's indoor market and would earn just under a pound for the whole day. This I would spend on fruit and vegetables to take home for the family. I am not sure thinking about it whether I ever was reimbursed. Actually, I would have worked there for free because the fruit stall just happened to be across from the record stall and half the time, I would be eyeing up the lads browsing through the records.

With the advent of the Beatles I learned to twist chiefly to Twist and Shout and I screamed my way through the film A Hard Day's Night at the pictures because that was what all the girls did. I and my brothers were frightened to death by watching an early 'Dr Who and the Daleks' film. It was bad enough seeing them on the telly but to have them life size appearing from nowhere on the panoramic cinema screen was enough to give us all nightmares.

Saturday evenings consisted of watching 'Dixon of Dock Green' (Evening all) and comedies such as Alf Garnett (who swore like a trooper) and Steptoe & Son. My funniest memory of Steptoe & Son was when 'arold had commandeered a water bed and brought it home to impress his latest girlfriend. He was showing if off to his dad who in true scathing style, screwed up his face and said, 'well at least you won't have any trouble with bed bugs—cos it'll drown the little bleeders!'

And then I met my first real boyfriend, a lad of mixed race, part Indian and part white, so good looking with light brown skin and gorgeous dark brown soulful eyes. I'm not sure we got up to much other than some kissing and cuddling in the field at the bottom of our very long garden. We held hands a lot and talked about all sorts but we split up when things got bad at home as I was too ashamed to tell him what was going on.

I also got some light relief during the school holidays when I went to stay with my cousins Philippa, Jane and Kathy in Stourbridge. I can't remember much of what we did other than play out on our roller skates, go up the Spinney, sleep top to toe in bed, do some praying and visit other family members in the area.

The family visiting my Great Aunt Margery (Gramps' sister)

Out of all of these relatives we visited, Gramps Cook, my mum's father, was the one to be reckoned with. He was such a character and had lived during and taken part in the First and Second World Wars. Here is his and his family's incredible story.

Chapter Two
Gramps' Story

1914-1918

British Stamp – To commemorate the Centenary of the First World War

Where to start when describing the incredible life of this wonderful man, William Ewart Cook, my maternal grandfather? I feel my Gramps has played a large part in my life, despite the fact we lived miles away from him. Whenever we got together, he would tell his wartime stories with such clarity and emotion but it was only as I got older that I realised the importance of the events that he had lived through and experienced. I'm slightly ashamed to say that when my brothers and I were younger we did not have the patience to listen to his tales as much as we should have done. I for one have always regretted this.

Well I guess to make it easier I'll start at the beginning. From details on his Birth Certificate, although he was known as Ewart, Gramps was christened William Ewart Cook and born to parents Charles Henry and Georgina Jane Harriett Cook (nee Cooke) on 22 May, 1898 in the town of Stourbridge. A Cook marrying a Cooke, whatever next.

Aside from when Gramps was away serving in the First and Second World Wars or training to become a pilot, his home remained in the Stourbridge area for the majority of his lifetime. When he was born, his father Charles was a Master Builder and was obviously a man who could turn his hand to anything because by 1901 his profession was listed as a Joiner/Carpenter and coffin maker working on his 'Own Account' which meant he was self-employed.

The census at this time shows the family living at 128 Lawn Street, Stourbridge. Charles was 29 years of age, his wife Georgina was 27 years of age and they had three boys fairly close together, the eldest being Frederick Charles Sydney, then came William Ewart (my grandfather) and then Ernest Baden arrived. They were aged four years, two years and 11 months respectively.

By 1911 Charles and his family had moved to South Street in Stourbridge, probably because they needed larger accommodation to house the additional children who had arrived by then. The census shows Fred aged 14 working as an assistant electrician, Ewart' aged 12 was a school newsboy and Baden aged 11 was a school garden errand Boy. They all learned to work at an early age and this work ethic was instilled, I think, by their father who appeared to work hard all of his life.

The family continued to expand and five more children had arrived, one on average every two years! And these were Elizabeth aged 9, Albert who was 7, Harry who was 5, Marjorie who was 3 and James (known as Jim) who was one-year-old.

Charles Cook's family – Back Row: Ewart Charles Baden Fred: Middle Row: Bert Bessie Georgina holding baby Tom Marje Harry: Front Row: Jim Wilfred

Out of all of these children the only Great Aunt we knew and visited was our Great Auntie Marjorie but there were reasons for this, which I will go into shortly.

When Charles (my great grandfather) was aged 39, he was working as an employed carpenter, whilst Georgina (my great grandmother) was busy looking after the eight children, three of whom were working, three were at school and two were at home. They would go on to have four more children, Wilfred, Robert born in 1915, Tom and Nancy.

Tragically, Georgina died aged only 44 years, two hours following the birth of her 12th child, called Nancy in July, 1917. This was still during the First World War.

Fred, Gramps' eldest brother, was born in 1896 and, although trained as an electrician, lied about his age in order to enlist as a sapper to fight in the First World War. He was in the Royal Engineers Corp (number 51171) but sadly was killed in action at Ypres on 19th December, 1915, at only 19 years of age. Fred is buried at Voomezeele Cemetery, which is a small cemetery some two-three miles outside of Ypres, the latter town is now known as leper. Many Canadian soldiers are buried there too as this was much fought over ground.

It is thought Fred was killed in a battle at or near the Cloth Hall at Ypres, a building that resembles a church, but we have no actual evidence to prove this place as being where he fell. A copy of the Corp's diaries show death from a gas attack may also have been a possibility, as this event occurred on or around the 14th and 15th of December. He was awarded the Scroll and Dead Man's Penny. Fred's name is highlighted on two memorials in his home town of Stourbridge, one being the War Memorial in Mary Stephen's Park and the other is in a Roll of Honour in St. Thomas's Church.

Frederick Charles Sidney Cook – Killed in Action at Ypres on 19 Dec, 1915

My Gramps' next in line brother Ernest Baden, known as Baden, who was born in 1900 also became a member of the Royal Flying Corp. He emigrated to Australia in 1922, living initially at Serpentine just outside of Perth. Baden was involved in the construction of water supplies to Perth and eventually went on to own a Cinema, of all things! He had a daughter and two grandchildren but sadly he committed suicide in 1956. Unfortunately, some years previously, when reversing his motor vehicle out of the drive, he had run over and accidentally killed his neighbour's young child. Understandably, he never got over it fully.

Ernest Baden Cook, Royal Flying Corp-Died in Australia in 1956

Albert, another younger brother, tragically died in 1914 following a heart attack when he was only ten years old. Four of his other brothers suffered from heart attacks later on in life too.

Wilfred, born circa 1913, went on to become the youngest ever manager of a grocer's firm called Wrensons and had three children, Graham, Colin and Philip. He gave up the grocery business and then ran a Public House but sadly his wife took her own life.

Marjorie born in 1908 moved to Sutton Coldfield and went into service, partly as a chaperone to her sister Elizabeth (known as Bessie) who was also in service. Bessie had met Fred' Grimshaw who owned a bike shop and who already had a child by his first wife Dora. (Sadly, Dora had died following a miscarriage).

Nancy, the youngest child born in 1917 eventually moved away from Stourbridge and lived in Derby. She went on to have three children. If you recall, her mother Georgina had died shortly after her birth. Nancy had considered moving to America with her stepmother Lily Link but for whatever reason this did not happen. Now, as we had lived for many years in Derby, I am surprised we never knew that Nancy and her family lived close by.

Robert, known as Bob, the youngest son born in 1915 got a job in a Butcher's shop and became a slaughter man. He lived for a time with his sisters Bessie and

Marjorie before moving to Yorkshire in the 1920s. During his lifetime Bob served in Wassistan, now known as Afghanistan. He played football for the Army and served in both Egypt and Italy before joining the General Post Office for the remainder of his career.

With all of these difficult events and tragedies, many happening in Gramps' early family life, it is a small wonder that he was able to cope with the immense pressures of serving on the front line and playing such an important part in the Battles taking place on the Somme. He enlisted in the Royal Engineers at the age of 16 in November 1914, just six months before his 17th birthday as he too lied about his age in order to go abroad. According to military records, he served in France from the 18th March, 1915. He was initially made a Corporal (number 30389) and his address was c/o 8 Beale Street, Stourbridge at that time.

I am extremely fortunate to have inherited some transcripts of interviews Gramps gave to a young student called Ursula who was studying for a degree in History at Cambridge University. Copies of some of his tapes were also donated to the Imperial War Museum in Lambeth, London but I have yet to listen to them. We have Ursula, amongst others, to thank for encouraging Gramps to talk about and give descriptions of life during World War One.

Lyn MacDonald, Author and Historian of the First World War also acknowledges her debt and the valuable assistance given to her by my Gramps and other brave men whose testimonies and accounts feature in her graphic and poignant book entitled 'SOMME'.

In addition, I am truly grateful to my cousin Sue's husband, Paul, who also conducted an interview with Gramps in the style of 'This is Your Life'. This was with a view to educating the children in his class about both World War I and World War II. I have also included part of this interview.

Gramps was initially a despatch rider and responsible for delivering important messages on the front line at Passachendaele. He describes how he was made a Corporal because a private wasn't allowed to approach the officers and he had to approach generals such as General French and General Joffre.

"Gramps Corporal William Ewart Cook, Dispatch Rider & Second Lieutenant in Royal Flying Corp

Apparently, you couldn't join up as a motorcyclist unless you took one with you, so he tells of taking (stealing I think he meant) a brand new one from his place of work but he claims no-one knew! He then went to Bristol for a Motorcycle Club test and upon arriving back home he received a telegram with the words 'Report at Bristol immediately for active service' so back he went to Bristol again.

Gramps was then sent to Aldershot where he expected to receive six months training. But Kitchener was short of men, so he went almost immediately to Farnborough for riding and shooting practise, passed out and within three weeks was in France in the Expeditionary Force. His brother Fred who had joined up in October, one month earlier, was in Kitchener's Army and this is where they split up as Fred remained in Aldershot initially whilst Gramps went off to France, ending up in Ypres on the French/ Belgium border. He spent three years on the front line experiencing the most horrendous conditions and every battle going. In his memories of the first gas attack at Hill 60 at Ypres in the April, he described it as 'terrible'. Gramps knew someone who was blinded by the gas, and some 50,000 men died.

The British Front was around 50 miles long and Gramps spent days and nights risking his life delivering messages along it. As a despatch rider he had to know the trenches like the back of his hand. At any time, the shells could have blown him up. Despatch riders were also at risk of being pulled off the bikes by the enemy placing copper wires across the roads, which the riders could not see as their bikes had no lights.

Meanwhile, Fred also spent time in the trenches. He was in the Royal Engineers on the Morse Code and had to travel with the Brigade in the dug-outs. Gramps managed to meet up with him once when Fred was located just outside of Armentieres with the 26th Brigade. He was sleeping in what was a ruined old picture house. They spent the night together sharing a blanket in the Orchestra Pit until shelling woke them at 3 am in the morning and they had to clear out.

Gramps also mentions the next battle in September 1915 which was the battle of Loos. By now he was attached to the 16th Lancers Calvary because they were in retreat from Mons. In the transcripts he describes the hell of the fighting, the mud and the poor horses who were painted brown to camouflage them so they matched the earth. The idea was to break through the trenches to gain ground. So, they looked for a gap in order that these horses could go through and trample down telephone wires and disorganise communications.

The initial battle was by the Guards Brigade, then the 9th Scottish Division; the Division that Fred was in would follow them through. Gramps got to go through with the horses and says it was a 'terrible do'. He saw dreadful sights of wounded and dying men of all nationalities, and complete carnage. Page 3 of the transcripts gives this in graphic detail but the injuries he witnessed are too upsetting to write about here.

By 1st July 1916, Gramps' battalion had made it to the right of Albert where a place called Verdun had to be protected from the Germans at all costs because if they made it there, then they could make it to and take Paris and the war would be lost.

His memories of this period are phenomenal. There were such awful massacres at Verdun that some of the French mutinied and wouldn't fight. General Petain got all the spare soldiers he could into Verdun to stop them losing Paris. General Haig moved his headquarters down the road leading out of Amiens up to St Paul (it's difficult to believe but the Western Front was some 430 miles long) and General Rawlinson was put in charge of the 4th Army nearby.

At this time my Gramps was fixed at a place called Morlancourt and it being summer the French were covered in body lice; the water supplies were really poor too. Prior to a proper supply being connected Gramps used to bring water to the 3rd Brigade Signal in 4-gallon petrol tins, which he had to clean out first, and then attach to each side of his motorcycle.

General Joffre was also involved in organising the troops and in one instance he decided to change the time frame for the attacks from 7. 30 am instead of the original 5 am. Gramps was responsible for informing everyone of the changes during the night prior. The first day 20,000 men were killed at Fricourt and Mametz. By the third day a German officer came forward with a rifle and white flag and asked for 48 hours to bury the dead because the stench was terrible. The main push was towards Perone from Albert and then towards Bapaume. The big explosion was at La Boisselle. All of these events took place from July 1st to November and then of course the weather deteriorated. On the Somme the soil is chalk and the transport could not get through this type of subsoil.

Gramps was then put in charge of getting the shells delivered by mules. Each one would carry 6 shells either side of their back. Sometimes the mules would sink in the mud and Gramps was under orders to shoot any that were up to their necks in mud because the shells could go off and kill their own men. And he ends this part of telling his experience by saying again how awful and terrible it all was, there were ambulances here there and everywhere.

One of his best-known stories was when Gramps was riding his motorcycle and was shot at by the famous German flying ace, Baron Manfred von Richthofen known famously as the Red Baron. Gramps was featured in the local newspapers fairly frequently telling this tale. 'The Baron was at 50 feet and his bullets were spurting up dirt either side of me like heavy spots of rain' recalled Mr Cook. 'I had to keep going straight or I would have been hit.' And keep going he did until his motorcycle hit a railway line and the Baron pulled away, leaving him for dead. I am fortunate to have a fuller account of this incident from one of the interviews Gramps gave at a school that my cousin Sue's husband, Paul, worked at as a teacher. It went as follows:

Paul – Just to give you an idea of what the battlefield looked like (shows a picture to the children) there is complete mud with just stumps of trees sticking out and wires

Gramps – Those wires were telegraph wires and the main road to Ypres was where I was going to a dug out

Paul – And what happened?

Gramps – Well on the Somme in 1917 the Germans had retired voluntarily returning to their concrete dugouts and trenches because the battle had lasted that long. One of our aeroplanes had been shot down, and we could see the pilot and observer get out trying to get to our line. Before they could get there, the Germans came around with fixed bayonets and took them away

Paul – So they captured the two pilots of the plane?

Gramps – Yes, that's right and Brigadier General Bellsmyre came to me and said, 'I want you to go straight down because I want that machine blown up before night fall,' so the Germans wouldn't capture it

Paul – So the Germans wouldn't capture it and use it for their own purposes?

Gramps – Yes. That's right, there might be messages or anything in it. So, I went, I put on a steel helmet and held a revolver. It was that quiet, it was deathly quiet, an unearthly quiet, I didn't like it quiet and my revolver wasn't loaded. I was going along (on my bike) and I looked down and bullets were coming, two guns about two inches each side of my foot and I had to keep dead in line. The Red Baron went straight along at 50 feet and then I heard a bang. Apparently, the gun that I was going to at St Emile had fired, tried to get him but it was too low an elevation because when I got there, they were just carrying out two of our burnt soldiers and the breach had blown.

Paul – So, Gerry was flying very low, and they tried to get the guns so low to hit the plane that the back of the gun had exploded out with the shell already in the muzzle hadn't it, and the two of them were killed?

Gramps – Yes. Well it smashed my front forks and I had to keep missing these bullets and I got in the shell hole. The shock absorber on the bike broke in two and I had to ride like that.

Then the Red Baron swerved around and there was a Barrage balloon with a basket on it, there were two parachutes on it, the only parachutes in the First World War, so if they got on fire they could jump out, you see. Well he hit the balloon that went up in flames, so that was me, the gun, the balloon, he killed whoever was in the balloon and I did not know who had gone down. I could see him getting out of the basket and jumping but he couldn't clear the strings on the basket so he was climbing back up into the basket when it disappeared behind what was left of the trees. And of course I went to the gun, not knowing who it was, and they told me it was Captain Whittaker

Paul – So it was a man you knew who was in the Barrage Balloon, Captain Whittaker whom you knew had been killed.

Gramps – Yes that's right, he jumped out and hit the soft ground first and the basket then buried him.

Paul – So, the basket landed on top of him and he was killed.

I will say that Gramps never spoke about any injuries but I understand he was slightly injured twice and had his boot burned off by a shell in one of the Battles of the Somme. He certainly had a few lucky escapes though as this next narrative with Paul Bell indicates:

Paul – Now tell a story you've told me many times of when you were in a town called Vlamertinge and you were standing on the kerb there and two horses came through pulling a carriage with ammunition on the back, and what happened then?

Gramps – Oh, well Vlamertinge is three kilometres (one-two miles) behind Ypres, and there were stone sets, like cobblestones you know, and I was stood on the corner and our officers were within the old house. They started shelling Vlamertinge when a carriage with ammunition on, and two horses galloping full out, came around the corner. The one horse fell, he lost his feet, flying, and the fellow went off, on the off side and he went into the wreckage and just at that moment a shell come over and went into what was left of a shop window, right where he was lying.

Paul – And made a nasty mess of him, blew him to bits did it?

Gramps – Yes, he was disembowelled, it was a terrible sight, right in front of you, and just at that moment an officer taller than you, cos I was only 16, he came round the corner and stood just like that, and he said, 'What a terrible sight.' and I said yes, then the officer fell on me.

Paul interrupts – He just collapsed on to you?

Gramps – Yes, and he put his arms around me and I said, 'what's the matter?' Another shell had come over and this was about ten inches long, red hot and jagged. It had gone right in his thigh from there down to his knee. He was unconscious and I dragged him, oh, 150 yards to a first field dressing station and legged him in. There was nothing you could do, you didn't have time.

Paul – So, if he hadn't have come and stood beside you, that would have been your leg wouldn't it?

Gramps – Yes, ten seconds was all it was, because all he said was 'what a terrible sight!' and he fell on me, he just shielded me.

Paul – Amazing really

Gramps – And of course when I got back, they had just brought a spy down out from the church with all his signalling apparatus, he had been signalling the German gunners where to put these shells. They shot him outside of the church.

Paul confirms – So in the tall church tower there had been a German spy who had been signalling to his own lines, and they saw he had a mirror, which told where to land the shells and they saw him, dragged him out and shot him outside.

Gramps – Yes, that's right. they shot him outside, because they had all the evidence you see, just as a civilian you see.

Paul – So, in both wars the penalty for spying was death wasn't it? You were shot.

Gramps – Yes, that's right.

Paul – But if you were in uniform you were taken prisoner. Right, after 3 years you returned to join the Royal Flying Corp. which was the start of the Royal Air Force wasn't it?

Gramps – yes that's right

And he goes on to describe his experiences in the Royal Flying Corp more of which is outlined later. I feel it is difficult for mine and younger generations in Britain to comprehend the horrendous sights and atrocities that Gramps and his brother Fred witnessed first-hand at such close quarters, let alone the constant news of bereavement within the family.

When Gramps was in the trenches in Arras in July 1917, he received a telegram from his father informing him that his mother had died two hours after giving birth to Nancy, his youngest sister. His officer said forget about it until we get relieved in two weeks' time, at which point my Gramps was then given 72 hours leave to travel from France to Stourbridge and return.

As mentioned earlier, his brother Fred also sacrificed his life in Ypres, serving his King and Country. How difficult it must have been for Gramps to hear this dreadful news of the loss of his brother, especially so early on in the War.

However, it was with a twinkle in his eye when Gramps told me that towards the end of the First World War, he was so good at riding a motorbike they figured out he would make a good pilot. So, at the age of 19, he was sent for training at Reading University. He was then made part of the Royal Flying Corp as a second lieutenant and showing off in practise he had a crash-landing! He made his first flight on Boxing Day in 1918.

He was assigned at first to submarine spotting over the North Sea. 'On the dawn patrol we'd take off in the dark and be flying by the time dawn broke.' Later he was assigned to bombers and returned to France for the anticipated bombing of Berlin. The pilots' pool, made up from all nationalities, were all ready and waiting to fly when the Armistice was signed. Gramps returned home to Stourbridge on the Monday and the following Friday he received orders to report to Dublin where he served as a flying instructor with 25 TD Squadron until he was demobbed in 1919.

I have a super photograph of him standing proud in front of the wing of his bi-plane at Tallaght Aerodrome in Dublin. I find it quite poignant that I have chosen to write his story in the year of the Centenary (2014) of the beginning of the First World War.

On Armistice Day, 11th November, 1918 my Gramps' father, (my great grandfather) Charles Henry Cook married again, this time to Lily Link at Stourbridge Registry Office. They went on to have three more children together who would have been half siblings to Gramps and his siblings. My Aunt Rosemary still has contact with one of their children. By now I am sure you can understand why my immediate family lost contact with the majority of great aunts and great uncles due to the circumstances outlined earlier.

Now aside from his military medals, in September 1980, Gramps' service in the Great War was recognised by the King of the Belgiums and he was awarded the Veterans Cross. Despite the time lag he said he was very honoured to receive it.

Once demobbed and back in Stourbridge he became a motor mechanic. He met and married my grandmother, May Elvidge who was 29 years of age, some 8 years older than my gramps who was 21 at the time. They married on 8th October, 1919 at the All Saint's Church in Stourbridge. Their marriage certificate shows that Nanna was working as a tobacconist's manageress. She also came from Stourbridge. I understand from my cousin Sue that Gramps had been engaged once before and he gave my nanna the same ring, which is unlikely to have gone down very well!

After the war, Gramps ran the Bell Garage (where the Bell Hotel is now situated in Market Street) but gave it up during the 1930s depression when he went to work as a bus driver for Midland Red. My grandparents went on to have five children. Paul, their eldest son was born in 1921 and went on to become a Professional Footballer. When he enlisted in the RAF, he played initially for Luton Town whilst stationed in Bedfordshire. I believe when he was younger, he was given the opportunity to be trialled for Wolverhampton, at the same time that Billy Wright was asked to trial for them. However, duty called and Paul then spent 5 years in India where he played football for Ceylon (now known as Sri Lanka). He went on to marry Joan and they had one delightful daughter, my cousin called Susan who I feel very close to, to this day.

Next Robert Anthony, known as Tony, was born in 1924. Sadly, it is around this time that my nanna was taken ill and spent time in Barnsley Hall in Bromsgrove, which was then an Asylum. As it was so close to Tony's birth, I am wondering whether she, like my mum had suffered from post-natal depression, which was not an illness recognised in those days. Tony went on to also serve in the RAF, despite the fact he worked at Baileys, which would have given him exemption from joining up. He was keen to go and my aunt Rosemary says it was the making of him because of the discipline instilled in all its new recruits. He went to New York, Miami, and the West Indies. In the latter location, where the Duke of Windsor's airfield was situated, the Duchess herself worked in the canteen. Back home, Tony met and married a young lady called Edna and they too had a daughter, my cousin Helen who was rather a minx when she was younger! More on that later.

Rosemary was born in 1929 and went to the local Catholic school, St. Joseph's, as did my mother and most likely all of the brothers in the family. Rosemary was very good at English spelling and with typing skills too, worked as a purchase ledger clerk for the Printers & Bookbinding firm, Mark & Moodies. I guess that made her fairly good at maths too! She met and married Tony Elwell and went on to have three girls, my cousins, Jane, Philappa and Katherine. Phil and I got on particularly well being of a similar age.

Patrick was born in 1932 and also served in the RAF during the Second World War, although at this point in time, I do not have any detail of whereabouts. He met and married Elsie and they went on to have a daughter, my cousin, Hilary.

And last but certainly not least, my mum Ann was born in 1935. She too was good at English and Maths and got a good report from the nuns at the aforementioned school. She left school to work as an accounts clerk for a Tailors and Drapers known as Scott & Bell and worked there from September 1951 until October 1953. By this time, she had met and fallen in love with my handsome and very clever father who was stationed at RAF Bridgnorth. They got married on 24 October, 1953. Mum was just 18 years of age when she left home and went to live in Nottingham, my father's hometown. They went on to have 6 of us children, Anthony, me Patricia, Paul, Peter, Ian and Kim.

The Cook Family: Back row: Tony, Paul, Pat & Elsie, Rosemary & Tony, Ann (my mum) Front row: Edna, cousin Sue with Joan and Nanna (Gramps must be taking the photo!)

The occasion is Uncle Pat's 21ˢᵗ birthday celebrations

So, taking a step backwards (metaphorically speaking) when first married, my grandparents lived initially at 4 Lawn Street in Stourbridge, together with sons Paul and Tony. As the family grew, they moved to 2 Prescot Road in Stourbridge and Rosemary, Pat (Patrick) and Ann spent their childhood and teenage years here. They had a decent life and every year Gramps would hire a car and take them on holiday to Rhyl. Prescot Road is where I recall my first childhood memories of visits to Nanna and Gramps' home.

I've digressed somewhat! Having qualified as a pilot at the end of the First World War, Gramps still remained interested in aircraft and used to organise trips to Heston Airport, now London Heathrow, for his colleagues where he hoped to set up a flying club of his own. He had the option to buy a plane for just £50. When Hitler came to power, he realised that we did not have enough planes to cope should there be another war. He began making collections from the Midland Red personnel raising £5000 to cover the cost of the prototype Bristol Blenheim twin-engine bomber. Gramps was 39 years of age by the time of the Second World War and on 26th August, 1939 he got instructions to 'hold yourself, in readiness to act promptly' should you receive orders to report for duty with the Royal Air Force.

A month later he received a telegram stating 'Report Air Ministry for selection board. October 3, 10.30 – no expenses'. On arrival he was told because he hadn't flown for one hour during the previous 12 months, he could not fly at present but could go out to France to help lay the airstrips. Gramps' reply was, 'I told them,' although they offered me the rank of Pilot Officer, 'I did not fancy a labourer's job.'

Returning to work on the buses he was visited by two military policemen with a request for him to go back into the Royal Engineers. During the winter of 1940, eighty officers including Gramps, two elderly home guards and a roll of barbed wire were ready to face the German air raids at Butlins at Clacton on Sea. Apparently, the joke was that they could never make out why the Germans didn't bomb Butlins until someone suggested if they ever came across, they would want somewhere to go for their holidays!

Sadly, the joke was lost when not long afterwards a machine gunner got the full force of a bomb blast which completely bent the barrel of his air gun back on himself and blew him to pieces.

In 1941, Gramps was told to report to Warwick where he was put in charge of the defence of Coventry by smoke screening. At this time the streets were lined with small containers of diesel oil which were set fire to, to produce the smoke screen. Now, 'had the Germans brought their tanks in, the streets were ready lined for them to refuel' observed my Gramps, 'we soon changed that though'. The diesel oil was replaced with a special chemical and the screening process was mechanised as the containers were moved off the roadside on to lorries. Problems arose however, due to trying to find suitable drivers and this was when Gramps called upon his bus driving experience.

In a local newspaper, in an article entitled *Memories of a war hero*, Gramps said his greatest achievement at this time was when he helped to fox Hitler at

Great Yarmouth. I never took possession of this particular article but I'm pleased to say the story is covered in Paul Bell's interview and here it is:

Paul – And then you were posted to Great Yarmouth, which is down towards London way, isn't it, on that coast

Gramps – Yes, that's right

Paul – Where the closest place is France, and you were put in charge of Smoke Screen Operations.

Now in order to stop the Germans spying on us and seeing what we were doing, we sent out smoke screens and this is a plan of Great Yarmouth and all the various points where they used to have these big cast iron pots and make smoke screens so that any Germans flying over couldn't see what was going on. And you can see at the bottom it says Most Secret, Paul emphasises Most Secret.

Gramps – Yes it was secret

Paul – Right, now in order to fool Hitler what you did at Great Yarmouth, you made some tanks, didn't you, which were not really tanks

Gramps – Oh dummies

Paul – Yes, dummy tanks, they were actually made out of plywood, so anyone flying over the top would think they were real tanks and think we had an enormous number of tanks and you went down and had a look at these tanks and

Gramps – They were landing craft on the Broads behind Great Yarmouth.

Paul – They were all made of canvas and plywood.

Gramps – They looked perfect until you went and touched them.

Paul – What was the profession of the men that were making these?

Gramps – I asked, said what Squadron are you, and they said all Royal Engineers and I said, where are you from and he said, every man in this Squadron is a man that in peacetime makes scenery for Pantomimes in London and Birmingham.

Paul – There you are then, they made all the scenery for Pantomimes

Gramps – They knew how to camouflage it all.

Paul – So, we've managed to bluff the Germans, with all these landing craft on our coast, that we were going to land, that we were going to go over the sea to France.

Gramps – On the racecourse we painted on the stands the red crosses and on the houses red crosses for our wounded to come back to, you see you're not supposed to bomb the Red Cross. Now, if you read the History of the Second

World War, Hitler said we should go across from there but Rommel said no, no go lower down the coast. Well it's a good job Hitler disagreed with Rommel

Paul *– Hitler was advised that that was a bluff and*

Gramps *–yes, we were bluffing and we'd got no real craft there at all. What happened, why we did this, was because at 9 o'clock in the morning from Norwich and that way (Gramps points to the map), everything imaginable had come in. Generals with flags flying, cars, gun carriers, tanks and they all had to go down into Great Yarmouth and practise driving out of the sea off the sands – as though they were going to do it the other side the Channel you see. Well, at 11 o'clock in the morning one of their planes used to come over.*

Paul *– A German plane?*

Gramps *– Yes,*

Paul *– Spying, yes?*

Gramps *– And he used to see all this and we used to fire but never fire at him, never intend (to hit him), let him get the photographs and, em, then at one o'clock in the morning, my job was then to fill all of Yarmouth with smoke. Then all them that came in at 9 o'clock in the morning moved out of Great Yarmouth and down the coast and hid in the woods, all round the east coast, until they got to the south coast eventually. The next morning another lot would come in and they would be photographed again and so in the daylight there'd supposed to have been thousands of troops on their photographs and yet at one o'clock in the morning, after this lot had moved out, there wasn't a soul.*

Paul *– They'd all gone. So, in the daylight all the troops moved into Great Yarmouth and the German planes photographed them and then at night time all the troops moved out down the coast, so we fooled Hitler because he thought we were going to land across the Channel from there.*

Gramps *– Yes, that's right, he could see all the landing craft being built and put on the Broads, camouflaged, and they looked perfect, as though we were going across in them.*

Just before the end of the Second World War, Gramps left the army because at the age of 46 years he was over the service age limit, but not before (it is reported) he received a request to return to flying! After he was demobbed, he returned to the Midland Red bus company as a foreman and remained there until his retirement at the age of 65 years. During this time, he made a full-sized First

World War plane with the children of Hagley Roman Catholic School which is now placed in the Flying Museum.

Whilst Gramps was busy doing his service for King and Country, my nanna must have been kept very busy looking after their children. My grandparents were relatively old when their youngest daughter, my mum Ann was born. My gramps was 37 years of age and my nanna was 46 years of age. She would have had to have managed her home in frugal times during the 1930s Depression and coped with rationing and the air raids during the Second World War as Coventry, situated fairly close by, was badly bombed.

I understand that from time to time Nanna suffered from poor nerves that sometimes resulted in jealous behaviour. Of-course my mum and her siblings would have been witness to these events as children. I don't expect it helped Nanna being married to such a charismatic man as my gramps. But despite all of the difficult times and experiences they endured my mum's family are the most loving, warm, kind and fun people and the welcome we received whenever we returned to her home town of Stourbridge was (and remains) wonderful.

In my earliest childhood memories of going to see Gramps and Nanna, I cannot recall either of them as younger people. Nanna would have been 66 years of age and Gramps would have been 58 years of age when I was born. All I remember was Nanna in her 70s and sadly she had suffered a stroke. She used to sit in her chair lost in her own little world. As mentioned previously, I did spend time with my cousins Jane, Philippa and Kathy during the school summer holidays from when I was about eight to twelve years of age. They lived just outside of Stourbridge and we had great fun together. I know I went to see my grandparents during these visits but I cannot recall any other image of my Nanna than the one described above, which is a real shame. However, I am delighted to say I do have one photograph which I would like to share with you of them both when they were much younger and here it is:

Left to right; Tony, Paul, Nanna (as I never knew her) and Gramps

As youngsters, I remember my three brothers and I used to play in their garden which had lots of shrubs and trees and still had an old air raid shelter in it. This conjured up all manner of games in our imaginations. It was perfect for hide and seek.

And of-course there was Gramps, always with that twinkle in his eyes! He had the best smile ever and life never seemed to get him down. By this time, he would have been in his late 60s, back driving the local buses and nearing retirement.

He had lost much of his hair, aside from that still surrounding his head. I shall never forget my younger brother Paul looking at him with curiosity and wanting to know 'why his head had grown up through his hair'! My grandparents' council home was very basic and there was only a scullery for a kitchen and a very old 1930s ground floor bathroom inhabited by the largest spiders I have ever seen.

Sadly, Nanna died on 7th June, 1973 when I was only 17 years old. It was some time after this that my Gramps moved to sheltered accommodation in the centre of Stourbridge where he lived quite happily in a self-contained bedsit.

He continued to give talks and lectures about his lifetime experiences, especially during the Great War and, as mentioned above, was often featured in the local press. I hope that I have been true in re-telling his tale.

As you've probably gathered, I am immensely proud of him and must admit I never miss the opportunity to tell friends about his escapades. I think true testament to his character was made by two beautiful eulogies when he died on Maundy Thursday 1991. The first was written by my cousin Sue's husband, Paul and the second by Ursula, the young student. Both had spent many hours listening to his amazing stories and enjoying his company. Reading both their letters makes me very emotional.

For they are not looking at my gramps, from a grandchild's point of view with rose tinted glasses, they are speaking from the heart. I would ask you to read Paul's thoughts of him, they truly capture the essence of the man. You too will be moved, I know.

On a lighter note, in the Summer of 1996, my great auntie Marjorie's children Mike and Carole Powell helped to organise a get together of the Cook and Cooke family descendants. Charles Henry Cook had two wives, Georgina and Lily and he raised 12 children with his first wife and 3 children with his second wife. As of the 5th of March, 1996, the descendants of the Cook family numbered 279 and Lily and Robert Cook gave everyone a handout of the names of all of the families involved. It was some get together, as over 100 family members attended! Gramps may not have been there in person but I bet he was there in spirit.

Paul's letter written to my Mum

Dear Ann,

A letter about Gramps and what he meant to me and indeed all of us is a mammoth task. It is not in any sense difficult except where on earth does one stop and feel that all has been said? One just has to accept the impossibility and write on knowing that any letter will never describe the stature of the man and the memories he has left with us.

We all have many personal thoughts of him and mine will always include the visits to the flat where he was always enormously welcoming even when he obviously was unwell. He enjoyed telling those remarkable stories of his youth and I thoroughly enjoyed listening—even though sometimes not for the first time. He had the amazing gift of being able to communicate with all generations, I never felt any age difference between us, any subject was discussed on equal terms. Gramps was a marvellous history teacher as witnessed by so many of us wanting to hear about those past days and his amazing role in them.

Whether at Hell Fire Corner 1916 or Hartshill Garage in the winter of 1947, on the motorcycle with Red Baron in pursuit or in the school meals' van, at Great Yarmouth smoke screening in 1944 or in the T Model Ford on an outing to Blackpool, on the Somme 1915 or the Prescott Road air raid shelter, reconnoitring over The North Sea or flying low over Dublin, Hill Street School or The Bell Garage, the stories never faded in the telling.

Amongst the many dramatic recollections were many humorous ones. Who will ever forget the false teeth finally being replaced on D Day, didn't they last well? The many antics of the bus drivers leaving the 'old boiling pieces' for each other at the bus stops. Bernard Griffiths and the circus elephant, Bernard Griffiths and the white mackintoshes cyclist and Ewart Cook crash landing after showing off his flying skills, these stories must take their places in the immortal memories of the man.

He was very much the centre point of the family, he drew all together over the threshold of the family H.Q., the 'operations room' at Flat 3. We shall all miss him from the youngest great grandchild to you the children. Sadly no more the welcome, the tea (with Bell's or without), the latest family news, the reading of proud letters received from Ursula and historian friends, the squirming on familiar seats, the upholstery aromas of the community room whilst enjoying Tuesday afternoon tea and the sounds of hard closed double doors in the distance.

The stick, the cap, the Royal Flying Corps tie, the blazer badge and the cigarettes were very much Gramps' trademarks and will form an important part of our affectionate memories together with his strong opinions when he felt something deeply or thought an injustice needed airing or rectifying.

He was a man who you would choose to have alongside in a crisis, his advice was drawn from his vast experience of life. He was not a man to criticise covertly, he was honest and open, a person of enormous reliability, a soul who has touched the lives of many for good and I believe I have been privileged to know him so well.

As he would say, 'Thanks for everything' and 'Chocks away'.
Farewell Ewart the pleasure has been much mine.
Love and best wishes Paul

Naive but Oh So Brave

Gramps and his brother each lied about his age
To fight in France, not worldly, nor sage
In going to the Front, Gramps even took his bike
To be a despatch rider, was better than a hike

To address General Haig, Gramps had a promotion
Propriety was all, gosh what a commotion
The terrain was tough, the ground mainly chalk
Horses nor mules, nor soldiers could walk

One day he was out delivering a message
When out of the clouds came a rite of passage
The famous Red Baron had Gramps in his sight
Bullets made him swerve, he was up for a fight

Gramps wasn't stupid, he laid down and played dead
The Red Baron claimed victory, not really ahead
But to go over the top to certain annihilation
No longer brave, but full of trepidation

With gas as warfare, little else mattered
It was different to shells, with limbs being shattered
For among the poppies in Flanders fields
With the death of his brother, heartbreak yields

For a few yards captured, thousands of lives lost
In the Somme, any small victory came at huge cost
Preparations were made for the big Push
By then the soldiers were not in a rush
They just longed to come home

This Poem is dedicated to my Gramps, William Ewart Cook, and my great uncle, his brother Frederick Charles Sidney Cook.

53

Chapter Three
Darker Times

1969

British Set of Stamps to Commemorate Concorde's Inaugural flight

At 12 years old, I truly became the 'little mother'. My sister Kim was only a baby when Mum fell pregnant again. Sadly, she was unable to carry this pregnancy to full term because of the danger to her health from a prolapsed womb. Unfortunately, the doctors took six months to reach their decision to allow her an abortion (these were illegal without some justification at the time). By then she knew she was expecting twin boys. Mum who loved children was devastated at this proposed course of action but there was no alternative. It was her life or theirs. When she came around from the operation a Catholic priest came to visit and told her what a wicked woman she was to have not tried to carry the children to full term.

Following this, Mum had a nervous breakdown and this is when I became the carer for my four brothers and baby sister. I was changing and washing nappies and helping look after the house. I'll never forget the twin tub washing machine. First of all, the poo was rinsed from the nappies down the toilet and then they were soaked in a bucket overnight. Then in strict order, the whites were washed first including the nappies, the coloureds went in next and anything really dirty went into the same water after that! The only saving grace was that we rinsed the clothes in the spin-drier following the aforementioned washing process. I should think we had the best immune systems going, especially as we siblings had previously all caught measles, mumps and chicken pox in turn.

It is not really surprising that I had little interest in having any children of my own. As much as I loved my brothers and, especially my little sister, I felt I lost a couple of years good and proper in my early teens, aside from all the earlier baby-sitting that is. That said, I've always been really close to my youngest sister Kim. When I got to the stage that I could go out of an evening, she would throw her little arms around my legs, saying, 'Don't leave me, Patty, don't leave me!'

Then Mum's obsessive jealous behaviour began to get worse to the extent that she imagined Dad was having an affair. I was accompanying my dad on the bus to work to ensure he did not speak to anyone else (by this, read any other woman). And I had to make this journey before I went to school in a morning. Oddly enough, I don't recall meeting Dad after school and accompanying him home on the return journey.

One lunch time Mum and Dad were arguing and fighting again and the chip pan got knocked off the cooker on to the floor. How it didn't catch fire I'll never know. We kids were shouting for them to stop and then the neighbours called the police. The fear that Mum and Dad would split up got very real. The final crunch came when a couple of weeks later, Mum turned up outside of Rolls Royce screaming the place down for him and his 'slut' to come out of his place of work. Poor Dad. He had been promoted to section leader and his career there was now at risk. At this point, Mum was sectioned and we children were split into two's and put into care for a couple of nights to enable Dad to get a rest as well.

All of this instability must have been our dad's worst nightmare. He was doing his utmost to keep the family together. As a child he had witnessed his own mother's unusual behaviour. In 1937–1938 his father ran a commercial hotel. My grandmother was a talented pianist and she played and sang to entertain the guests. Unfortunately, she began to imagine different men fancied her. Things came to a head when the Brewery chief, a married man, became involved in her flights of fancy. My grandmother wrote him letters and this caused huge problems and my grandfather got the sack. As a consequence, my grandfather split up with her and Dad was then brought up by his grandmother. He knew what it was like to be separated from both his mother and father and he told me in later years he didn't want this to happen to his children too. For Dad, life with Mum, was like history repeating itself.

Following this latest episode, my mum had the worst of worst treatments for her mental health illness. She was given electric shock treatment, which dulls the brain and affects the memory. It was pretty barbaric in those days. When she came home, Dad took voluntary redundancy in 1970 and time off work to look after her. If you recall from Gramps' story, my grandmother on my mum's side also suffered from depression and experienced similar traits of jealousy that my mum appeared to have inherited.

And so, as a family, we needed a new start in life. And where better than Perth in Australia? As mentioned previously, my dad was a really intelligent man and his forte was solving problems with the aid of mathematics. He actually made up formulae to resolve an engineering dilemma and at Rolls Royce he was much respected for his designs and early work on the Concorde aeroplane engines and RB2-11 casings. He was an extraordinary scholar. I have in my possession all of his certificates, merits and records of achievement.

Dad (in the middle) with colleagues at Rolls Royce

The Apprentice Board recommended that Dad's name be added to The Roll of Merit as the Best Apprentice for the year 1950.

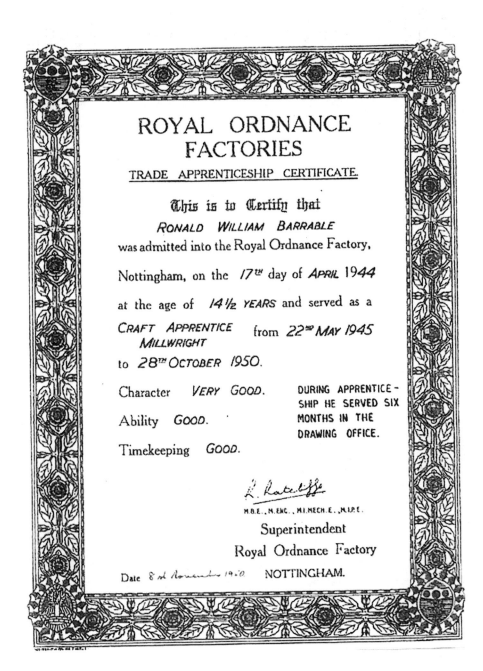

ROYAL ORDNANCE FACTORIES

TRADE APPRENTICESHIP CERTIFICATE.

This is to Certify that

RONALD WILLIAM BARRABLE

was admitted into the Royal Ordnance Factory,

Nottingham, on the *17th* day of *APRIL* 1944

at the age of *14½ YEARS* and served as a

CRAFT APPRENTICE MILLWRIGHT from *22nd MAY 1945*

to *28th OCTOBER 1950*.

Character *VERY GOOD*.

Ability *GOOD*.

Timekeeping *GOOD*.

DURING APPRENTICE-SHIP HE SERVED SIX MONTHS IN THE DRAWING OFFICE.

L. Ratcliffe

M.B.E., M.ENG., MI.MECH.E., M.I.P.E.

Superintendent

Royal Ordnance Factory

Date *8rd November 1950* NOTTINGHAM.

R.O.F. (N) Form 14

(Postage must be prepaid on all
Letters, etc., sent to this Office).

ROYAL ORDNANCE FACTORY,

KINGS MEADOWS,

NOTTINGHAM..........26th Feb., 1957

Dear Mr. Barrable,

     I should not like to let you leave the Ministry without expressing on behalf of the Minister of Supply, appreciation of the loyalty, diligence and devotion to duty displayed by you during nearly thirteen years in the public service.

     May I add my personal good wishes for the future.

               Yours sincerely,

               Superintendent

Of-course the only downside to this was when I asked for help from Dad with my homework. If I didn't get the point of what to him was obvious straight away, he would be throwing his hands up in frustration. The more he did this the more my mind seemed to close down. Quadratic equations were a good example. I really took to Geometry but Algebra seemed like another language altogether and one that I did not get to grips with until my late 20s when, as a mature student, I was studying to become a surveyor. So, at the time of the 1970s Rolls Royce 'crash' when Dad took voluntary redundancy to care for Mum, they spent the next year together having sold their house in Shelton Lock going out on day trips to the Peak District and anywhere else that took their fancy.

Visiting Beresford Dale in 1972
Baby sister Kim, Mum, Dad, Ian and I

Mum gradually got over her 'therapy' and we moved to a rented three-storey maisonette, which for the eight of us was something of a squash. I think I have blotted out much of this time because it really wasn't a normal way of carrying on but still it was seen as a temporary measure. Until we got the go ahead to move to Australia that was. Dad had a talent that firms in Australia wanted and they offered emigration sponsorship schemes to a favoured few. As a family of eight we were given special dispensation to go because my brother Tony and I were soon to be of working age; usually the limit was for families of six or less. Well the forms had been signed, Mum was doing well and I had visions of a future with an Aussie sheep farmer. Unfortunately, our dreams of a fresh start were not to be realised. My parents, being honest Catholic folk, had mentioned my Mum's nervous breakdown on the emigration forms. Once the references were taken their application was refused on the grounds that Mum could become a liability should the going get tough upon arrival in this strange and foreign land.

And so, another year went by. My teachers at school had requested to see Mum and Dad with a view to me staying on to do my '0' levels. In those days you either remained at school studying these exams until you were 16 years of age, or you left at the age of 15 and generally went on to do an apprenticeship, or learn office or factory work.

Well, as the equity monies from the house were dwindling fast, (Dad had been out of work for nearly two years by then) my parents would not give permission for me to carry on with my education. I left school at 14 years of age thinking we were on our way to Australia but the Authorities visited my parents and I had to return to school until the following March. The only thing I achieved in these latter months was opening and closing the curtains at the end of term school play. My brother Tony, following a disappointing foray into plumbing, was then taken on as an apprentice for British Rail where he learned to renovate the carriages and seating at the local Derby coach works.

What were the choices for a girl of 15 with no qualifications to her name? Well, there were two, one I could do some office work and attend college part time learning to type or two I could go to work in a factory. Nottingham was famous for several things, lace making, Raleigh Bikes, Triumph undies, Boots the Chemists, Robin Hood and there being four women for every single man. It was 1971 and the government had just introduced decimal currency, which confused everyone no end! The main difference in earnings at that time was four pounds a week for working in an office or seven pounds plus a week for doing 'piece work' in a factory. Dad gave me little choice, I had to help keep the family going and so the factory it was. I began my working life as a sewing machinist making baby clothes. I can only be grateful that they'd stopped sending children down the mines, otherwise that might well have been my fate.

Still, what a culture shock! There were a few tough cookies working there I can tell you. At coffee break you dare not glance too long at anyone and if you did, as I soon found out, you were treated to the threatening words, 'what the hell are you looking at'? We started work at 8.30 am, had half an hour for lunch, two 15-minute coffee breaks and worked through until 5.30 pm late afternoon. Living on the outskirts of Derby, I caught the bus at 7 am in the morning to enable me to get to work in time and then caught the return bus at night leaving the bus station in Nottingham at 6 pm to get home at 7 pm. I gave my weekly earnings to my parents and was given 50 pence for bus fares and 50 pence spending money, the rest going into help with the weekly grocery shop.

I don't think I'd realised what hard work was until I began working at Stevex Ltd. I even did overtime on a Saturday morning working until one pm, although I did have a vested interest in doing this. After finally overcoming the prejudice of a fellow machinist and convincing her I wasn't that posh, or after her bloke, (one of the material cutters) I began staying at this young lady's house on a Friday night. We would go out together of a Friday evening, with full make up on so we looked old enough to gain entry to the Nottingham Palais Dance Hall. It was a great place to be with a glitter ball hanging from the ceiling and the first revolving disco bar floor in the country. We often didn't roll in until 4 am in the morning but my mum and dad knew nothing of these shenanigans. As I worked overtime on a Saturday morning, they were none the wiser when I arrived home from work at lunchtime.

Gosh, did we think we were the bee's knees. Strutting around town in our Oxford bags (trousers in case you were wondering) and crop tops we thought the world was our oyster. The sewing training really came in handy as I was going through my 'hairy stage'. Strangely enough my friend, whose name escapes me now, was classed as a skin-head so if that wasn't a clash of cultures, I don't know what was. Anyhow, we used to have one drink each to last us all evening. We gave up on having a Babycham, which didn't last five minutes, and went in for drinking half a lager instead.

Going back to the sewing practise, Mum had bought a sewing machine and somehow thought I would wish to do even more sewing when I got home from work having had my tea at 8.30 pm at night. I admit it did help with not having much money. I was able to make myself smock tops and put triangles of material in a variety of trouser bottoms to turn them into flares. But as for making things for the rest of the family, forget it! I was so **not** interested.

It was around this time that I started to become aware of my own sexuality. I had ditched the braces when I was 15 years of age and was thrilled with my nice even teeth, long flowing hair, enhanced with a blondish colour home dye and dark pencilled eyes. I was 15 going on 18 really, or so I thought. We were still living in Borrowash in the dreadful 3-bedroom maisonette with the warm air central heating. Next door lived a young man and his girlfriend, together with his mother.

Well this young man was in a Pop group with three other young men, called Hare, a pun on the word Hair I think because they all had long hair. The lead singer was the spitting image of Marc Bolan from T Rex but he already had a girlfriend, so that put paid to any designs I may have had on him. But I began to go out on their gigs with them on a Saturday evening. The lead singer's girlfriend and I would watch them set up their equipment in working men's clubs and get free musical entertainment. They sang *Born to be Wild* as good as any band I've heard and from then on, I got hooked on heavy rock music. I did briefly go out with the Marc Bolan lookalike but he actually wanted to go to bed with me, as this was what his ex had done. But I was having none of it. Mum had instilled it into me that sex, or making love as she described it, was something to be enjoyed but only if you thought a lot of one another and there was a future together. I really respected that idea—for a time at least.

I was gaining in confidence and one morning whilst I was waiting for my bus at 7 o'clock in the morning, a handsome young man in a red sports car drew up to offer me a lift into Nottingham. He said he had noticed me quite often waiting for the bus and seen me walking down Maid Marian Way on my way to work. Feeling chuffed I got into his car and after nothing untoward happened he dropped me off in town. Then the next time he stopped, he asked me out for the evening but this was mid-week, generally a 'no' as far as my parents went. Obviously, I couldn't let on that I intended on going out with a man who was quite a bit older than me, I would think in his mid-twenties. So, I let Mum and Dad assume I was going to see a girlfriend for the evening and was very sketchy with the actual details.

He called for me at the end of our road and off we zoomed into Nottingham to a nightclub. I was trying to act all grown up and drank three Babychams rather quickly. I needed the loo so off I went and when I got back there was another drink waiting for me. I didn't like to admit that I didn't usually drink (aside from the half of lager on a Friday night that is) so gulped it down.

The last thing I remember as I got to his car was of me holding the door handle waiting for it be unlocked. The next thing I knew I woke up outside on the ground and was frozen stiff with cold (it was during the winter months). I felt as if I was dreaming. As I looked around, I registered that I was in the parking area of the coach station at the end of our road so I realised I was near home. Staggering up the road I saw all the lights were on in our house. As I got to the driveway my dad came out of the house with a policeman hot on his heels. 'Where the bloody hell have you been?' shouts my dad. Luckily the policeman restrained him and said I looked as if I was not well and needed to be treated gently. You can imagine how my parents must have felt. It was 2 am in the morning and they had no idea where I was, so to admit this to the policeman must have made them feel really irresponsible. The fact I'd been economical with the truth didn't help. The next morning, I was made to see a doctor to see if this guy had had his wicked way with me. Thankfully he hadn't but this didn't stop my parents going down all of the workplaces in Maid Marian Way dragging out unsuspecting dark-haired young men to see if they were guilty of drugging their daughter and leaving her dumped on the ground in an unconscious state. I was grounded for a month. Nonetheless I had learnt pretty quickly that I couldn't take my drink, although it was thought he may have slipped me a 'Micky Finn'. I also learnt that I possibly shouldn't trust dark-haired, good-looking men in fancy sports cars that I didn't know from Adam.

I worked at the factory for just over a year and although I would never have gone into sewing by choice, I discovered I was rather good at it. I began making my own clothes from patterns by Vogue and really enjoyed the experience.

Now ironically enough, on my dad's side, my great grandfather William Henry Barrable and 2nd great grandfather Henry Pethick Barrable had been Tailors in their lifetimes and their amazing stories follow next.

Chapter Four
Henry's and both William Henrys' Stories

1840

British Stamp of Queen Victoria—Tuppenny Blue

According to Parish records Henry Pethick Barrable (my paternal 2nd great grandfather) was born on the 14th April, 1854 in the village of Holsworthy, Devon to parents Henry Pethick of Marhamchurch, Cornwall and Ann Barrable, spinster of Holsworthy, Devon. The local register shows that Henry junior was baptised on 13th May, 1854. He was of illegitimate birth, which in those days I'm sure would have been frowned upon.

His father, Henry Pethick was born in 1816 and was some 19 years older than his mother Ann Barrable. I cannot help but think that Henry senior may have taken advantage of a woman so much younger than himself.

I have recently discovered that Ann's first cousin, Mary Ann Barriball (sic) married into the Pethick family. This could be how Ann, my 3rd great grandmother, had met Henry; possibly at a family gathering, say a wedding or a christening.

However, Henry Pethick does not appear to do the honourable thing when Ann became pregnant with his son. So, she went on to marry William Jordan of Holsworthy some two years later on 7th August, 1856. She had 6 further children with him; Richard, William, Fanny, Matilda, Alfred and Annie were all born in Holsworthy. Sadly, Richard died aged just 3 years 9 months and was buried on 2nd January, 1871 in the Parish Churchyard. Hence, I must have links to another step family out there somewhere.

It is likely that Henry's father, Henry Pethick (try to keep up!) left for Ontario, Canada not long after his son's birth because the 1861 census shows him, at the age of 43, living in Hope, Durham West, Ontario with his occupation listed as a farmer. Henry's grandparents had already emigrated to Canada in former years and his grandmother Johanna died in Canada in 1858 at the age of 63. Henry senior must have travelled home at some point following his father Robert's death because passenger records show him returning again to Canada on the ship Damascus in 1868. Five of his brothers also emigrated there some three years later. In 1871, Henry senior is shown as Head of the Household, now married, and a farmer being of Wesleyan Methodist religion. I cannot help but admire the bravery of these intrepid families setting up home thousands of miles away in foreign lands. The journey alone, sailing across vast oceans on Schooner type ships, must have been an ordeal in itself. Oddly enough, Henry Pethick died in October 1892 in a place named Peterborough in Ontario, Canada. I say oddly because my father, Ronald William Barrable, Henry's great great grandson died in October 2013 in a village on the edge of a town also named Peterborough, but in the country of England, not Canada!

So, returning to Henry junior's early days, in the 1861 census in England, it appears that he temporarily took on William Jordan's name because he is registered as Henry P B Jordan, son aged 7 to the Head of the Household, William Jordan, agricultural labourer. Of course he was really William's stepson and the family lived in Little Holsworthy in Devon at this time.

It is interesting to note that, by comparison, the Pethick family must have been fairly well to do because they have several headstones in the local church at Marhamchurch in Cornwall. Nonetheless, Henry was raised in a Labourer's household. His maternal grandfather was Richard Barrable, who was also noted as a labourer at the time of his daughter Ann's marriage to William Jordan.

By 1871 Henry was listed on the census as a lodger and had regained the use of his mother's maiden name, Barrable. He had also become a Tailor and I am

65

guessing he left school at an early age and entered into an Apprenticeship. According to records there were several Tailors, Dressmakers and Shoemakers trading locally. I've also been told by the local townsfolk that the town of Holsworthy did have buildings that bore tiles below the eaves. These are a sign that they were occupied by the Flemish cloth makers in days gone by, so this is almost certainly where he learnt his profession.

By now Henry lived at 96 North Street, Holsworthy with his mother, step-father (who still worked on the land) and half-brothers William (13 years of age) and Alfred G Jordan (one month old) and half-sister Matilda (5 years old).

Henry finally left home and must have had reason to travel because at the age of 22, he married Miss Ellen Turner (1854 – 1939) at Winchcombe in Gloucestershire on 3rd June, 1876. I have obtained a copy of the marriage certificate and there is no mention of any witnesses from the Barrable side of the family. In fact, Henry's father is shown as William Barrable on the certificate, a detail which is not true as Henry Pethick was Henry's real father. He appears to have used William Jordan's first name but put Barrable as his surname. It also states his father was a farmer rather than a labourer. This indicates to me, how illegitimacy was a stigma at that time and Henry appears to be marrying into a fairly well to do family. He is not keen to reveal all!

The marriage certificate provides details of Ellen Turner's family who I have also traced through the census records. Her father's name is also William and he is listed as a Builder, but more than that, he was also a Stonemason. His children, Ellen's siblings, Susanna and Charles are listed as witnesses to the marriage and Ellen's family originate from Grafton in the Parish of Beckford, Gloucestershire. By 1881 Henry and his wife Ellen have moved on. I am assuming that, as this is the time of the Industrial Revolution which took place in Victorian England from the early 19th century onwards, the family were moving to places where mills were being built and towns were growing in population. They now live at number 6 Great Francis Street, Aston, Warwickshire. Ellen had by this time given birth to a son William, (my great grandfather) now four years old, and two daughters Nellie Maud who was aged two and Bertha Ann who was still a young baby. Henry is working as a tailor and they are sharing the household with Catherine Hughes who is a domestic servant with her young daughter Ellen and a school master called Thomas Daffern.

In 1883, Ellen's father dies leaving a will to whom Henry Barrable, Tailor is shown as one of the executors. Her father, William Turner, my 3rd great grandfather had a personal estate of £487 7s 11 d, which was a princely sum of money in those days.

Within the next seven years and by 1891, records show that the family have moved again, this time to 74 Palmerston Road in St Giles, Northampton. Henry is now a Tailor's Cutter and William, Nellie and Bertha have been joined by Frederick T, 8 years of age and Lilley, the youngest daughter at 3 years of age. There is no room for lodgers here!

When Henry was 47 years of age and his wife Ellen was 49 years of age, they were living at 63 Windsor Terrace, South Gosport in Northumberland. William Henry, the oldest son, had got married and left home. Surprise! He was a Tailor's cutter too following in his father's footsteps. Frederick at 18 years of age was also listed as a tailor in the 1901 census but he still lived at home with his parents.

The census shows the family have grown again and there were now 4 additional children, Frank aged 9, Kate aged 7, Percy aged 5 and Florence aged 3. Florence had been born in York so it would appear there had been yet another move for the family since living in Northampton, unless Ellen went away to have the child. The older children including Bertha aged 20 are also still living at home.

Henry would have been too old to take part in the First World War as the conscription age was 17 to 30 years, as would possibly (I thought) his 2 eldest sons, my great grandfather William Henry and his brother Frederick. However, I have subsequently traced some documents. These enlistment papers show that Fred later enlisted on the 23rd May, 1916 with the Northumberland Fusiliers. And this was during the First World War. His trade was stated as a master tailor, he was 33 years of age and he was married at the time, living at 35 Napier Street, Newcastle. Perhaps he was making or repairing the Regiment's uniforms.

By 1911 Henry, now aged 56 years, had moved with the remainder of his family to 18 Day St in Newcastle Upon Tyne. Records show that his wife Ellen, aged 58 years, was still (thankfully) living with him as was his eldest daughter Bertha aged 30. By this time, she is a vest maker working from home and Kate, her sister aged 17 is working as a packer for a wholesale chemist. Percy Albert, her brother is an assistant at a Jewellers and Florence, the youngest sibling being 13 years of age is still at school. Although there are only 5 rooms in the house, they have a lodger by the name of George Percy Hall who at 48 years of age appears to be living separately from his wife and works as a house painter for a Building Firm.

At the moment, I've been unable to trace any further information about Henry Pethick Barrable but my, how he worked hard all of his life. He raised 9 children with his wife Ellen and moved to better himself and accommodate his growing family at least six times since leaving the small town of Holsworthy in Devon. He took advantage of the changing times and the boom in industry but still to travel as far north as Northumberland in the latter part of the 19th century showed immense guts and determination.

Henry died at the age of 75 years on 1st August, 1929, just 3 months prior to my father, his great grandson, being born. He was living at 9 Belle-Grove, West Spital Tongues, Newcastle-Upon Tyne leaving his widow Ellen, who lived for another 10 years, the tidy sum of £80 two shillings.

Meanwhile, returning to Henry's eldest son William Henry Barrable, my great grandfather; he had married Emma nee Jones who was 3 years older than him. The marriage was held in the Spring of 1900. William and his new wife now lived at 59 Nursery Road, Aston Manor in Birmingham. He was by now a Tailor's cutter himself so he too had followed in his father's footsteps. By 24 years of age it appears William had left Northampton and returned to where he lived as a young boy.

How he met Emma currently remains a mystery yet she was trained as a machinist, so they may have worked together at some point. She is reported to have been born in Leicester and the county of Leicestershire borders Northamptonshire. This is where my great grandfather was living prior to their marriage. I do remember my father telling me Emma was known as 'The Duchess' and he felt sure his grandmother had family in the Birmingham area. Apparently, she did not take kindly to her husband's 3 brothers (William was the oldest child of 9 offspring) as they frequented the local snooker hall and pub following church services!

Within a year of being married, my grandfather, also called William Henry Barrable, was born. The household was shared with Sarah E Jones, aged 19 years who was listed as daughter-in-law, together with a Mr Thomas R Panton, a boarder aged 44 years. As William was only 24 years old at the time, I'm positive the stated daughter-in-law relationship is not correct. My aunt tells me that Sarah Elizabeth Jones was Emma's sister and known as Lizzy. This would make her

William's sister-in-law. Emma had two other sisters, Sally and Rose but sadly Rose died as a teenager.

William and Emma were (unusually for the times) to only have the one child, so William Henry Junior remained with no known brothers or sisters.

The 1911 Census tells me that the family had by then moved to 5 Fowler Street in Gainsborough, Lincolnshire. In addition to his young son, William aged 10 years, my great grandfather now shared his home with John Robert Jones (I know this is Emma's brother although he is listed as a Boarder) aged 23 years and a machine labourer, and Sarah and Nellie Fidell, both listed as visitors and aged 47 years and 35 years respectively.

Unfortunately, there is a bit of a gap in my knowledge now as I've yet to trace what happened in the intervening years but I do possess a copy of my grandfather's marriage certificate, which gives his home address at that time as 33 Market Street, Gainsborough. Of-course he may have left home before he got married but if not, it appears that my great-grandfather and his family moved yet again from 5 Fowler Street to this address. His profession is listed on the certificate as an outfitter but at what exact date he opened up his businesses is yet to be discovered.

What I do know is that my great grandfather William Henry Barrable and my grandfather, also named William Henry Barrable (in case you've forgotten!), owned two businesses in Ollerton, near Gainsborough during the 1920s; one being a bespoke tailor and the other whereby his father diversified into an 'Off the Peg' shop selling ready-made suits. There is a super photo' of my grandfather as a young man standing outside the Tailors shop with the fascia displaying Barrable & Son. It was situated next door to the local Billiards Hall and so had a good passing trade. It also had a telephone and I possess a pencil advertising the shop's name with the local exchange and number on it.

Grandad Barrable standing outside of the family business – Barrable & Sons Tailors

During this period, my grandfather married Lilian Maud Makin on 10 February 1926 and his marriage certificate (details of which are also outlined above) indicates he was still a tailor and outfitter at that time. Indeed, he was still trading as such in October 1929 when my father Ronald William Barrable was born. Dad always said he came into the world with a bang as the day he was born, 29th October, 1929, was the day that the Worlds' Stock Markets crashed and thousands of people and businesses went bankrupt. Dad's sister, their first-born child, was my Aunt Margarita. She was born on 14 August, 1926, and it would appear that Lilian must have been expecting Margarita when she got married (if my sums are correct).

Sometime later, William (my grandfather) started up another business, which included electrical and mechanical repairs and sales of electrical goods; also sales of bicycles and motorbikes. This was in the 1930s at a time when radio's, Hoovers and the suchlike were just being invented. There is a great photo of my grandfather as a young man with his parents on a motorbike with side-car.

Grandad as a young man with his parents, William Henry and Emma Barrable.

Unfortunately, according to my dad's account of things, my great-uncle by marriage, who was brought in to manage the 'Off the Peg' store was (allegedly) found to be stealing clothes and takings from the business. The story goes that he got away with his crime because it was considered a scandal in those days to report family to the police. But his actions resulted in my great grandfather being made bankrupt in 1936. Thankfully, my great grandparents' home at that time (a bungalow in Walesby) was in my grandmother's name so they did not lose their home as well. This was a blessing really because my dad and his sister, who were eventually brought up by their grandmother, lived there too.

I'm not sure my great grandfather really recovered from these events and sadly, only seven years later, in 1943, he died from Tuberculosis. His wife Emma (nee Jones) lived to the grand old age of 84 years but her life is yet another interesting story.

Briefly, I do know that in November 1890 she sailed to New York, America with her mother Elizabeth Jones and 5 siblings on a ship called the Majestic. Her occupation was even then listed as a machinist. There's definitely a bit of theme going on here. My auntie Marge has confirmed that Emma's father went to America to open a factory but what became of this intention I do not know as both Emma and her brother Robert had returned to England by the year 1900. Prior to this Emma's father worked as a Watercress salesman so it was no mean feat for him to speculate on opening a factory in a faraway country. Whether their parents remained in America or not remains a bit of a mystery as tracking down the name Jones in genealogy is the stuff of nightmares. On her return, Emma became known as 'The Little American' so I guess she was there long enough to take on an accent and gain some airs and graces.

I can only think that I took to sewing and making my own clothes in my younger days, thanks to the genes I inherited from this side of the family. Likewise, my dad Ronald and my brother Paul inherited their engineering skills from my grandfather, William Henry junior who, following the demise of the businesses, obviously decided bespoke tailoring wasn't for him. As a civilian engineer, William went on to explore the Eaking Oil fields in Nottinghamshire on behalf of the British government just prior to World War Two. Once he had discovered the oil his job was done. William was then moved on to work in the Royal Ordnance Factory in Nottingham, which chiefly made guns and other weaponry. As described earlier my dad followed in his father's footsteps and worked (whilst studying in the evenings) at the Royal Ordnance Factory from the tender age of 14 and a half years until 1957, except for a two-year break when he undertook his National Service in the RAF.

So, the chain of tailors in my dad's family line disappeared for a couple of generations until yours truly became a sewing machinist (not quite in the same league admittedly) many years later.

Chapter Five
Moving to the South East

1972

British Stamp – Britain's Entry in to the European Communities

I was finally released from factory life in the summer of 1973 when Dad got a new job in St. Ives, Cambridgeshire. The family, minus older brother Tony, who was still serving a five-year apprenticeship with British Rail, moved to a house situated on the edge of the Fens. I had never seen such large fields on even land, not a hill or much foliage in sight. Although I understand that the world is round, I could appreciate folks in the Fens possibly thinking it flat. It was odd to drive for miles on end along dyke edged roads and then all of a sudden come across a picturesque village without warning. The skies appeared vast with nothing but the odd tree to break the monotonous horizon.

We had relocated to a village called Bluntisham and I didn't like it one bit! I was a townie, not a country girl at all. There was one bus a day that went into the market town of St Ives and one bus that came back and that was it.

I also missed my brother Tony who I was closest to in the family. Then things got even more weird when he started dating a girl called Trish. When he brought her home from Derby to meet us all, he just sat gazing into her eyes. He wanted nothing more to do with me! There was a definite shift in the dynamics of our relationship. He was also going through his Genesis stage in music and had shaved the front part of his head into a bald triangle aka Peter Gabriel. Well, when we went to collect him off the train one time, my mum didn't know where to put herself with the embarrassment of it all. I think part of him was rebelling somewhat. He credits his now wife Trish with saving him from going completely astray, his words not mine. When they got married, I and my sister Kim were bridesmaids. Their wedding remains one of the fairy tale ones as far as I'm concerned. The nuptials were held the week before Christmas and their reception hall was decked out with lights and Christmas trees and everything was so festive, it was magical.

1975

Brother Tony & Trisha's wedding, Kim and I are bridesmaids (note the fashion!)

Dad began work at a firm called Industra designing the machines that wind the copper wire onto electric motors. It was great for him to be back in his profession again. He was well thought of and the firm's order books grew mainly down to his expertise. He went off to Europe as part of the marketing team much to all of our surprise because before Mum wouldn't have wanted him to be let out of her sight. His colleagues were all men mind you.

Initially, it was my job to stay at home and take care of my younger brother Ian. Mum was required to go out to work and retrieve the book-keeping skills she had last used as a teenager. I think this was the making of her after all of those years of staying home and keeping tabs on us children. She even learnt to drive, which in her forties was pretty awesome, and to her credit she finally passed her test on her third attempt. I'll never forget when Dad bought her a Bubble Car, a kind of three-wheeled vehicle when we lived at Sawley, with the intention of her learning to drive then. He was reversing it out of the garage with Mum gamely indicating that he was good to go, when all of a sudden, she let out a piercing scream because Dad had run over her foot. Somewhere along the line she had forgotten it was a three-wheeler, hence the painful misjudgement that the back was narrower than the front, in terms of wheels that is. Still, after finally passing her test in St. Ives, there was no stopping her and boy, did she love driving fast. It was definitely not a calming experience being a passenger. My dad also drove fast and sometimes they would play games of dare (this is true) and Mum would leave it to the last moment before telling him to brake at a crossroads. I'm only amazed they didn't kill themselves and anyone else in their path long before their eventual demise.

Ian, my youngest brother, was born with asthma and when he had one of his attacks, this was pretty scary to witness. The ambulance was called on more than one occasion. Unfortunately, when he got nervous about anything this brought upon an attack and he really didn't like school. So, yours truly had the job of taking him to school and sitting with him in class until he had settled down. Then it was back home to deal with the boring chores. I was not happy with my lot at this time and felt isolated stuck in the back of beyond.

That was until I met the local baker, a young man who had a mop of curly light brown hair and a great smile with dimples in each cheek. Yes, I was rather smitten and being lonely and bored with the house to myself for most of the day, he became my first lover. Now this state of affairs was all well and good until I had the fright of my life when I didn't get my period. I will say this for him, he was prepared to do the honourable thing and marry me. Yet I knew deep down my dad was disappointed that I had not met someone academic and clever like him. He certainly didn't think I should be thinking about tying myself down. Thankfully, the marriage situation didn't arise because my period eventually arrived late, the relief being palpable, and I broke it off with him as I could see he was more attached to me than I to him.

Mum and Dad then decided I shouldn't be left to my own devices at home so I went for an interview at Charringtons, Gardner & Lockett Coal Merchants, my mum's place of work. There I took a test to prove I could do the maths and began work in the Accounting Machine room where I learned a lot about accounts and book-keeping.

It was while I was working there in St Ives that I met the most gorgeous looking fellow ever. He had the most startling blue eyes I have ever seen in a person and I must now be sounding quite fickle as I tended to get smitten fairly often. He too was in to heavy rock music but he was also in to drugs. It was the flower power period as highlighted in the film of the Woodstock festival. When I went to his friend's house they would all be sitting around on the floor, off their heads saying intellectual things like 'Yeah Man', whilst listening to loud music. I was never tempted to take drugs myself because I was scared of not being in control but I was heartbroken when this boyfriend finished with me for no particular reason. At 16 years of age I was growing up fast.

But then, to my dismay, my front teeth started to protrude again. It wasn't until I had an X-ray that it was realised, I had impacted wisdom teeth. So in to hospital I went to have them removed, which was quite a tricky procedure as they weren't fully formed. Where they cut into my gums I bled like crazy. When I woke up my face was so swollen, according to my dad, I looked like a chipmunk. Back on went some new braces for a further year or so I think.

It was around this time that I got friendly with a girl called Lynne who originated from South London. She had more than a hint of a true cockney accent. I'd never come across a person with this accent before but she became my closest buddy for a while. I was allowed to go and stay at her relative's house once, in order to watch the Four Tops live at Fairfields Hall in Croydon, and that was one of the most exciting nights out I'd ever had.

In 1971, I was asked to be my cousin Sue's bridesmaid. Sue lived in Kidderminster at the time and I think I was chosen out of all of the female cousins on mum's side because she felt I lived away from the rest of the family in Stourbridge and could do with the attention. Well I soon made the most of that idea and flirted outrageously with the best man, despite the fact he was married. My cousin Helen obviously wasn't keen on me being the centre of attention either because at the reception she asked me to go outside to see the swimming pool in the grounds of the Hotel. Me, being my gullible self, stood on the edge of the pool and with one hefty push she shoved me, wearing dress and all, head first into the pool. I must have screamed for England as I still wasn't the World's best swimmer unlike Helen who was a County swimming champion. Thankfully, my screams alerted all and sundry and I was rescued forthwith. To say I looked like a drowned rat was yet another understatement and my cousin got the worst telling off ever. In fact, I then got even more attention so her little plan failed miserably, but not before ruining my outfit good and proper.

It was around this time when I discovered the Alconbury Base where the American soldiers were stationed during the Second World War. It was here that any vestiges of nightlife could be found and boy, did I need some of that. There was a disco held there every Friday or Saturday evening but the drawback was there was no transport to get to and from it. Hence, I was dependent upon lifts from Dad; well until I got myself a boyfriend with a car that is. I think in the main it was good that Dad was around in a way because I did end up having a one-night stand with some guy who lured me into his car following one drink too many. It was one of the most unpleasant experiences of my life and I felt ashamed about it for a long time afterwards. The only saving grace was that he did think of some form of protection amidst all his fumblings.

On a lighter note, in 1973 at one of these dances I met my first fiancé, a chap named David. He was not my usual type; he didn't have dark hair or dark eyes but he was handsome in a different sort of way. He had longish (as was the fashion) light brown hair, blue eyes, a strong straight nose and a fantastic smile with super even teeth. I always noticed the teeth; and he had dimples too. Unfortunately, he smoked but I suppose I was used to this habit thanks to my Dad smoking Players cigarettes in the early days and a pipe later on. David drove a Morris Minor car, which added somewhat to his allure.

We went out together for about three years and initially things were great. We had fun times together going up to the Peak District for long romantic walks and off to various motor racing circuits because he was a big fan. Twice we camped out for the week at two of the British Grand Prix where the Red Arrows and The Harrier Jump Jet gave displays as additional entertainment. Once we went over the Channel to the Nuremburg ring in Germany to see the Grand Prix being held there. My favourite driver was James Hunt and I secretly wished I was one of his groupies. David supported Jody Scheckter. In Germany, the circuit was some 14 miles long so you had plenty of time to sun bathe before the cars came around again and for a short period (well two laps to be exact) James Hunt held the lead. This led to me jubilantly jumping up and down on top of a wooden seat in a sea of Ferrari supporters until I suddenly realised his car had disappeared from the race and the Ferrari driver, who I think was Nicki Lauda, was now in the lead. At this point I felt rather silly and sheepishly got down from the wooden seat.

On my 19th birthday David proposed to me and as I was hopelessly in love with him, I said yes. David's father was a squadron leader in the RAF stationed at Brampton. David himself was training to be a NAAFI manager. Although his store was on the RAF base, he himself was not enlisted personnel. His family were quite well to do and I felt a bit overwhelmed when I initially met them. I remember attending the Officers' Christmas Party with David and feeling somewhat out of my depth. His elder sister and her friend kept making the odd snide comment within hearing distance at the time but I was determined to hold my own. Looking back, I suppose my northern accent may have had something to do with their disdain and 'Hey up me duck' and 'Ta ra a bit' may have seemed a tad alien. However, I knew my manners were good and how to behave in company. Thankfully David's father took to me, although I'm not so sure about his mother. I've always been fairly outgoing because when you are part of a large family, if you don't speak up, you basically don't get heard!

In 1975, David was moved to RAF Brize Norton, located mid-way between Farringdon and Shrivenham in Wiltshire to continue his training there. I was bereft. I so missed him and although I too had moved jobs, I was now working as a Punch Card operator within the computer industry, I only saw him at weekends. Of-course we spoke on the phone but we didn't have a phone at home and it meant me hanging around outside the local telephone box waiting for his call on a Friday evening. He would then turn up on a Saturday lunchtime and lounge around full length on our settee whilst I waited on him, hand, foot and finger.

My mum and dad were not impressed by this behaviour and rows would begin the minute he left our house. I would defend him like mad as I couldn't see him doing any wrong but my parents were having none of it. In the end, Mum said unless things changed then I should leave home and find somewhere else to live.

So that was it. After successfully getting a job at Hambro Life Assurance in Swindon as a Visual Display Unit operator, and fixing myself up to share a house with 2 other girls, 2 chaps and a dog, I left home with as much dignity as I could muster, carrying my belongings in a few cardboard boxes and several black dustbin bags.

Chapter Six
Moving Further South

Mid to Late 1970s

Arnold Machin British Booklet Stamps ½ Pence And 1 penny

I really enjoyed working at Hambro Life Assurance as they did reward hard work and loyalty. I remember one year when the legislation was changing regarding pension plans. We had to get all the details of the ones sold onto the computer by the end of March in a particular year. Well we worked until 10 pm at night, over several weekends and got triple time in pay and steaks for dinner in the canteen! They even paid for a yoga teacher to come in and give tuition one night a week and this interest has remained with me ever since.

But then, having been a VDU operator for three years and despite liking my work mates, I got bored of doing the same thing. I felt capable of so much more. So, I applied for a position in the Marketing Department, running what was grandly known as the Professional Registration System. I had to take two sets of tests, one English and one maths because I had been allowed to originally join the firm with no qualifications; other than previous accounting, touch typing and Punch Card operating experience.

With relief I passed the tests and went to join the folks, including the directors, on the top floor of the building. I literally felt as though I was going up in the world. I had to speak on a daily basis with the Associates who needed to check whether professional people like Stockbrokers, Accountants or Solicitors were already registered with another Associate before they approached them (the idea being for each of them not to tread on one another's toes and put off prospective clients and their professional advisers).

I really loved this job and the contact with staff around the country at the various branches. But this was all well and good until once a month a group of Associates were brought around the Head Office for a tour. I was the one meant to give a small talk about the department. And this is when the nerves got the better of me. I would disappear to the loo as soon as I saw a group of disembodied heads above the office partitions coming in my direction. I felt physically sick as any anxiety attack always went straight to my stomach- and worse was yet to come.

I was asked to stand in for my boss as one of the speakers at one of the annual conferences being held in Liverpool. The night before the event we were treated to a scrumptious meal out at a Greek restaurant together with the associated Greek dancing and plate smashing that went with it. Well it would have been a super night out if I had not been so scared at the thought of standing up in front of everyone the following afternoon. I was unable to eat or really enjoy anything.

The following day I could not get an ounce of breakfast or lunch down me. Then one of the girls felt a brandy would help to settle my nerves that were getting wildly out of control by this time. The moment arrived. I got up to speak and just prayed for the floor to swallow me up. Of-course nothing that wonderful happened and you could cut the atmosphere with a knife, so palpable was my fear. My mouth got drier and drier and my voice got deeper and deeper, a bit like a distorted tape recording. So, I suddenly stopped my planned speech and looking down at my 32a size chest said, Gosh, my voice is getting deep, perhaps I'm changing sex! Thankfully everyone laughed. The relief I felt at this interaction went a long way to helping me proceed with a modicum of intelligence and I was able to complete proceedings. However, it did nothing to instil any future confidence and luckily my public speaking days came to an end for the foreseeable future.

Whilst living in Swindon, I moved house a number of times, once to share another house with two other girls, and then on to a bedsit so David and I could have more time on our own. This sub-divided house wasn't in great order and the electric fire in my bedsit was lethal and gave off fumes. If I had been more savvy, I could have reported the landlord for faults like this and got a rent reduction into the bargain; but I simply ignored the problem and shivered rather a lot instead.

One night, at David's suggestion we went out for a drink with his assistant manager, a pretty young female, and her boyfriend. Suffice it to say, the boyfriend and I may as well not have been there, so taken up with one another were David and his 'colleague' from work. And the boyfriend noticed it and said so too. I was rather naive in all this but I must admit to being rather jealous of all the attention she was getting. Later that night, following a blazing row, David confessed to having an affair with her. I was devastated. I broke up with him shortly afterwards and have never felt so lonely in all of my life. Living in the bedsit didn't help. Even though I managed to get through the week at work, being alone every weekend with no one to talk to really exacerbated how sad and unhappy I was.

It was during the hot summer of 1976 and I can honestly say I felt physical pains in my chest so upset was I to lose this guy. To have my trust betrayed like that was one of the worst things that could have happened to me. When '*I'm not in Love*' by 10 cc came on the radio or something equally poignant by Neil Young, Bread, The Carpenters or The Eagles I would burst into tears beyond consolation.

Then one day soon after, I saw on the notice board at work someone looking for a person to share a flat with. And that person became my dear friend Terry. The first floor flat we rented together was not far from the locomotive carriage works in Swindon and it was located over a car sales showroom. We didn't register it at first but it had a red-light bulb in the hallway and had previously been used by prostitutes we think! We reached this conclusion following one night when I was frightened out of my wits by someone trying to open the front door with a key. Well, the door was on a chain thank goodness so whoever it was, was unable to get in. We guessed afterwards that he or she didn't realise it was no longer a place of ill repute. We changed the colour of the light bulb *tout suite* after that incident.

Terry was a dark haired attractive young lady of Irish Catholic descent. She had qualified in Cordon Bleu cookery at college and it was from her that I learnt to experiment with food. At home, due to Dad's fussiness over different foods, we had never eaten anything that didn't comprise of meat and various veg. And as to anything 'foreign', look out! I began cooking and eating things as exotic as spaghetti bolognese, chili con carne and curry. I appreciate none of these items were French in origin but Terry did give me lots of tips for making sauces and desserts, and one especially delicious recipe involving tenderloin, oranges and green peppers. We didn't live in one another's pockets but it was nice to think that on some nights at least she might be rumbling around in the flat with me.

I was still generally miserable, moping around, and tempted at one point to forgive David for what had happened, even to the extent that I got in touch with him again via his sister. Having moved back home to Sheffield, he was going to come and see me.

To compound matters I had remained friendly with my friend Lynne back in Cambridgeshire and she was getting married. Guess who was to be her bridesmaid? I should have been awarded an Oscar for trying to look happy for her on that day when deep inside all I could think about was how this was meant to be me getting married to the man of my dreams.

Just before any arranged meeting with David could take place, I met up with another chap called Stirling who drove a bright red Frog eyed Sprite sports car. Stirling was the archetypical tall, dark haired handsome bloke with stunning blue eyes, an athletic body and a really nice personality. In fact, he was too nice but following my disastrous affair with David, I needed someone who thought the world of me for a change. And I think it's fair to say he worshipped the ground I walked on. We had a whirlwind courtship, I convinced myself I loved him, and yes, I got married on the rebound.

We got engaged on my 21st birthday. David my ex-fiancé rang my place of work that very same day but I never got his message until a couple of days afterwards and the deed was done. Seven and half months later in June 1977, we got married in my parents' home town of St Ives, Cambridgeshire. I can still recall saying to my mum, 'Mum, I'm not sure I've done the right thing,' on my wedding day, to which she replied in a bid to give me some assurance, 'Oh, darling, we all feel like that!'

Writing this now. I wonder what it was I was searching for, some form of security I'm guessing, and an end to the dreadful loneliness too.

Meanwhile, Mum and Dad and my four younger siblings had moved into a super new semi-detached 4-bedroom Council house in Hemingford Grey. This village was beautiful with the River Ouse running through it. It featured many historical properties including the oldest occupied Norman Manor House in England, that even had a moat surrounding it. This house was owned by an authoress named Lucy Boston who wrote children's books. She was famous throughout the world. Strangely enough I had never come across her works but she wrote the Green Knowe series and also her own autobiography entitled 'Perverse and Foolish'.

Circa 1980

Lucy Boston's Manor House in Hemingford Grey where brother Ian was a gardener.

My youngest brother Ian worked for her for a time as her gardener and also a chauffeur, taking her on trips into Cambridge. As a family we were all invited to her home, to have a tour around, and it was fascinating. The original part to the rear was Norman built whilst the frontage was Elizabethan. Lucy refused to have central heating installed as she knew this would dry out the clay fabric of the Norman part of the house. In the front garden grew the most amazing box or yew hedging in the shape of chess pieces. I'm not sure she ever let my brother loose on these masterpieces of topiary but she did try to train him to trim them in this respect.

Her good friend was an artist called Elizabeth Vellacott who also lived in the village. She became well known for her paintings of figures without any faces. Any expression from the figure depicted came from the person's posture. Once, she and Lucy Boston featured in an episode of the South Bank Show with Melvyn Bragg. Even my brother Ian was caught on camera walking through the gardens. Lucy must have been fond of him because Elizabeth painted a picture known as Lucy and the Gardener, which went on to sell initially for £2,000. I would so love to have had the opportunity to view this picture. But I digress (again!).

My husband Stirling, like me, came from a large family. He was one of five children and they too were Catholics. Sadly, his father had died when Stirling was just a young teenager. His mother had since remarried a 'well to do' man who owned several jewellery shops in the Wiltshire area.

Stirling's stepfather kindly loaned us the money to buy a two up, two down, 200-year-old cottage, which had no bathroom or kitchen and was in a semi derelict state. It was located in the village of Shaw, some 4 miles outside of Swindon. We were unable to get a mortgage on it until it was renovated.

1977

Our two up, two down stone-built cottage at Shaw, prior to renovation

But it was whilst we were engaged and during the making of our wedding plans that two difficult things occurred. One, I discovered I was pregnant. This

84

was not a good time for this to happen as we planned to move into an old mobile home that would be situated in the garden of the cottage. It came with no running water, sewerage pipes, or mains electricity. The aim was to live on site and do up the property in our spare time, as and when we could afford to.

Sadly, when I was 3 months pregnant the unthinkable occurred and I had a miscarriage. I often feel guilty about this loss because part of me was not ready to be a mother. I'm not sure whether I sub-consciously willed the baby away. I know I started to lose blood and was told to slow down and I sometimes wonder if I ignored this advice. Or whether it was my good old Catholic conscience coming to the fore again.

Being practical about it, I'm not certain how we would have managed had we had to raise a baby in this mobile home. We had an Elsan portable loo that made your eyes water big time, a stove with two rings, that was run off a gas bottle and a fan heater as our only form of heating. We had to fetch any water from the tap in the cottage and had a single electric wire to provide some power and lighting.

Twice a week we went to Stirling's mother's house for a shower or bath and to watch some television as we did not own one ourselves. Any monies we both earned went into this property and we did without any holidays, new clothes or anything else for that matter for the majority of our married life.

The second sad thing to happen was that my father was rushed into hospital and nearly died from Emphysema. The hospital staff needed to drain his lungs, but because he could not breathe under anaesthetic, they were unable to carry out this procedure. It was touch and go at one time but somehow, he made a miraculous recovery and was able to walk me down the aisle and give me away (with some relief I should think) at our wedding.

And I can honestly say, for the three years I lived in this mobile home I was really happy and content. In the summer, it was just like camping, with me ironing outside in the garden and helping out with the removal of any rubble that Stirling had created from knocking the cottage into shape. He was extremely clever with his hands and a cabinet maker by trade. In fact, both of his brothers were also creative, one being a goldsmith and silversmith, and another being a clock and watch repairer.

In the winter months though, life in the mobile home was tough. As mentioned previously, our only form of heating was a fan heater and often our bedclothes became damp from the condensation that formed on the walls. One morning I couldn't get out of bed due to my bones setting in a fixed position and I think this was down to the continual cold and wet. Another morning with frost hard on the ground I fell over going across the garden to the car and really injured my lower back. As I lay there on the ground, I did have some misgivings about our crusade to create this perfect little home.

On other occasions I would arrive home from work doubled up with stomach pains. They were so bad that I was being sick bringing up this awful green bile. To explain further; when I was a youngster I had been diagnosed with Colitis, an extremely painful tummy condition which often meant I was unable to go to the loo. The chosen remedy for this condition at the time was for my mum to sprinkle raw bran purchased from the local pet shop all over whatever food we were eating for the day. Now this was what rabbits ate and to say it was repulsive and near impossible to swallow doesn't even begin to cover it! If I'd be made to eat sawdust, I'm sure it could not have tasted any worse. I don't recall sticking with this treatment for long.

I also remember in the past when I worked at Photo Precision as a Punch Card Operator being rushed into hospital on more than one occasion. I would experience a flare up once every 6–8 weeks. The pain was so bad I would inevitably be sick and again bring up a similar strange sort of green bile. This continued to affect me for six years in all until eventually when I was living in the mobile home, and after yet another bout of illness, I was finally diagnosed with grumbling appendix. I was rushed into hospital and my appendix was removed. I can honestly say that was one of the best things to happen to me as I was free from suffering from this type of debilitating pain for evermore.

On a further bright note, it was whilst living here that began a chain of events related to my love of stamp collecting. I had in my possession two of my original albums and a shoebox full of the stamps I had acquired over many years since my childhood. With nothing else to do in the winter months I began to take more of an interest again. I started to buy the latest issues of stamps and send first day covers addressed to myself.

Now there was a certain coincidence in this because at that time my married name was Patricia Machin. For those of you not in the know, the man who had designed the style of the Queen's head to feature on a stamp issued firstly in 1967 was called Arnold Machin. And just like me, his wife was named Patricia and she lived in Derby too!

Christmas 1979
Post Office First Day Cover

Arnold Machin OBE was born in November 1911 in the town of Stoke on Trent. He was a sculptor, artist, coin and stamp designer and he came from a long line of potters in the Stoke on Trent, Staffordshire area. My husband's family came from the adjoining area of Birmingham, which in those days was also classed as being in the County of Staffordshire. I am convinced there is a link between these two families, as Machin is quite an uncommon surname, although I have yet to find the exact connection. In the 1881 census in High Street, Burslem, there were four families with the surname Machin living next door to one another. Also, the two branches of the family share many of the same forenames. For example; Stirling's great uncle, born in 1875, was known as William Machin. Likewise, in Arnold's family, his father born in 1872, was also known as William James Machin. Often children would be named after parents, grandparents or aunts and uncles. When Alfred Machin, Stirling's Great Grandfather was born in 1841, in the same civil birth registration list there was a William Machin born in Stoke on Trent the same year. Arnold's son was called Francis Machin and I believe that Stirling's brothers have Francis and James as second names too. In addition, both families shared many creative talents, all being good with the use of their hands.

All that aside, it was around this time that Stirling's stepfather asked Stirling and I to go to the various auctions being held in the Wiltshire area. He wanted us to bid for items of silver that he was interested in, to sell on in his shops.

In 1978, at one of these auctions, I purchased for myself a job lot of a bundle of envelopes for not very much money I know. The majority of the envelopes either had Queen Victoria's British Guiana Jubilee stamps stuck on them or late Victorian British stamps stuck on them. Although I managed to mislay them for a long period of time, I've kept hold of them to this day. They became a part of my stamp collection but I didn't take a huge amount of notice of the envelopes at the time other than to read that they were chiefly addressed to either Mr Edward C Luard of La Bonne Intention Estate, Demerara, East Coast or to Mrs Edward C Luard or his solicitors at various addresses in England. In to a box they went, not to surface for another 40 years.

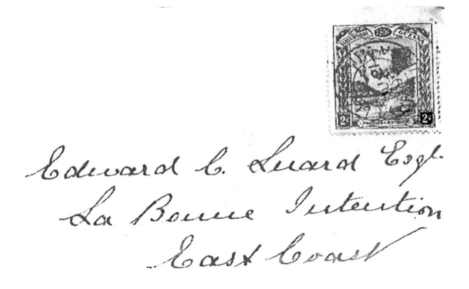

Stirling and I were now busy pulling out all the stops to finish the major works on our cottage in time to move in for Christmas 1979. And move in we did. We celebrated our achievement with our respective families over the Christmas period and the future looked good. But we weren't destined to find true happiness together in our little country cottage because soon someone else entered my life who I fell for hook, line and sinker. And this person was Arthur Morgan.

Chapter Seven
Arthur's Story

1937

British Coronation Stamp – King George VI And Queen Elizabeth

To understand the rather deep and complex character of the man that is Arthur William Morgan you would have to go back to his fairly harsh 'Victorian like' upbringing. His mother Lillian was born in Wellington, Somerset in 1902 and his father Francis was born in Richmond, Yorkshire in 1897.

I well remember Lillian being a rather dominating figure and she was not given to showing much love or affection towards her two children (or me for that matter!). It used to amuse me that she called Arthur, Arthur Morgan all the time as if she wasn't quite sure he really was her son!

Sadly, his father Francis died before I could meet him. I understand that he was a gentle and clever man raised in later years by his aunt and her husband Arthur Carver, because he was of illegitimate birth. When he was about 8 years of age, Francis's mother (Arthur's grandmother) Elizabeth Morgan had decided to get married. It appears to have been a condition from her new husband that Francis would not form part of his new stepfather's household. Arthur's grandmother went on to have 3 further children with this man.

Arthur was born in March, 1936 in Shepherds Bush, London and his twin sister Margaret was born some two days later. Following this second very protracted birth his mother was, understandably, not keen to have any more children. They were initially brought up in South Ealing, at 46 Creighton Road, which was a Victorian terraced house.

Arthur and his twin sister Margaret with their mother and father at Teignmouth in 1940.

In 1939 the 2nd World War began so at three years old, in early 1940, the family moved to Somerset leaving his father behind. At this time all children were being evacuated from London and Arthur still possesses the small brown suitcase that held his worldly possessions. His father worked for an engineering company in Acton and remained there in order to continue supporting the family.

The rest of the family came to live with Arthur's grandfather, William Flay (sadly his grandmother, Susan Flay had died before then) at his house in Springfield Road, Wellington. His grandfather was fairly elderly by then as Arthur's mother was the youngest of the three children, and he died in 1947.

Due to bomb damage to his father's works in Acton and the family home in South Ealing, his father then joined the family in Somerset in 1941. Shortly after Arthur's father arrived, they moved to The Manse at Norton Fitzwarren, which was a stone built detached property occupied by no less than three families. As a family they shared two rooms, one upstairs and one downstairs with a gas cooker in an alcove in the hallway. There was no heating, no mains water (there was a pump in the garden) and no electricity. They used oil lamps and used to go to bed by candlelight. The toilet was in the garden and although it was on mains sewerage there was no water to flush anything away so one had to take a bucket of water to flush it manually. The three families shared this facility, so times were tough!

Arthur first attended the primary school at Norton Fitzwarren but later changed to Corams Lane school in Wellington. He and his sister Margaret travelled daily by train to get there. Sadly, Margaret suffered from epilepsy from a young age, most likely due to such a difficult birth; eventually forceps were used in her delivery. She frequently visited the Great Ormond Street children's hospital in London for treatment but unfortunately there was no cure and it plagued her life thereafter. Arthur looked out for his sister for the majority of her life and when her marriage broke down, he took care of her until she died in 1999.

Their parents were relatively old as his father Francis was 38 years of age and his mother Lillian was 34 years of age when the twins were born. In fact, his father had served during the First World War at the Battle of Jutland and his amazing story is told elsewhere. Needless to say, Arthur remains proud of him to this day.

In 1947, Arthur won a scholarship to Wellington School, which he had difficulty settling into and quite frankly he tells me he couldn't wait to leave. The long Public-School hours, particularly with travelling times during the winter made for arduous days. Despite this, he managed to achieve a school certificate that is today the equivalent of 4 '0' levels. He did enjoy playing sport there, especially rugby and cricket.

During the school holidays he would catch the bus to a village close to his uncle's farm, that was tenanted and owned by the Roper family of nearby Forde Abbey. On the farm, Arthur would spend long days playing with his two cousins and no doubt getting up to all sorts of mischief.

When he left school, he adopted a Golden Labrador from the Vicar of Kingston St Mary and Marcus, as he named him, became his best friend. Arthur also met his first true love called Jean Baker who worked in a chemist shop but this relationship was not to last.

Knowing that he would be facing his National Service in two years' time Arthur took a job working for the Great Western Railway in the Telegraph Office, which he recalls as being a lot of fun. After that he went to work for the Bus Company for about a year.

In 1954 when he was 18 years of age, Arthur got called up to do his National Service with The Somerset Light Infantry. He did his basic training at the barracks called Jellabad located in Taunton and was there for 10 weeks during which time he learnt how to shoot, march and fight any given enemy.

Following two weeks' home leave, he found himself on a train to Liverpool where upon he transferred to a troop ship called Empire Clyde. The ship left Liverpool at 6 pm on Christmas Eve 1954 travelling down the Irish Sea straight into a Force 10 gale that continued all the way to Gibraltar. You cannot begin to imagine 1000 troops being seasick but a full description isn't warranted here (!)

Once passed Gibraltar they sailed through the Mediterranean and stopped in Port Said, Egypt and spent three days aboard there due to an accident between two ships colliding in the Suez Canal. Conditions were very hot and cramped but worse was to come.

They set off down through the Suez Canal into the Red Sea whereupon their troop ship engines failed and they were stranded aboard in temperatures exceeding 120 degrees below deck. So, most of them were glad to sleep on the top deck to get some respite. At least rations were good. It was a couple of days before the engines were repaired and they set sail again. Their next stop was Aden in the Middle East.

At last the troops could disembark and were allowed to go ashore for a short visit. This was Arthur's first time abroad and everything seemed very different and exotic to him then, especially the bazaars. They took on water and fuel. 36 hours later they set off across the Indian Ocean. Conditions were benign and he doesn't recall anyone being seasick at this point, Thank the Lord.

Their next port of call was Colombo in Ceylon (now known as Sri Lanka) but again they weren't allowed to disembark. Following this the troops finally arrived at Singapore after thirty-one days at sea. They then transferred to a transit camp and the next day were put on a train to Kuala Lumpur, which is the capital of Malaya. As they were now in a war zone, they had to have guards on each end of each carriage.

At this time, following the Second World War, the Chinese attempted to take over the country of Malaya. This started roughly in 1952 and didn't end until around 1961. Many of these communists were hiding out and fighting in the jungle. They were well equipped with guns (ironically) supplied by the British during the Japanese occupation of 1942 to 1945.

Arthur then joined the Somerset Light Infantry Battalion whereby he was interviewed to ascertain where his main strengths lay. It was suggested he become the clerk to A Company but being young, headstrong and possibly foolhardy he decided he would rather be an active soldier.

As a consequence, he was sent on a 6-week jungle training course at Jahore. After a couple of weeks there when he was spending more time in the jungle this was a bit of a wakeup call. Arthur decided to see whether the initial post of clerk to A Company was still open but was told he had had his chance!

Arthur tells me that the worst things about being in the jungle were the mosquitoes, the leeches that went right through any item of clothing and the constant heat and humidity.

At the end of six weeks training Arthur joined Support Company at a camp near the town of Bentong in the state of Pehang. The Support Company was made up of the Mortar Platoon, of which he was a part, the Machine Gun Platoon and the Pioneer Platoon.

Their Mortar Platoon consisted of approximately 30 soldiers and was commanded by a Lieutenant Ogilvy to whom everyone took an immediate dislike. There was also the Platoon Sergeant, Bob Hembrow, who had fought as a Chindit during the war and they all had a lot of respect for him, plus two Corporals. Arthur's rank was as Private.

30 Aug, 1955

Arthur in Malaya forming part of Guard of Honour for General Bourne

The Platoon had two functions; one was jungle patrols and the other was fighting with mortar bombs. The jungle patrols usually lasted 4 to 5 days, although sometimes they lasted as long as 10 days. This meant the soldiers were supplied rations and rum by parachute. Each night they took off their wet clothes in exchange for the one set of dry clothes in their backpacks. It was at this point they burnt the fat leeches off their bodies. The following morning back on would go the wet clothes from the day before. One-night Arthur had an unwelcome visitor in the shape of a large snake that slithered over the bottom of his legs. He has had a distinct dislike of snakes ever since, although it was unusual to have sight of these reptiles.

They would camp at 5.30 in the morning and were dropped off by a rubber plantation to enter the jungle before daylight so, hopefully no-one was aware they were in there. On these jungle patrols Arthur carried a Bren gun and it was extremely heavy. Through intelligence they were trying to locate the enemy camps. He had to discharge his Bren gun on several occasions and he tells me his saddest memory is when one of their soldiers died due to friendly fire. By this he meant one of their own soldiers accidentally killed him. They wore hats with different colours on for each particular day so they could be identified and the Gurkhas who fought alongside did the same. But the jungle was so thick it wasn't always easy to discern the enemy and the communists wore similar style hats too.

On one such patrol they came upon what they later learned to be a camp used by Colonel Spencer Chapman. He had spent three and half years in the jungle during the war fighting the Japanese with the help of Chinese guerrillas. Now the British were fighting the Chinese. His wartime experiences are told in an excellent book called 'The Jungle is Neutral' and it is well worth reading.

The Platoon's second aim was to set up 3 mortars by the side of a road, usually at night and they would fire approximately 1000 bombs into a certain area where it was thought the enemy was in hiding.

On one occasion the Royal Artillery were firing shells from one end of a large area and The Somerset Light Infantry were firing mortar bombs from a different direction. Then a Canberra Bomber dropped bombs in the same area too. It was the first time this plane had ever been used in open warfare.

The sound of the mortars going off was deafening and it was Arthur's job to load them into the barrel and once the mortar hit the bottom, off it went, in very close proximity to his head. There were no ear defenders in those days, hence the reason he is now profoundly deaf.

Every few months the soldiers had rest and recuperation and went to a place at Kuantan on the east coast of Malaya for a week. All they had to do was a few chores in the morning and the rest of the day was theirs. This is where Arthur saw his first giant turtles on the beach.

1954-1956 Arthur taking centre stage!

He also went on leave to Penang Island, which was very beautiful, and spent time in Singapore. Like every other tourist, he went to the Long Bar at the renowned Raffles Hotel.

This was much needed light relief because there were several times when the they came under fire from the Communist Guerrillas and sadly they lost one of their Platoon, a Geordie called Smudger Smith. Arthur attended 3 funerals in all held in the Military Cemetery in Kuala Lumpur. One of their grislier duties was to retrieve the dead bodies of the enemy that had to be taken back to camp for identification purposes.

It was a great relief when his two years National Service came to an end and their return journey was much easier than the outward one. He came home on the troop ship called the Devonshire and eventually received his Campaign Medal, the GSM.

Arthur on his return from Malaysia

When Arthur got back to the barracks in Plymouth, he contracted Glandular Fever and spent about a week in the Naval Hospital before going home on sick leave. In those days Glandular Fever was considered contagious and so he had to spend time in isolation. He then returned to Plymouth and was sent to a place called Millom in Cumbria on a civil defence course. Despite the beginning of the Cold War he didn't take the contents of the course very seriously; What to do in the event of a Nuclear War. He was then finally demobbed.

Back in Norton Fitzwarren Arthur had to try and piece his life back together. He re-joined the Bus company as a clerk as they were under a duty to keep your job open for you during National Service. That didn't last long as he didn't like being in an office. So, he took a job selling electrical goods, mainly televisions, twin tubs, and radiograms, as these had just become popular. This was in a shop in Taunton.

He had his fair share of girlfriends before he met his first wife Shirley. She worked as a nurse at the Old Taunton Hospital and he just happened to be a patient there because of undergoing an operation on his knee. Arthur asked her out and they got married about a year later. Stephen, their son, was born in 1959 and they lived in Taunton.

Unfortunately, that marriage wasn't to last and Arthur met his second wife Heather in 1961, who just happened to walk past the electrical shop on a frequent basis. They eventually got married and Arthur was then promoted to manager of another store within the John James Group, based in Honiton. Heather also worked for the John James group in a store in Exeter, in charge of the records and L P's section. Their son Timothy was born in Honiton in 1967.

Arthur first started playing golf at Honiton Golf Club and remains in contact with many friends he made there until this day. He managed to acquire a not too shabby handicap of 12.

Shortly after Timothy was born, Arthur got a job with Western Credit who were owned by Farleys Rusks and Hambros Bank. He worked at the Taunton branch. Hence, the family moved to Upper Cheddon and Timothy went to Kingston school. Then his youngest son Jonathan was born in 1969 at Musgrove Park Hospital. And so their family was complete.

In the early 1970s they moved to Swindon where Arthur became manager of the local branch of Western Trust & Savings. He also became a member at Marlborough Golf Club. It was in Swindon where he met me, his third wife, Patricia, known as Pat or Patsy. With some trepidation, he has given permission to let me relate the rest of our story.

Chapter Eight
Moving On

1980

London International Stamp Exhibition 50 pence

Whilst still married to Stirling, I began to find my work in Registrations a bit tedious. I was also getting restless at home as we had moved into our dream cottage and completing the work in doors was coming to an end. Stirling was by now toying with the idea of building a further extension to the rear of the cottage. I must admit to not being too enthusiastic about this idea.

And so, began my foray into Music and Movement. I had loved to dance, albeit mainly of the disco type with a bit of ballroom thrown in, since I was a teenager but Stirling had two left feet and then some. I recall how, with a massive amount of persuasion, I had signed us both up for some ballroom dancing lessons. But whilst I glided around the floor partnering the male teacher with very little effort, Stirling possessed no rhythm whatsoever. I frequently ended up with two bruised feet. So, ditching this attempt to join the 'Come Dancing' crowd, I enrolled with a class that did a form of moving to music unlike anything I had done before.

Our teacher was a very imaginative soul and I soon realised that there were lots of these all lady groups around the country. Our class entered a competition to perform at the Royal Albert Hall (RAH) doing a piece to *'Pomp and Circumstance.'* This involved some ambitious lifts and lots of swathes of red, white and blue ribbons which were meant to end up signifying the Union Jack. I personally thought this routine would look great from an aerial view in the RAH. As I was still rake thin at that time, I was the one that got to go up in the air. My head for heights has never been the same since. Alas, we didn't qualify for the final and so any bids for lasting fame died in that moment. The next show we put on was to the music of War of the Worlds. This is still one of my favourite records to this day. Justin Hayward's, *Forever Autumn* is such a contrast to the rest of the album too. I also adore Richard Burton's deep voice telling the story in such an emphatic way. I had three roles to play, one was being a Red Weed, secondly, I was part of a crowd but thirdly, my starring role was that of the lead of the Tripods. We had to wear these specially made leotards and goodness knows what we must have looked like as these silver costumes hugged every contour of our bodies. But hey, the music was so great I don't think anyone took much notice.

I was also learning to drive and that was a challenge in Swindon. You may not have heard of this but there is a roundabout like no other in the country situated in this railway town. It was affectionately known as the Magic Roundabout. There was no centre to speak off but it was made up of about six smaller roundabouts forming a huge circle. In addition, you could drive through the middle of the outside lanes of these roundabouts, should you feel brave enough to do so. As to who is giving way to whom was more luck than judgement. I had to cross this dreadful conglomeration in my driving test. I'm not sure who was more scared, me or the test inspector.

I did fail my first test due to a ridiculous way (in my view) of learning to reverse around a corner. According to my instructor you had to judge a pavement's width in the rear window before turning the wheel and all would be well. Yet when I came to my test there was a shop set back on the chosen corner with no fence boundary to show this ideal pavement's width! I knew as soon as I turned the wheel, I was going to mount the pavement. And mount the pavement I did. Getting hot and bothered I asked the test inspector whether I should attempt the manoeuvre again. He sternly said, 'You're the driver.' So, I tried it again, trying to estimate this imaginary pavement's width and proceeded to mount the pavement for a second time. I knew then I'd failed miserably. Still success was to be had on my second test attempt.

Then began my search for a new job. In those days there always seemed to be lots of employment opportunities and the thought of not being successful, without hopefully sounding too big-headed, never entered my head. I spotted an advertisement for a job working for Western Trust & Savings Ltd, who at that time were part of the Royal Bank of Canada. The job itself was described as banking clerk based in the Swindon branch of the firm. This was a new concept in banking with open plan branches and folks being interviewed for new current accounts, savings accounts and loans in the front office. You had to have the required number of '0' levels to apply, yet even this criterion did not deter me. I rang up and spoke to the branch manager who said he had already short-listed applicants for the job. Yet something made him hesitate and he agreed to see me that Friday evening after I'd finished work.

That particular evening Stirling and I were going up to Cambridgeshire to visit my family for the weekend, so whilst Stirling sat in the car, I made my grand and confident entrance into the branch office—and into the life of the branch manager, Arthur Morgan. We sat and chatted about all and sundry and it was one of the most informal interviews I've ever attended. We got on really well together, although I had to confess to my lack of academic qualifications. I sold myself by saying that I had passed relevant tests in both maths and English at Hambro Life Assurance and went on to describe my previous Accountancy and Visual Display Unit experience.

Arthur said he would need to consider my application along with the others. He would let me know the outcome early on in the following week. And, lo and behold, I was successful! I was so pleased to be changing jobs. Then, whilst serving my notice I began training the person who had applied for my job. Funnily enough, I discovered she had come from Western Trust & Savings, and I was taking up her position! Naturally, I was really surprised about this and I did have some misgivings as to why she was leaving the place I was going to, as it all seemed a bit vague. When I asked if she knew Arthur Morgan, she nodded wisely and said, 'Oh yes, I know Arthur Morgan,' but wouldn't say any more than that.

In my first week at my new job in January 1980, I soon learnt that Arthur had a low tolerance level. Should anything be amiss, then Rosie his assistant would be the first to know about it, following his usual semi anguished cry of

'Rosie, what's gone on here?' She was a lovely petite young lady with long blonde hair and big blue eyes and for some reason she seemed to be his whipping post. She had the most patient of natures and would just shrug her shoulders saying she didn't know what had gone on, until Arthur registered actually nothing had gone on at all. It (whatever 'it' was) was not as he'd first thought. Rosie, whose surname was Rainbow, and I became great friends and a more loyal colleague to Arthur I've never known. Oddly enough he did possess that ability to inspire folks to be loyal to him.

Within my first week, he took it upon himself to show me how to credit score a new loan application that had come in. Now I had never heard of this kind of rating system and to be fair to me, he didn't explain anything about it, so I must have seemed a bit slow to begin with. I think he wondered whether he had made a mistake in taking me on but once I grasped the meaning of it all my confidence grew and I loved the job. Each day was different. Despite not possessing any of the qualifications the others had, I soon realised I appeared to be the only teller who knew how to work out percentages without the aid of a calculator and do the maths in my head. I was soon bringing in the business and opening new accounts on a daily basis. I enjoyed the interaction with the customers and life was great.

But pride comes before a fall as they say. It was a Saturday afternoon and I was paying out a loan of £3,000 to a middle-aged couple who lived on the outskirts of town. Well, I had the total sum ready and following procedure, I had another member of staff watch me count out the payment of cash. Then as I'm ready to put it all into an envelope the customer asked if I could change some of the notes into other denominations. It was during this process that I must have got muddled up with the amounts received back and then given out. Unfortunately, this further transaction wasn't witnessed as my colleague had gone to answer the phone. Thankfully, I had recorded all of the notes I'd exchanged as requested but didn't register my mistake until I was cashing up at the end of the day. I was £500 short in my till. I felt sick. I counted and recounted my cash sheets and monies left over. Then, when I looked at the back of the loan cheque that had been cashed earlier that day, I saw where the error lay.

To my huge relief Arthur wasn't in that afternoon but Sue, who was the most senior cashier at the time, took the matter in hand. She rang the couple up who were back home by then and we arranged to go and see them. I'll never forget sitting at their kitchen table explaining the situation. Well they got the remainder of the monies out as they'd already spent some of the balance and it appeared at first that they were not admitting to having received £500 more than they should have done. By this time, I'd gone deathly white and felt faint until the woman realised that they had been in to some place or another and had put a £500 deposit down, on what I can't recall. I was in tears by this time with gratitude that they had at least registered my error and were willing to return the additional monies. This was a good lesson for me to learn because quite frankly I was probably a bit of a cocky young thing and this taught me to be more vigilant. When Arthur learnt what I had done he was fine about it but whether he would have been if the money hadn't been returned, I am not so sure.

The days went by and the only weird thing in working at Western Trust was I remember feeling slightly uncomfortable whenever Arthur was present in the office. I didn't have a clue as to why. I actually felt relieved that he was out a lot of the time. He had lots of management meetings that always meant a couple of days away including golf at some venue or other and at other times he was out visiting business clients. At 45 years of age he was a very charming man but not in a 'stick your fingers down your throat' kind of way. He took a real interest in anyone he met and with dark curly hair, tanned skin and brown eyes he wasn't bad looking either. He certainly looked a lot younger than his age.

I was totally unprepared for when Cupid struck. That particular day I was completing some filing at a cabinet situated in front of the manager's desk at the back of the office. Well I happened to glance up and at the same time Arthur happened to be looking in my direction. And wham (for want of a better description) I felt as though I'd been hit by a bolt of lightning. I was mesmerised by him and just stood there like a rabbit in headlights. After coming over all unnecessary I rushed out the back to the loo to try and recover myself, but things were never the same again. I was acutely aware of his presence all of the time and went out of my way to look the best I could at work. To my extreme embarrassment now, I recall the following summer cycling into work from our cottage in Shaw, arriving in shorts and a small top all flushed and breathless. Blimey, Barbara Cartland couldn't have described me any better!

To Arthur's credit he didn't fall for my charms immediately. I think I should set the record straight by saying that Arthur was married with two teenage boys at this time and I cannot believe that I made such a brazen play for him. I was so besotted and in love with him it was as though I didn't care. I consoled my guilty conscience with the fact that I wasn't the first woman he had had an affair with.

Indeed, I later learnt that I was at the end of a number of affairs and how his wife coped with this behaviour I will never know.

We started seeing one another after the Christmas Do in 1980. Arthur gave me a lift home and unexpectedly he kissed me good night. I was on cloud nine. Following this, the secrecy of our illicit meetings just seemed to emphasise our passion for one another. But he told me quite clearly that there was no way he would be leaving his wife and children for me. As I worked Saturdays, I was able to have a day off during the week so we were able to continue our liaison without too much worry and spent delightful days off together. One sunny day we made love naked on the edge of a field much to the surprise of the pilot in a passing light aircraft that did a double fly pass. On another occasion I pretended to Stirling that I was going to visit my relatives in Stourbridge for a couple of days. I spent the first night with Arthur in the Cotswolds before turning up as an unexpected visitor at my aunt's house in Kidderminster to spend the second night there and give some credence to my lies. She was not without her suspicions I have to say. Arthur had tied up his getting away with a golf trip but I'm pretty sure he didn't play his best golf the next day.

One night after going for a drink with Arthur to a local pub, I set off for home and being unfamiliar with the road took a right-hand bend at some speed and ended up in a ditch. This wouldn't have been so bad if I hadn't found the only tree growing in this ditch that managed to carve a large 'V' shape into the front of my bonnet. I had not had this fairly new Mini for long and I was truly shaken up. I then had some explaining to do as to why I was even driving along this road, as I should have been returning from my Music and Movement lesson. I'm not sure anyone was too convinced by my 'cock and bull' story.

Then eventually, at a party at Arthur's house, we were discovered in a passionate embrace on the landing by his wife. My husband was devastated but didn't realise yet how serious things were for me, and Arthur's wife was understandably very hurt and angry too. Somehow, Arthur managed to convince her that our relationship wasn't anything special and nothing was really going on. Yet I knew deep inside it was special to me.

Stirling was prepared for him and I to carry on together and he convinced me to go on holiday with him. So off we went to Crete in August of that year. Yet despite this being our first holiday since our honeymoon in Scotland, and first holiday abroad together, it was to no avail. We were trying to pretend things were all right but we had a gulf between us that was difficult to bridge. All I could think of was Arthur at home. Shortly after our return I made the decision to break up with Stirling because I didn't think he deserved to be with someone who didn't love him as they should do.

Thankfully around this time, I was head-hunted by a Chartered Surveyor called Frank who used to visit our branch to undertake property surveys in respect of our secured loans. He needed someone to work in a new Estate Agent's office that he and his partners were opening in North Swindon. And in terms of my career this was an enormous door opening for me. Frank was inspirational and sometimes he used to take me out with him when he undertook structural surveys. I found the work so interesting, I decided this was the way forward for me.

I really enjoyed being involved in this new set up and began by typing up the details of new properties taken on to sell and then accompanying interested parties on viewings in the hope of making a sale. I had really found my forte. After a couple of years' experience I was going out and valuing domestic properties myself. Thus, began my long academic journey to become a general practice surveyor. I attended evening classes for two years in order to gain three '0' levels and one 'A' level. I also gained a merit in Construction Drawing, which was another evening class I thought would come in useful. I think I must have inherited some of my Dad's drawing abilities and found it really enjoyable.

In my personal life, when I first joined Cox & Billingham, I was well placed to look for another house to live in. When I split from Stirling, I knew he would wish to keep the cottage that he had put some much care and effort into. Unfortunately, he couldn't wholly afford to buy me out. With this in mind I had to purchase an older Victorian property in need of renovation and Stirling agreed to undertake some of the necessary works. In one sense this was a big mistake as we were still seeing one another on a regular basis. His heartache was beginning to turn into resentment. In another sense though I ended up introducing him to my young neighbour who he eventually married and with whom they had, at the last count some six children together!

It was whilst he was doing some decorating for me that Jenny spotted Stirling walking down my path. 'Who's he?' she asked, really interested. Well that's my ex-husband I told her. Thinking I was doing them both a favour, I offered to treat Stirling to a meal to thank him for doing the work on my new home and I invited Jenny along too. Well they got on like a house on fire but I have to say it was very strange when Jenny invited us both in for coffee on our return. I refused but he accepted! And that was the start of a beautiful relationship for them both. This happy outcome was about the only thing that salves my conscience over my dire treatment of my very first dear husband.

Our divorce came through in March 1982 around the time of the Falklands War; the latter had the whole country in a frenzied state of fear and excitement. It was one of the first times that I recall war being so vividly portrayed live on television, which made it seem unreal somehow. Argentina had threatened to take back the Falkland Islands which were classed as British Territory. Thankfully for the people of these islands our defence of them came good. Sadly, the sinking of the Belgrano brought about many casualties so this war was not without its heavy price—on both sides. Maggie (Margaret) Thatcher, who was Britain's first elected lady Prime Minister, was in office and a more formidable woman to come up against, you wouldn't have wished to have known.

It was also around this time that Ice Dance skaters Jayne Torvill and Christopher Dean (from my home town of Nottingham) became Ice Dance World and European Champions, then two years later in 1984 Ice Dance Olympic Champions. Their routines to the music from Mac and Mable and Bolero have become legendary to us Brits. I for one never tire of seeing them.

Where was Arthur during this time? Well, he was asked to open a new branch of Western Trust in Cheltenham but our separation didn't last long. Within months we began seeing one another again, albeit, on his terms. I actually put up with him visiting me on his way home from work, fitting me in on fleeting visits on my day off and of course with no commitment to change the way things were. We did get to go out together on occasion but not very often. He seemed very taken up with his new life and new colleagues and friends in Cheltenham.

I began to realise I would have to make some sort of separate life for myself so I started to go out on a platonic basis with a guy called Chris. He intimated that he would like us to become an item but I was still infatuated with Arthur so that idea was soon squashed. Together we would play pitch and putt of a summer's evening and at weekends we would go out somewhere as company for one another. On one outing we visited the Arboretum in Gloucestershire where the Army had a display wall erected for anyone who wished to go climbing up and abseiling down. So, as a dare, yours truly decided to give it a go. Nothing to do with those rather fit young soldiers giving you a leg up or a hand down, I hear you say!

Because cats had played a large part in my earlier life, I found a pair of kittens who were the best company ever. They were both ginger Toms and I named them Bubble and Squeak. One was more adventurous than the other and sadly he was only young when he got run over. I found him dead by the front door. I was so upset. As I sat there crying and cuddling the surviving kitten, he actually began to lick my tears as if to say, don't worry you still have me! He may well have been after the salt but it wasn't long before Bubble became known as Bubbly Boy. He was truly the soppiest cat I have ever owned. He was pure mush—with a capital M.

And as ever when going through tricky times I found solace in my stamps. I've often thought of them as some kind of comfort blanket under which I could lose myself for hours at a time. In addition to this I found a guardian angel living next door but one, in the shape of a dear lady called Nita. In her late fifties, this cherub faced, slightly rotund, salt of the earth woman had a heart of gold and took me under her wing. Her generosity of spirit and joy for life was incomparable with anyone else I've ever known. When she learnt about my passion for stamps, with no hesitation, she gave me her collection that included examples from South America, the Middle East and Europe. It was years before I integrated her stamps with mine because somehow, they were always known as Nita's stamps. When I went through an especially bleak patch later on in my

106

life, she was the one to pull me through it, even though she was not aware of her influence at that time.

In November 1982, I went on holiday with friends to Marbella and all I could think about was Arthur. I really don't know how they put up with me. I have photographic evidence of us on a beach, me sporting my latest perm, trying to smile and look as though I was enjoying myself for the camera. We did have a bit of an adventure whilst there though. One day the five of us decided we should go off for a day trip somewhere. Four of us voted to go to Tangier for the day, yet my friend Marion wanted to go to visit Seville. Now Seville wasn't deemed exciting enough for the rest of us so Tangier became the chosen destination. We were sold tickets to travel by boat and visit the local souks. As a consequence, we showed all five of our passports, albeit three of them were one-year visas, in order to make the transaction.

The following day off we sailed on the boat from the South of Spain to the North of Africa, which seemed a really exotic thing to do. When we arrived in the port of Tangier, we all had to produce our passports to be allowed to continue with our excursion. Unfortunately for us political relations were not good between our British Queen and the King of North Africa, although for the life of me I can't recall why. As a result, the three of us holding our annual passports were not allowed to disembark. Worse still they confiscated our papers and we were left on the boat under the guard of a man with a rifle over his shoulder. It just happened to be myself, my friend Marion who hadn't even wanted to visit Tangier (!) and her lover Gerry. Well she was spitting feathers to say the least. The temperature got hotter and hotter as it hit midday and we worried whether we would be formally arrested and held captive for good. Marion glibly suggested I might be taken away and sold to a white slave trader, which did little to relieve my anxiety. Eventually some African guy came and demonstrated that he could get us a drink if we wished. We had little choice but to hand over some cash and hope he'd return as promised. Well he did thank goodness and that was the best can of orange juice I've ever drunk. Nothing more happened for the rest of the day and the hours dragged by. We were so pleased to see the return of the others, retrieve our passports and get back to the relative safety of Marbella. That was a lesson hard learnt.

Then Arthur did the unthinkable. He had a dream about me one night and started talking in his sleep. This obviously did not bode well for his relationship with his wife and he finally confessed to her that we were still seeing one another.

So, she did the only wise thing she could ever have done and threw him out. Well, all of my hopes and dreams, or so I thought, were going to be realised. However, instead of him rushing over to be with me, he went off to stay at a friend's house in Cheltenham. I was perplexed, very hurt and really upset. Deep down this is what I had been hoping for all along and it wasn't going to plan.

In fact, I think Arthur was so shell shocked at the break up it took him some time to come to terms with the situation. He suddenly realised what he had lost and then began his campaign to blame me for what had happened. I really don't know how I lived through that period. You may well be thinking I deserved all of the unhappiness I got but I was still holding out for some dream future that was now not going to materialise.

Arthur did move in with me after several weeks but carried on as he had done before, in as much as he went off on his golfing trips without any consideration for me, he flirted outrageously with the girls in the Cheltenham office and ignored me entirely when I turned up at his birthday celebration with Rosie and another friend Linda. It was like he was trying to lash out at me for all of the hurt he was feeling. One time he went off to Devon and I thought he was coming home that night and he didn't bother to ring to say he wasn't. I spent all night worrying as to whether he had had an accident until in the early hours I rang up his friend's house and got a very frosty reception from his friend's wife telling me Arthur had decided to stay the night. I felt dreadful going into work the next morning as I'd had little sleep. I wondered if I could take any more of his poor behaviour. On top of all this he would take different women out to lunch and treat them with more respect than he ever did me. He finally admitted he was deliberately trying to make me jealous and I soon realised this was a very destructive side to our relationship.

And then came another bomb shell. Arthur and the whole tier of management at his level were made redundant. The Royal Bank of Canada had sold the business on and the company that took over decided that the branches could still work with only the assistant managers running them. This redundancy knocked Arthur for six. All of his previous security had disappeared, together with his carefree lifestyle, and he really didn't cope well at all.

We had a massive row one lunch time as he was out of work and I'm guessing he was feeling sorry for himself. He said he didn't get this sort of aggravation from his wife, so in a rage I suggested he go back to her then. When I returned home from work that evening there on the kitchen work surface was a note to say that that was what he had done. It was bizarre really because my initial reaction was one of pure relief. Needless to say, this feeling didn't last long because despite everything I was still obsessively in love with him. I took some time off work and slowly sank into the depths of despair. I just didn't want to get up in the morning and didn't know how to function without him being a part of my life any more. I even rang him at home one time to ask him whether he now had what he wanted. I had no self-respect left whatsoever.

Frank, one of the partners from work, was wonderful and truly understanding of my predicament. No-one at work, aside from my little YTS (Youth Training Scheme) friend, Teresa, knew who I was dating because I had kept his name a secret. It was a bit of a standing joke as my immediate boss Andrew called him Mr X, yet I still didn't share his identity with anyone else. Teresa was a brick and listened for hours on end whilst I went on and on about how desolate, hurt and let down I felt. I remember one day bumping into Arthur in the local post office and as my heart began beating really fast, all I could do was leave the queue and run away from him.

1982

Teresa and I at Rosie's wedding (we've remained friends to this day)

And then slowly, I began trying to pick up the pieces. As I had enjoyed pitch and putt so much with my friend Chris, I started to have golf lessons at the local municipal golf club and driving range. I was hooked and spent three months developing a swing before I felt ready to go out and play the course. To my surprise I was reasonably good at it and won the Novice Trophy in my first event. Having never been that competent at sport I had found my niche and realised there were all manner of chaps willing and ready to give me some additional coaching! Things were looking ever so slightly up.

I dated a guy called Alf but my heart wasn't really in it; although I did happen to bump into Arthur at the driving range when I was with Alf, I don't think Arthur liked seeing me with him one bit. Finally, a role reversal!

In early summer I went down to Torquay to stay with our mutual friend Linda for a few days and Arthur happened to ring her up whilst I was there. Well Linda went to town telling him she had seen me recently and I was fine. She said the boys were buzzing around me 'like bees round a honey pot' (slight exaggeration I know) but I think she was trying to make him see what he'd been missing.

And I'm guessing he was missing me because not long after this he came to see me to ask whether I would take him back. He had finally realised that his relationship with his wife was beyond repair and his boys had their own lives to lead. After all, he had hardly been a pipe and slippers kind of guy so when he had returned back home to them his boys carried on as normal, doing what they always did, thinking I'm sure that he would do the same. I do know that he has never truly forgiven himself for the hurt he caused his family. And for that matter neither have I.

But with much apprehension, some conditions, and lots of reassurances I agreed to take him back. Arthur arrived with his tool box. Now this was rather amusing because I wasn't sure whether he knew how to use any of the contents. I thought things must be serious. He helped me buy some decent furniture for the sitting room and he set up an office in our front room because after losing his job he had gone self employed as a financial consultant.

He also helped me to decorate the rear bedroom. Well this was a feat in itself but wanting to do it properly, after fiddling around with the pipework, he decided to lay the radiator down on the floor so we could paper behind it. Unfortunately, during this manoeuvre, Arthur had managed to split the pipe ever so slightly and then water began to spurt out and down between the floorboards. Luckily, my ex-husband Stirling was now going out with Jenny next door and he happened to be in with her at the time. I ran around to ask him for his help much to Arthur's chagrin. It was a bit like that 1980s comedy T V programme called '*My wife next door*', albeit Stirling only stayed over for the odd night or two with Jenny as he would not give up his beloved cottage for anyone. So, Stirling came to our rescue with the leaking pipework. I swear he felt rather smug about doing this.

Meanwhile, Arthur hadn't realised how hooked on golf I'd become in his absence and suggested I join Marlborough Golf Club; or else we'd never see one another! He even joined in with the Mixed Golf competitions, and he and I managed to win the odd trophy. We also played in mixed matches together and visited many different courses in the Wiltshire area. It was whilst at Marlborough Golf Club that I was to meet a girl who would become a very close friend for many years.

I had entered a ladies' competition and was right at the end of the field waiting for a lady called Mary who was meant to be joining me, to turn up. I was pacing up and down on the tee, patience not being my strongest suit, when an out of breath attractive blond ran over with her clubs, apologising for being late. I was not impressed but I learnt that she had delivered her two sons to Badminton on the way and then upon arrival realised she had forgotten her golf shoes. So, she had had to buy a new pair. What a scatterbrain I was thinking to myself. Anyhow, we took the golf seriously but while waiting on the 5th tee, I suddenly thought how she reminded me of someone I used to work with at Hambro Life. I remarked upon this and said, 'Well this girl I used to work with was Polish and called Maria.' Mary looked at me amazed. 'That's my younger sister,' she said! You could have knocked me down with a feather.

And thus began our on/off journey through life together. I supported her through her divorce, her husband regrettably went off with another women, and we spent hours putting the world to rights over the years. I was delighted when she met this chap called Daniel, whose father she had worked for when she was a teenager. Eventually they got married. This was one of the best weddings I've ever been to for copious quantities of champagne. There were only eight of us to celebrate these late nuptials in life and we drank champagne from early morning till nearing midnight. Surprisingly, I didn't have a hangover but perhaps over the length of a day and evening, I drank myself sober again. I've digressed, *again!*

Actually the comedian Ronnie Corbett used to do this rather well. He'd begin to tell a story, go off on a tangent and then come back to finish his original story at the end. The main difference between him and me was that he could always remember what he was talking about in the first instance. He was also much funnier. Gosh, we did watch some great comedies in the 80s. Another of my favourites was 'Only Fools and Horses' in which actor David Jason was hilarious, especially in his famous leaning on the (missing) bar scene. Ronnie Barker in 'Porridge' and Frank Spencer in 'Some Mothers Do 'ave 'em' were other great series. I think we were spoilt for choice.

In the summer of 1984 Arthur and I had our first magical holiday together in a place called Calpe situated in southern Spain. My head for heights was sorely tested as we climbed to the top of the volcanic rock located there. We also visited the local town of Guandalest, this too was perched precariously on top of a rocky mountain.

Who was this reformed man? By now Arthur was aged 48 and I was aged 28 but our age difference didn't matter to me at all. In the early days Arthur was always more conscious of our age gap but he was and always has been so young in his thinking and relatively fit and able. Now enough of the trials and tribulations of our early years together but you can see it was hardly the ideal start.

After nearly five years of working at Cox & Billingham the partners had a huge disagreement as to how best to run the business. The office that I had helped set up was transferred to one of them, whilst the remaining three partners continued to operate out of the main Swindon office. Then the father fell out with his son together with Frank, the chartered surveyor who had been the inspiration for all of my studies. And then, my boss and I were made redundant. Finally Frank and the son had a disagreement and the whole partnership disintegrated.

Swindon, an old railway town at the time of my arrival was, during the 80s, to become the fastest growing town in Europe, with all manner of new firms springing up along the M4 corridor. It boasted the largest expansion of housing in the West, mainly due to the ripple effect out from the towns of Reading and Newbury.

Hence, I had to decide what to do next. It was deemed that I had the necessary experience and qualifications to begin a part-time two-year surveying course at Reading College. Once completed and having sat more exams, this new qualification was recognised as the equivalent to level one at chartered surveyor status. I had also joined the Incorporated Society of Valuers and Auctioneers (I.S.V.A) as a student member in the hope of gaining their qualification too.

However, attending college meant I had to get a Friday off work. I finally decided that I would try temporary work and began a temporary contract with Texaco UK Ltd dealing with their customer accounts. Before being allowed to join the firm, I had to have a medical. It was then that my own personal inherent defect was discovered; I had a crooked spine. Now funnily enough, in 1986, I was able to truthfully say that my kypho scoliosis had never given me a day's trouble in my life; although this enviable position was not to last.

For the foreseeable future, I undertook to do five days work in four long days and then had Fridays off to attend college. At this time, I was driving an old second hand car as I had to return my company car when I left the Estate Agents. Arthur remained in possession of a huge square automatic BMW, built like a tank.

In the winter months Arthur decided that as he was working from home, I should drive his car up to Reading College as it would hopefully prove more reliable on the motorway. One frosty morning, I set off down the narrow alleyway behind my house. Not being a morning person, I took the rather tight corner too close to the left-hand side. As a result, the car got jammed against the edge of the concrete block wall. Try as I might I couldn't seem to go forward nor backward. I got hotter and hotter. Then with a loud, graunching sound I managed to drive forward leaving some of the body paint and possibly some of the metal work behind on the aforementioned wall.

In a state of panic, I drove all the way to Reading and could not concentrate on my lessons at all. Eventually one of the tutors asked me if anything was wrong and bursting into tears, I told him, between sobs, of the earlier accident with my partner's car. My tutor suggested I ring Arthur from the office because as he rightly pointed out, there was no point in my being there if I wasn't going to pay attention. I have to say Arthur took the news surprisingly well but it did take a while for me to live that particular incident down.

After about a year at Texaco my contract wasn't renewed. Not because my work was unsatisfactory but my colleagues had gotten fed up with having to answer my phone when I wasn't in on a Friday. So, I left there and went to work, on a temporary basis as a secretary to one of the bosses at Intel Corporation, one of the giant computer firms. My new boss was happy for me to continue on a four days a week basis. I was offered a full-time job there but my heart was set on becoming a surveyor. When my two years of part time study at Reading was up, I took six weeks unpaid leave from temporary work in order to prepare for the I.S.VA.'s exams. I had been sent some past papers and the contents made me realise how unprepared I was! I revised day after day until the week of my eight exams arrived. These included the subjects of valuation, economics, building construction, contract, tort and property law, accounts, land surveying and planning with its associated history and legislation. Bearing in mind I had followed another curriculum at college it was with some trepidation that I set off to Bristol to sit my exam's.

I will never forget my first exam which was the subject of different Valuation methods and formulae plus influencing factors. As was customary I felt sick with nerves. Upon opening the paper all reason fled and I nearly fled too, out of the examination room. Instead of taking time to look through the whole paper, all I could see was the first question. This related to understanding the Investment Valuation formulae when applied to rental properties and involved taking the formulae apart and explaining how it worked. As I read and re-read the question, I couldn't understand what it all meant, such was my anxious state of mind. After about 20 minutes of nervous flux I decided I wasn't brave enough to walk out, and with another two hours 40 minutes to go I began reading the rest of the paper. And bingo, there was a question I could answer. Off I went; scribbling furiously trying to make up time. I then went back to the first question in a much calmer state and managed to answer that one too. To my sheer amazement I passed the exam!

A week and eight three-hour exams later, I felt like my brain was full of cotton wool yet I was so full of adrenaline I couldn't sleep. And then I was exhausted and full of temporary relief that my first level of exams was over. Returning to college my tutors decided I should also take the Chartered

Surveyors Level One exams. This I did managing to get a pass in this curriculum too.

I can't begin to tell you how proud I felt in undertaking this academic work (and yes, I know pride is one of the seven deadly sins). But as a reminder, I did leave school with no qualifications at all. To achieve these passes whilst still working full time was, I think, testament to my sheer determination and hard work. I think being a mature student helped in a way because I was not only paying to take these exams, I had a positive goal at the end of it all.

1988

Celebrating my passes with Mum and Dad for Level One on both Chartered Surveyor and I.S.V.A Curricula

Arthur meanwhile put up with me studying evenings and weekends and continued to work from home on a self-employed basis.

It was during this period that we took Arthur's youngest son, Jonathan then aged 16, together with his friend, on holiday with us to Sitges in Spain. It is a super destination boasting a fabulous long beach with an Art Deco styled hotel at one end situated next to a golf course. Arthur and I had been there once before and played golf with some of the residents at the hotel. With two independent teenagers, this wasn't a golfing holiday but we gave them some space to do their own thing. To Jonathan's credit he did not seem at all resentful towards me, for which I was truly grateful.

Whilst they went off for the day, Arthur and I caught the train to Tarragona to explore some ancient Roman amphitheatre. On the edge of Sitges was a nudist beach and from the train we were treated to some rare sights. On the return journey we must have hit the rush hour because we never thought we'd make it aboard with all the folk and animals waiting to get on. At one point, standing up squashed in the luggage area, over our heads came a cage full of chickens who had to remain at this elevated point as there was no space for them on the floor.

Timothy, Arthur's middle son, visited us quite frequently and he too, appeared to accept his father's new life with a younger woman. As a consequence, he and I have always got on well together.

Arthur was estranged from his oldest son by his first marriage but we tried to remedy this yet again by inviting him and his then girlfriend to stay with us for the weekend. Regrettably, things did not go according to plan. Following a steak dinner, we took them out for a drink to meet up with his half-brothers Timmy and Jonathan. Unfortunately, as usual Stephen drank too much and turned on his father with all sorts of untrue accusations. This final act of aggression squashed any chance of a reconciliation between them and we never saw him again. Arthur remained in contact with his ex-wives and learned from Shirley, his first wife, that Stephen became more and more agitated as time went by, often spoiling any family get together.

It was also around this time that one of Arthur's best friends suddenly died from a heart attack. I had had the privilege of meeting Gerry when Arthur and I first got together. A nicer guy you couldn't wish to meet. Whenever we visited him and his wife there would be Gin & Tonics the size of which I'd never seen and large chunks of tasty strong (tongue curling as my mum would say) cheddar. Arthur met up with another old friend called Mervyn, when we all attended Gerry's funeral together. Arthur had known him from way back in the 1950s and Mervyn now spoke with a strong American accent. Mervyn had set sail on the Queen Mary in 1954 to join his sister who was a GI (American Forces) bride. He had been there ever since but travelled all the way back from America, which was now his home, to pay his last respects. Well this meeting between the two of them led to a friendship that has lasted to this day. Mervyn invited Arthur and I to go and stay with him and his girlfriend Rachel the following year for a holiday. They both worked at an upmarket resort called Longboat Key Club in South Florida not far from the Florida Keys. They lived close by in Sarasota.

On these holidays, we had the time of our lives and were spoilt rotten. As Rachel was front of house manager, she was head of bookings. Her task was to keep the resort as fully booked up as possible. To this end she worked 24/7 and often worked 10 days on the trot before getting one solitary day off. Because of this she didn't cook and they would eat breakfast on the way out to work and dinner on the way home. We were treated by Mervyn to play on the local golf courses, one being Harbourside. And he would get time off to play with us whilst Rachel just kept on working. She didn't play golf but was quite happy to walk around listening to us moaning about any poor shot or missed putt. She often said she couldn't understand how we all enjoyed the game with the amount of self-berating going on!

Rachel loved deep sea fishing and this is how she spent her odd days off relaxing. She had in the past caught a shark about four feet long and had had it stuffed. She proudly got it down from the loft on one of our earliest visits. Well, after watching the film Jaws, I have never paddled, let alone swum in the sea since. I was highly relieved they didn't carry out a prank to rest it on the pillow next to me whilst I was still asleep! Mervyn later told us of how, when they moved apartments, they had finally decided to get rid of the shark. He put it in the communal dumpster with the head facing upwards and then waited for a young lady following him to open the lid to get rid of her rubbish. Her screams at the sudden sight of this creature could be heard for miles around, so we're told.

We visited Disney World, the Epcot Centre, the various Film Studios, the Kennedy Space Centre and Sea World, which contained a huge theme park somewhere just outside of Orlando. Some of the rides were so scary you could have suffered a heart attack just standing in the queue, let alone getting on board. I was quite ambivalent about going to America initially, thinking it a somewhat brash country but I soon realised anything in the entertainment world they turn their hands to was of the highest calibre. The spare ribs in barbecue sauce, French fries and sweetcorn has to be the tastiest meal ever.

As Longboat Key Club was owned by the Arvida Corporation (who also owned Disney World at that time) Mervyn and Rachel would call in favours from friends in other resorts. On one of our visits they arranged for us all to stay at the resort of Sawgrass in Raymond Floyd's villa. We got to play on the Championship golf courses there before being taken out to eat in top class restaurants.

Of-course this type of treatment and treats were very hard for us to reciprocate. Nonetheless, nearly every other year from the mid-1980s to the mid-1990s Mervyn and Rachel would come over to stay with us for a few weeks. Until then Rachel had never been to England before and she was ecstatic over our pubs and narrow little streets with quaint little houses. And boy could she drink! She loved white wine and it took several months to stock up enough supplies in readiness for their visits.

Over the years we took them up to the Lake District, going on to stay in Scotland, visited parts of Wales and Herefordshire, and did a tour of the West Country going down as far as Devon and Cornwall (at the time we were still living in Swindon). Mervyn loved the opportunity to play some great British courses including the famous links courses Carnoustie and Royal North Devon and the championship course of Blairgowrie. We all got on so well together albeit the trips were planned mainly around Arthur and Mervyns' golfing dreams.

If all this sounds too good to be true, then possibly it was. Despite the good times Arthur hadn't had a personality transplant; he was still as charismatic and flirtatious as ever. Often, I would feel envious of the attention he would pay to other women. If we went to a party, especially with his older friends present, the minute we arrived off he would go to circulate leaving me alone to make the best of it. I know I was the object of some curiosity, especially to the older women Arthur knew but the men did their utmost to make me feel welcome.

But in 1988 I was destined to move again. Two of Arthur's oldest friends and colleagues from Western Trust, upon being made redundant at the same time as him, had set up an Insurance business, which they ran from their home in Somerset. They were fortunate to live in a large Georgian style detached house which had a basement in it that fronted onto the street. This was where the general public could come in and their insurance or assurance needs be met. In November 1988, Arthur bought into the partnership owned by Barry and Jeanne; and down to the West Country we went.

At the time I didn't have any particular ties with Swindon. I was still working on a temporary basis if you recall and had completed my Level One studies in September that year. I knew I had to get a job whereby I was in partial training to become a surveyor in order to embark upon my Level Two studies as this formed part of the criteria for the course.

So, I applied for an assistant valuer's job at the County Council. Although I was unsuccessful due to a lack of experience in gaining this post, I was then contacted by a person from Human Resources to see if I would accept the position of valuation assistant instead. I was thrilled and jumped at the chance because it meant not only 'on the job' training but I could also apply to the University of Reading to undertake a correspondence course to continue my studies. The assistant valuer's post went to my now very good friend Wendy as she had had more experience on site searching and acquisitions than I at the time.

Arthur and I spent several weekends looking at property in the surrounding areas of Taunton and fell in love with a little thatched cottage located on the Brendan Hills in the village of Lydeard St Lawrence. From the gardens we had views of the Quantock Hills and we were not far from the edge of Exmoor and only some 20 miles from the nearest coast. It was idyllic and our cat Bubbly Boy thought he had died and gone to heaven. And so did I. For Arthur moving to Somerset was like coming home.

Chapter Nine
Moving to the South West

1988

British 18 pence Stamp – Sports Series

But the issue of commitment, of the lack of it, continued to affect our lives again with this next move. There was no way Arthur would be marrying me (in his own words) and yet I was putting down the (then) large deposit of £32,000 from the sale of my own home in Swindon on our dream cottage. Arthur's monies were going into the new business he was joining. Trust me when I say, that in true American terms, the alimony due to ex-wives and children can amount to a lot. Yet it was my decision to get mixed up with a married man so I really had no-one to blame but myself. I honestly didn't resent any monetary awards made to his family at all, possibly due to my Catholic conscience, and knowing that this was the least they all deserved.

However, when we had moved down to Somerset, one of Arthur's partners said they wished to join up with an Estate Agency team in the area as 'It was money for old rope'. Now, as I had not only been an estate agent but also done the books for Cox & Billingham in recent years, I knew he didn't understand the concept of the business. This decision was also making Arthur nervous as he had purchased 40% of their partnership. We had come down to the South West on the basis of him continuing to be involved in something he was familiar with, i.e. the Insurance business.

Moving into our Dream Cottage in Lydeard St. Lawrence on 18 November, 1988
(our 2/3rds of the cottage is on the right)

Being associated with this new team of estate agents meant Arthur, and his two partners taking out a huge bank loan to buy new computer equipment, pay out for extra staff and purchase a new lease for an additional office in Williton. As collateral both his partners' home and our cottage were meant to be secured against all of this finance.

Thankfully, as I wasn't a part of this new business, the bank was under a duty for me to obtain independent advice because I would be adversely affected in the event of a default. So off I went to see a solicitor. He asked me what our relationship was like and whether Arthur intended to marry me or not. All I could do was be truthful and say that he hadn't the slightest intention of marrying me. The solicitor said I would be foolhardy to let the cottage be secured against the business loan. And that is 'the best piece of financial advice' I think I have ever received. Naturally, I had still put the cottage into joint names but as things turned out the bank could not retrieve more than 50% of the equity in the event of the partnership defaulting on the repayments.

The timing of this new venture couldn't have been worse. Despite my decision not to back them with the security of my investment in the cottage, the depression of the early 90s set in not long after the new office opened. We were losing money at the rate of £1,000 per week at one time and the banks were threatening foreclosure. Not to dwell on too much detail but Arthur and I lost £40,000 on the business. Even worse his two partners had to sell their home in order to find their combined share of the losses.

In the end, in 1997, we had to move from Lydeard St. Lawrence to Taunton to a less expensive house. We did 'ride out' the recession, eventually managing to sell the cottage for the same amount of money we had bought it for, namely £89,000. As far as the banks went, because it was a partnership, we paid every single penny back, going for months at a time eating beans on toast or cheese in jacket potatoes. We had no social life except for the purchase of a £2 bottle of Bulgarian red wine once a week in order to retain our sanity.

All of the above happened over an eight-year period. When things were at their lowest ebb, Arthur told me he had considered ending his life, he felt such a failure. Yet really, he is the most cautious man I know. He had been unsure of the expansion plans from the start. Unfortunately, by that time we were committed to moving down to Somerset. I think Arthur just saw this as a new beginning, and let's face it, if we could all foretell when a recession was coming along, then no-one would suffer as a consequence.

I often think that this experience was the making of Arthur. He realised he wasn't infallible and he appreciated how much I had stood by him, through thick and thin. I still think to this day if he had made a success of this venture, we may not be together now.

Whilst all the uncertainty about Arthur's new business was going on, I also suffered some personal consequences during this recession. And this may have had a profound effect upon Arthur too.

When I initially joined the County Council, I was so happy in my work. I was asked to join the Site Survey team and become the county surveyor's assistant. This was the best working experience of my life. Colin Ewan, who was the County Surveyor at that time, had never worked with a woman before and it was hilarious. On one occasion during a site visit, I had to change from wearing a skirt into trousers in the back of his car. I think it took him some getting used to. He was in charge of assessing acquisitions of land and property for the various departments in County Hall, primarily Highways and Education. If numbers were dwindling for attendance at a village school or the running of the school was no longer financially viable, then he would be looking out for new sites and all that that entailed. One day I would be looking at maps for evidence of Roman platforms, the next I would be going out with Colin; walking the lines of new highways to assess new chosen routes and decide what compulsory purchase acquisitions would be required. Because I had construction drawing skills, I was given small traffic schemes to design. In addition, I would negotiate any small acquisitions of land within the confines of the relevant legislation.

I would occasionally venture out with two of the land surveyors to gain experience in the use of a Theodolite. This instrument was initially used to measure the different levels and plot the whereabouts of existing buildings on land set aside for any scheme the County Council wished to embark upon. I got to visit most of the schools in the Somerset area when I undertook site surveys on all of the playing field areas allocated to each of them. This is when I realised what a diverse county Somerset really is. You have the Mendip Hills, Cheddar Gorge and Quantocks to the north, the Levels running through the middle of the County, Exmoor Country Park adjacent to the north-western coastline, and the Blackdown hills located to the south. The countryside is so varied and beautiful. I never tired of going out and visiting the historical towns of Wells, Glastonbury, Shepton Mallet and Frome. Taunton itself is a market town and the main industries in the area are agriculture and tourism. Apparently, there is a local saying that 'Somerset is a graveyard to many a man's ambition'. And I truly understand why. I wouldn't wish to live anywhere else.

Upon arrival in the County, Arthur and I had both joined Taunton & Pickeridge Golf Club. At 34 years of age, I was one of only four younger, working lady members. Arthur's friends said I had managed to reduce the average age of the ladies' section to about 60! Once a month, the four of us would try to get out and play our monthly medal, often amongst the men, many of whom were extremely chauvinistic about us being on the course at the same time as them.

Other light relief came in the form of gardening and recreating new areas in our large corner plot. I had caught this particular 'bug' from my mum who thrived in her own garden and was equally willing to give advice and help in mine. One summer her and Dad visited and she even got our dear neighbour and friend Stewart involved in the reconstruction of a pond. Ever after he wished to know when they would be visiting next so he could plan to be away! We spent many a happy hour after work winding down sat on the patio with a gin and tonic or glass of wine together.

On those glorious summer days, I would get up early on a Saturday, get the washing sorted and the basic chores done; and then spend the rest of the day digging, weeding and planting all manner of herbaceous plants and annuals. The latter would spill out of all sorts of tubs, baskets and anything else empty and worthy of filling. I found being outside with nature one of the best ways to relax.

It was on one of these idyllic days, when I had roped Arthur into helping me create a new path, that a young man cycling past our cottage, happened to stop on the road outside to catch his breath before continuing up the hill out of the village. Arthur and I were laughing hysterically about something, possibly the way in which he was about to tackle this awesome DIY task. I was later told by this same young man that that was the moment he had fallen for me. He too worked at County Hall but in the architects' department. He had recognised me from working there in the property services' department. I had met him briefly once when visiting his office for advice but had no idea he had any feelings for me. He was a really nice chap, clever and good looking too. When we went on a course together, he gave me a lift and during a drink in the local pub afterwards, he revealed how he felt. He said he had even written a song about me; gosh, how romantic was that? With Arthur being so involved in his new set up, and showing interest in any new woman he met, it was really flattering for a man to pay me some attention for a change.

I realised that he wished to take things further but despite going full tilt into an affair with Arthur, I wasn't the sort of person that could have a fling just for the sake of it. However comforting that might have been at the time! I had to tell him that I wasn't interested in him in that sense but I would like for us to remain friends. Regrettably this wasn't enough for him so I discouraged his attentions as best I could without hopefully hurting his feelings too much.

In 1989 Mervyn, our friend from America, finally proposed to Rachel and she was so happy. Mervyn had been married before and had three daughters by his first wife who was American. Rachel's dream was to get married over here in England and so Arthur and I set out to see if this was possible. Strangely enough, although Mervyn had worked in the States for over thirty years, he was still a British citizen. I think he must have slipped through the net somehow because I'm sure his employers thought he was an American citizen by then.

Anyhow, we made all the relevant enquiries and found out that they could get married in our Taunton Registry office. This was to be followed by a blessing in Kingston St Mary's local church. Ten folks were to come from America, mainly family including Mervyn's daughters and their respective partners together with Rachel's brother and his wife. Loads more people were invited from England, chiefly Mervyn's family here and old friends too. What I hadn't realised was that the American side of the families needed to be looked after day and night during the course of their holiday! They were here for a week in all and we organised most of their accommodation, trips out, a steam train ride, skittles and pub evenings etc. I was highly relieved when we discovered that Mervyn's daughters all intended to visit London for a few days because by now I was suffering from nervous exhaustion. Following the wedding Mervyn and Rachel went off to Devon for a couple of days to be by themselves. Arthur and I collapsed in a big heap. We then joined the happy couple for a short tour of Cornwall and I know they were really grateful for our help in making this happen. I had used up nearly all of my leave in order to ensure everything went according to plan. Then I returned to work feeling anything but rested!

By this time and after taking a year out from my studies, I enrolled on a distance learning course at the University of Reading. I began studying for my Level Two surveying qualification in my own time. This meant most of my evenings and weekends were spent with legs twisted in a spiral with all my books laid out before me. With lots of assignments to complete I wasn't great at utilising my time. Often, especially in different areas of law, I would look at the question and then research the answer, drifting away from the original point because one interesting topic led to another. Then I would read the question again and discover I had gone way beyond the limits of information required for that particular answer. Still I absorbed a lot and I really enjoyed learning about the different aspects of each subject.

Because I had to be in training on work relevant to becoming a general practice surveyor, my days in the site survey department came to an end. I then worked as a valuation assistant undertaking tasks set out by the various valuers. During this time, I shared an office with Wendy, who has remained a dear friend ever since, and a guy called Andy who I really liked too. We did have a laugh and used to help one another out with any queries or feedback we required.

My Level Two exam's loomed. I was relieved to be able to sit the Incorporated Society of Valuers and Auctioneers exam's locally in the Registration office. The nerves were still there but I had learned a lot. This time I read through the whole paper before deciding which questions I knew the answers to best. I managed to pass all of the papers except for the Building Construction one and I was allowed to re-sit this paper in the Autumn. Thankfully, I managed to pass this exam on the second sitting, which meant I was all ready to take on my Finals.

It was then I got promoted to assistant valuer and became the area valuer's assistant concentrating largely on cases in the district of Mendip. This promotion meant I was responsible for hitting various targets. Each case would be charged to whichever department had requested the work, for example, education or probation or social services. I was allocated many minimum fee cases. For instance, it could be a case of one department letting part of its premises to another department. This meant the annual rental on a particular property may not always be a market rent and it could be relatively low by comparison. As a consequence, the fee was low too. At the same time, the area valuers were on performance related pay so this naturally led to them taking the highest fee earning cases.

This wouldn't have been an issue if it were not for the fact that I was allocated some of the most complex and time-consuming cases to deal with. One example was of the local town hall, owned by one department who wished to sublet some of its office space to be used as a Cop Shop by the local police authority. Setting the rent was the least of my worries. The town hall was a listed building so I had to not only get planning consent for a part change of use, this consent was also subject to Listed Building Planning Permission. Well, suffice it to say this case went on forever. The £200 minimum fee for setting the market rent plus £200 for liaising with the relevant departments **and** sorting out the relevant permissions made little dent in my target level of £20,000 income.

In another example, I was given a case to deal with of an old disused Quarry let to a national Electronics company wherein the tenant wished to purchase the Freehold interest. Well, rental evidence and yields for disused quarries are not that easy to come by, especially with this specialised use of the land. Not only was there the difficulty in setting the Freehold value, part of the quarry was subject to collapse. This meant that the local farmer who had a right of way along the track which ran on the edge of the quarry needed an alternative route. Also, there were other easements to negotiate, and restrictions and conditions on the sale itself, as the Quarry was situated in an Area of Outstanding Natural Beauty. I'll never forget attending a meeting with two of the directors of the company, their valuer and Uncle Tom Cobley and all being present for their side and it was just me representing the County Council! Needless to say, I needed a few glasses of water on that occasion to steady my nerves and retain my voice. I am pleased to say that two years later all issues had been resolved but it was a really complex case to deal with and the area valuer knew he had off loaded a time-consuming one too.

I was also dealing with small Compulsory Purchase acquisitions of land in connection with road widening schemes or road strengthening schemes, or low rental commercial rent reviews, whereby again, not much income was at stake. Yet all the relevant terms and conditions within the leases had to be gone through in detail. I got really anxious at one point and went to see the chief valuer to explain why my target income levels appeared to be lower than they should be. He was not at all concerned and said I was doing a good job and not to worry about it.

So, on I went, thoroughly enjoying the challenges of valuing so many different types of property and interests and keeping a journal to go towards my Professional Assessment, which would follow my Final exams. I was thrilled when I managed to pass my Final examinations, again sat in a local hall. At last I was able to begin work on my Professional Assessment. This comprised of keeping the aforementioned journal highlighting the different aspects of work I had been involved in during training, a precis of aspirations and goals, and lastly a project, which involved a development appraisal and valuation of a real 'live' property. In this case it was an Art's Centre situated in a medium size town in Wales. I worked on the latter in my spare time, taking leave to visit the site and survey the grounds that contained wonderful old trees, mainly Cedars of Lebanon. I took external measurements of the existing property so I could draw up various plans, and visited the local planning office to discuss potential permissible changes of use. I got really involved in this project to the extent it became my pride and joy. So keen was I to present a professional document containing my findings, valuations and conclusions as to the most viable proposition.

But then one day something rather scary happened. At the time, I was in my office trying to make an alteration to a plan I had drawn, that was laid out on my desk. I should really have fixed it back on to my drawing board so I could amend it there, but I was being impatient. As I was leaning over the desk at full stretch, I suddenly developed this horrendous pain in my chest. I must admit I initially thought I was having a heart attack. Well, I cried out to attract someone's attention as I had got very breathless and was frightened. It was suggested that I go and lie down in the first aid room but lying down made the pain worse. A colleague rang Arthur to come and collect me. He felt it might be something to do with my kypho-scoliosis, although this had never given me any problems before. Off I went to see Arthur's friend and Osteopath, Steve. He confirmed that my vertebrae had gone completely out of line and needed manipulation. Then began the rather painful process of getting my back into good shape.

And then I had another accident at work. I was up a stepladder inside the safe in the county solicitor's office lifting a very heavy box of deeds off a top shelf, when suddenly I couldn't hold the weight of the box. I turned, still hanging on to the box, in order to drop it onto the nearby table. Well, I thought nothing more of it, until the next evening when I was food shopping. I bent down to pick up some biscuits from the lower shelf and got stuck there. My lower back had locked this time and I needed help to get back up on my feet. Hence began my problems with recurring sciatica.

Subsequently, I have spent a small fortune on private therapy including Bowen treatment, manipulation, physiotherapy and more recently, Craniosacral therapy in order to keep myself active and still able to work.

Anyhow, going back to my career in County Hall, the only fly in the ointment that I could see, was that there would be no advancement for me once I was qualified because the only step up from assistant valuer was to become area valuer. We had four of these, all men who had been in their jobs since time began.

They were totally in their comfort zones and appeared to have no aspirations to move on. And I suppose I couldn't really blame them!

However, us four assistant valuers were slightly disgruntled with our pay scale, as we were gaining in experience. Once qualified we wished to have the opportunity to have our roles reassessed. Then along came a job re-evaluation scheme, so we impulsively jumped at the chance to take part. Unfortunately, I have never been backward at coming forwards and so I became spokesperson for our group. I put forward the necessary arguments to support implementing a new tier of valuer status and also a new pay band.

Well, I ended up fighting our cause against the head of Property Services, one of the most autocratic and chauvinistic men I have ever met. He wouldn't listen to our side of things at all and most people were afraid to speak up to him. When we had monthly meetings, he would break these down into three groups. On one occasion he had asked a pertinent question about the accountability of the department. I asked what I felt was a reasonable query to clarify things in response. Well, the head took umbrage at this and leapt down my throat in the most unprofessional manner in front of everyone. When the next group came in for a similar lecture, he put the same question to them; no-one dared answer. So, this man said, 'Come on now, you can say what you are thinking, Pat Machin did and she is still in a job.' One of the participants in this group later told me what had been said. It was at this juncture that I registered I was not his favourite employee. What happened next certainly proved this point.

Chapter Ten
Bleak Times

1992

British 18 pence Stamp – 'Wintertime in the Four Seasons' Series

Literally, out of the blue, came the news there were going to be redundancies made within our department. Ten people would be going overall and whoever was chosen would get a telephone call before 10 am the next morning. When my telephone rang, I was stunned. I knew that due to being conscientious I worked harder than my male counterparts. Two of them would often skive off work when out on site visits and one was a part time fireman. When his beeper went off, he would just leave his work and run out of the building. I do know that their respective area valuers had given them properties with higher rental values. This in turn meant they could charge a percentage fee rather than when dealing with the minimum fee cases I seemed to be constantly working on. Yet, if you remember, I did have the chief valuer's support in that achieving my own personal targets was not deemed to be a problem.

The head of Property Services summoned me to his office. I was in such a state that I couldn't really take it in. I certainly wasn't thinking straight. I asked him why I had been specifically chosen out of all the assistant valuers. He replied, 'You have not hit your targets in the past year'. When I defended this by telling him of my previous discussions with the chief valuer, his response was that 'I could take him on if I wanted to'. I went to see the chief valuer in the hope that he would support me if I challenged this reasoning. But I learnt that he was also being made redundant and he didn't see what he could do to help. He was coming up to retirement age so I'm not sure it was such a blow to him, other than to his pride of-course. I went home devastated. As with the other nine unlucky souls, I had been given six months' notice. This in itself was awful because I now remained working with all my colleagues who were staying on. I felt the lowest of the low, and my self-esteem hit rock bottom. When I went shopping one night after work, I had a panic attack.

In those days there was no chip and pin. You had to sign for your goods and this signature was then compared to that on your debit card. Well, my signature was queried by the checkout girl and so I was asked to sign again. With shaking hands, I scribbled my name again and it was subjected to even more scrutiny. It was at that point I couldn't breathe. I felt rooted to the spot but wanted at the same time to leave my shopping and run out of the store. It was as though the checkout girl was questioning my whole being. I later learned that this was a typical 'fight or flight' response. From that moment onwards I couldn't sign my name. I just froze and would only use my card providing Arthur accompanied me so he could verify who I was in the event I was questioned again.

I went to the doctors and whilst waiting to be seen I began to cry and cry and cry. One of the receptionists took me into a small side room, made me a cup of tea; and I was still crying. The doctor who saw me was amazing. He prescribed me some mild anti-depression tablets to help me stay calm and then he said he was going to sign me off work for a month with stress. I said he couldn't sign me off because I needed to be working; and had to be able to get another job once my notice period had expired. To make matters worse, Arthur's business had by this time closed down and I was now the main breadwinner.

My doctor insisted and said he would not record stress as the reason for my time off. So, I was able to stay home and try to come to terms with what had happened. I became a bit of a zombie, not I'm sure due to the medication, but I had lost all interest in doing anything. I didn't want to see any of my friends, in fact I didn't want to see anyone at all. A meal out for those leaving the council had been arranged but I didn't go to it. It was like I wasn't worthy of mixing with anyone. I spent hours lying on the settee watching the hands on the clock go around. And Arthur didn't know how to deal with this sort of mental breakdown. He felt he should chivvy me along and encourage me to do stuff I didn't want to do. He invited friends round to talk to me, when all I wanted was to be left alone.

It was not a happy time for either of us. In addition, Arthur's sister Margaret became extremely ill and we thought we were going to lose her. Then his mother began to suffer from forgetfulness. For instance; putting on the high-level gas grill and leaving a tea towel draped across the top of the cooker, then going off to do something else—not recommended!

Somehow, I returned to work at County Hall to finish serving my notice. Just before my six months was up, in March 1993, I was notified by the I.S.VA. saying that I had won the prestigious Hammerson Award for the Best Professional Assessment from any student in that particular year in the whole country. I couldn't believe it but the County Surveyor, Colin Ewans and my colleagues were delighted for me. I and my former area valuer attended a Presidential Luncheon at Cadogon Gate in London where I was presented with a cheque for £250 by the chief executive of the Hammerson Group. This enabled me to pay my first year's annual subscription to the I.S.VA.! I won't pretend that either of us were not overawed by the occasion and we probably drank a bit more wine than we should have done.

Following my notice period, I then transferred to the typing pool as they were short of a person to work in there. This did nothing to boost my self-esteem. All of a sudden, I was typing up reports for my fellow valuers, instead of being involved in writing them. I had applied for a couple of jobs but there were not many in the offing. I had qualified as a valuer in the middle of a recession.

And then I got a phone call from the Valuation Office Agency in Taunton. In the past I'd had dealings with several of the valuers from this office when negotiating various cases that cropped up with their clients and ours from time to time. The District Valuer himself was calling me asking if I would go along to see him as they needed qualified valuers to deal with Council Tax Appeals. I was flattered but terrified that I wouldn't be up to the job and able to cope.

But this was the boost and change in direction I needed. As they say, when one door closes another one opens. And this is where I met the incredible person that is Hazel Gaul. She was like a breath of fresh air; in charge of this whole new division set up to deal with Appeals under the new legislation of taxing properties by way of Council Tax. This system was brought in to replace the disastrous Poll Tax formerly introduced by Maggie Thatcher's government.

Hazel was a very experienced valuer who had previously worked in the City dealing with multimillion-pound properties on behalf of the government. She was a Christian who had extraordinarily long dark hair which she wore up, wrapped around in this sort of circular bun affair. It looked as though she was wearing a hat but it suited her striking features. She would go around the office singing songs out loud! Hazel was in charge of training all new employees to attend Tribunal in the event we were unable to settle an appeal by mutual discussion. She immediately recognised that I was still fairly vulnerable at this time; she said to me, 'I feel your confidence has taken a knock.' Well a bit of an understatement as far as I was concerned but she was the person that helped me on my way again. She even arranged for the photograph I had had taken when I went to London to receive the Hammerson Award, to be published in the Valuation Office Agency national magazine. I got to hear that my dear friend Colin at County Hall had cut it out and stuck it on the notice board outside the head of Property Services' office, bless him!

The other truly sad event that occurred to make me realise I needed to start living life to the full again was the sudden death of my dear friend Nita who still lived in Swindon. She had been diagnosed with cancer and within months she was dead. This woman loved life and would have given anything for more time on this earth I know. The shock of losing her made me realise that I was wasting my life with too many negative thoughts and really not doing it justice.

And so I slowly got to grips with things again. Despite the nerves in attending Tribunal to represent the Listing Officer, I gradually regained some confidence thanks to Hazel's wonderful support and help. With the aid of a thicker ball point pen, I also managed not to shake so much when I signed my name, although Arthur still had to chivvy me along to get over my fear of facing work some days.

Since the business had folded, he too, was offered a temporary contract at the Valuation Office Agency. Arthur took on the role of valuing, under the legislation, new properties being built and coming on to the Valuation List. He loved working there and made many new friends almost straight away. It was good he was taken up with this job satisfaction because we were still making payments to the bank for the considerable debts we owed.

After eighteen months of three renewable six monthly contracts, I realised one of us needed to get a full-time job. As I was the youngest, I felt I stood more of a chance. Thus in 1995 I applied for a post in the housing division at The Borough Council as a housing assistant. I was really over-qualified for this post but I was desperate.

So, I attended an interview with an armful of qualifications and answered many questions, explaining to the two managers there why I was the right person for the job. Thankfully I must have managed to convince them of this as I was offered a permanent role in Lettings. Although I was not using my valuation experience to the full, at least I was still dealing in property management.

What was never explained to me was the fact that my new manager within the department had been off sick at the time of the interviews, hence why she had not formed part of the interview panel. In addition, no one thought to tell me that two of the more junior members of staff had also applied for the role. They were both obviously extremely disappointed in not being successful. Within my first week I had one of the most disheartening experiences ever. One of the aforementioned junior members of staff was a very young and attractive girl and she worked within the same department. I was senior to her and had asked her to undertake an urgent task. Well, she didn't bother to do this straight away and time was getting on so I asked her to please sort the matter out. For a moment I thought she was going to rebel and if looks could kill, I'd no longer be here writing my story. That same day when I was returning from lunch, she came walking towards me. She grabbed my arm saying she needed to speak with me now and then practically shoved me into one of the interview rooms. She then said because of the way in which I had spoken to her that morning, she was going to report me to our (mutual) manager. Little did I realise that the manager was very friendly with this girl to the extent that she did not ask for my side of the story at all. The manager proceeded to say I needed to watch my step because she had not been happy about my appointment. In other words, if it had been down to her I wouldn't have got the job. My heart was pounding and I felt really sick because sensing a barrier from her side, I had genuinely tried to be tactful in the way I had dealt with this young lady. But she seemed determined to dislike me no matter what. The second girl who did not get the job was also unpleasant and resentful towards me and this made the situation seem even worse. Thankfully she was located in the office next door and left to work elsewhere not long after.

I can truly say the first year there was one of the most miserable of my working life (aside from when I had been made redundant and was working my notice at County Hall of-course). And then this same young lady took a dislike to another girl within our department and so I got myself an ally. I worked like a trojan because I felt that the manager was possibly looking for any excuse to get rid of me. Ironically, she called me her 'rock' in the end and said she didn't know what she would have done without me. I wonder now whether possibly one of the young ladies in question had some insecurity issues. When I met this same boss later on in life, she did have the grace to apologise for being so taken in and blinkered over the whole situation.

So how did I manage to last eight years working there? Well, even my antagonists got around to liking me in the end. But sadly, I felt I could never wholly trust either of them again. I felt so shaken by that experience. Especially as it had come at a time when I was feeling fragile and in need of a job so badly. It was with some relief when, once again, life finally began to take an upward turn.

Chapter Eleven
Happier Times

1995

British 1st Class 'Greetings in Art' Booklet Stamp

Eventually I was promoted and my title was upgraded to Allocations Officer. I had been responsible for getting our vacancy rates down to a really low level and we successfully hit the government targets set for turning empty properties around. I really enjoyed meeting the different people who so needed our help. From families who required larger houses, to priority homeless people who didn't get any choice as to where they lived, to those on Probation who wanted re-housing or those Social Services' cases whereby more suitable accommodation was needed on medical grounds. I loved going out and about on home visits, carrying out inspections and undertaking accompanied viewings.

I did have some hairy moments though. I recall one guy who I had re-homed following a stint in prison after a violent attack on someone. He had done his probation and was known to be still fairly volatile. Alas, this information wasn't transferred to his new file, so when he applied for alternative accommodation several years later, yours truly took him out alone in her car on an accompanied viewing. I remembered his face but not his name and it wasn't until I was driving him out into the countryside that I recalled his dubious history. I can honestly say the hairs stood up on the back of my neck. I was highly relieved to deposit him back on his own doorstep despite the fact he now appeared relatively docile.

My confidence gradually returned during this period and life resumed on an even keel again. I made four good friends within the department, two of whom, Michelle and Tottie, I still see to this day. We did have some fun together. Actually, dealing with some of the unfortunate and angry folks that we saw day in and day out you needed to be able to laugh about things now and then.

One day, the housing receptionist who happened to be a rather short rotund chap was ordering in a loud voice some poor applicant **'to take a ticket and seat'** and to **'not push to the front of the queue'**. Well, this person didn't take kindly to this approach and shouted out, 'Who do you think you are? the Fat Controller?' For those of you not in the know this was a character puppet off one of the children's television series at the time. Well, the rest of us were in stitches at this exchange of words although I'm not sure our colleague found it quite as funny as we did. (Nowadays this would be deemed to be politically incorrect).

Around this time, I seemed to develop some form of dyslexia myself. I was on the phone one day answering an enquiry and I asked for that person's 'Coastal Pode'. As we worked in an open plan office, everyone had heard this remark and fell about laughing at my mix up on words. Thankfully the person on the other end of the phone thought it was funny too. So, I tried again and said the same words again! Luckily the caller got the gist of my request. Not long after, I visited the doctor about my herbaceous (rather than sebaceous) cyst, which amused him somewhat too. And I shan't be recounting the full story about getting the word orgasms muddled up with organisms; I expect this latter mix up would be known as a Freudian slip!

Then early in 1996, to my complete astonishment, Arthur proposed marriage to me! All along I had said, should he ever get around to asking me, I would say no; but that notion went right out of the window I'm afraid. I don't think it was the most romantic of proposals because it was made first thing in the morning when he had woken me up with a cup of tea. As a consequence, I had no makeup on with hair sticking up on end and my mouth feeling like the bottom of a bird cage. Stupidly I felt embarrassed at this declaration of love and commitment whilst being in such a dishevelled state. Trust him to take advantage of me not being a morning person!

Coincidentally, we had been contacted by our friends in America, Mervyn and Rachel, who wanted to know when we would next be going out to see them. So, Arthur rang them back to see what the possibilities were of us getting married over there. They said they would be delighted to arrange our nuptials in America, especially as we had gone to so much effort to make their wedding a success over here. We left everything to them and gosh, did they do us proud. However, things did not get off to an auspicious start as a hurricane was blowing into Florida during the week of our arrival, which meant our plane got diverted to Atlanta airport. Mervyn and Rachel were not able to hire a car due to the storm and arrived to collect us in their small 4-door saloon. How we got everything in I'll never know but we did; and we had to spend the night in a hotel close by as parts of Florida had been evacuated. The next day we were driven back to their home in Hilton Head Island. Thankfully, the storm passed over with not too much damage.

We had to register our intention to get married in the Beaufort County Court, South Carolina. The ceremony itself was to take place in the grounds of a local hotel recently built in the colonial style located on Hilton Head Island itself. And it was magical. I had tears running down my cheeks all the way through taking our vows. So much so that the journalist from the weekly newspaper ended up by taking a photograph showing Arthur hugging me at the end of the service with my face stuffed into his chest! I guess he got tired of waiting for me to smile. It was the one day in my life when I actually felt beautiful. I was really happy we were finally making this commitment to one another, and I'm still not sure why. After all, we had stuck together through some pretty trying and tedious years with the emphasis not on the words for richer but definitely **for poorer**. There were just the four of us at the wedding, together with the new manager and his wife from the hotel who also agreed to be our witnesses. Afterwards we enjoyed a scrumptious high tea with champagne.

Following our Wedding Ceremony on Hilton Head Island

An amazing honeymoon followed and Mervyn and Rachel came too! I suppose they felt, after thirteen years together, we were not in need of some time on our own. They had organised some fabulous treats for us all. We left our wedding venue and went to a nearby jetty whereby we were taken by boat to Dufusky Island. This was a private resort and yes, you've guessed it, it had fabulous beaches and a golf course, called Bloody Point. After a superb evening meal, we stayed overnight in a villa overlooking the sea.

Returning from Dufusky Island to the Mainland by boat

We then travelled on to visit the famous Pinehurst Golf Club in North Carolina. The next couple of days were spent in a pine lodge at a resort called Pine Needles. It teemed down with rain during the first night but as this was a championship course built on sand, we were able to go out in buggies and play 18 holes of golf the following day. We then went on to visit the historic and picturesque town of Charleston in Georgia. Rachel and I also took a boat to Savannah, whilst the guys went off to play golf elsewhere. No sooner had we sailed out of the bay then the skies got darker, the water got choppier and frankly, even my seafaring friend Rachel wondered whether we would survive the journey. Our next big surprise was a visit to Kia wah Island, the famous Ryder Cup venue and resort in South Carolina. Whilst Rachel and I rode in the buggies, Arthur and Mervyn tried to bring the course to its knees. The wild life was pretty scary and alligators as usual were in abundance so there wasn't too much searching going on for lost balls. We ended our time there by going down to the beach, which had white sand in abundance. Then we had our most romantic photograph ever taken together. All in all, we would never have had wedding celebrations like that without the generosity and kindness of our two friends who couldn't have made it any more special.

The following year in July 1997 we held a marriage blessing for family and lots of friends who had been unable to share our happy wedding day abroad. I was cooking and preparing food for several days beforehand. We were to be blessed in Lydeard St Lawrence village church, have cocktails in our garden and then food and drinks (including our friends' homemade white wine) followed by dancing in the local village hall. Dear friends including Ros, Mel and Janet helped us to get the hall spruced up and decorated with bunting, balloons and suchlike. Arthur and I even had the first dance to Wet Wet Wet's, *'Love is all around'*. It was tremendous fun and I'm told by some; it was the best hangover they'd had in years. My mum and dad, brother Tony, Trisha, Carly and Kirsty came (Kirsty being my maid of honour); brother Pete, Gail, Clare and Mark came too, together with my sister Kim and Arthur's son Timmy. Ian and his family broke down on the motorway half an hour before the blessing began and Dad (being Dad) bailed them out once again with funds to get them home. Arthur and I felt very honoured that so many had made the effort to be there.

The month before our blessing, Mervyn and Rachel took the momentous decision to move to England to see if their futures lay here rather than in America. Arthur and I did have reservations about whether this was the right thing for them to do. We felt visiting a place on holiday is wholly different to living there. We also realised, that after spending many holidays together, Rachel appeared to suffer sometimes from a mild version of depression. When she was up, she was really up but when she got low that was something else altogether. Mervyn, on the other hand, thought he was returning home to a country similar to the one he had left behind in 1954. He was soon disillusioned as to how much everything had changed since he had been away. Still, Arthur found them some rented accommodation on the edge of Taunton to live in and Mervyn set about doing it up. The other concern we had was that whenever they had visited us in the past, we had spent all of our holiday time together. Now Arthur and I were certainly not in any position financially to give up work and spend lots of time with them. We were also fortunate to have many other dear friends that we socialised with too. Initially Mervyn was going to join our golf club Taunton & Pickeridge. Arthur proposed him and got a friend to second him. Then without telling us he had changed his mind; Mervyn joined another golf club that his cousin belonged to. Arthur didn't mind this a jot. What he did mind though, was not being told by Mervyn that he had changed his mind and was no longer going to join our club!

Sadly, life in England didn't turn out as Mervyn and Rachel had expected it to and within a year they had packed up and returned home to America. They didn't tell any of their friends that's what they were doing. We were both flabbergasted and really hurt by their actions and lack of communication.

Meanwhile, circumstances for us were marching on. Just one month after our blessing in August 1997, we moved out of our thatched cottage at Lydeard St. Lawrence to a 1930s three-bedroom semi-detached house with a lovely big garden on the edge of town. The house, which we bought for the reasonable price of £72,500, needed some modernisation but it was basically clean and tidy, aside from a doggy smell in the carpets. We knew we could live with it until the day we could afford to do something about it; the lack of renovation that is, not the doggy smell! And Arthur managed to do a deal with the bank. Because we had moved to a less expensive house, we were able to release some equity and finally pay off the balance of the loan. What a relief it was to no longer have the burden of debt from the business hanging over us. For several years we had endured mortgage rates of 15% and loan rates even higher. We were so grateful to survive the 90s recession and all it threw at us.

Now, since living at our current home we've had the pleasure all these years of some wonderful neighbours in the shape of Nan and Les. They are an elderly couple and the week before we moved in, Arthur went around to introduce himself; and to ask if they had any soap he could borrow. He and a friend had been taking up the carpet in the living room and decided they would have some fish and chips for lunch; hence both needed to wash their hands.

Nan answered the door and a short time later she came back to hand over the oldest piece of lined soap you could ever imagine. Years later, Nan told us that when she went back in to the house from this encounter, Les said to her, 'We're going to have to watch them!' Having celebrated their 70th wedding anniversary several years ago, complete with a telegram from the Queen, Nan has achieved 97 years of age. Sadly, Les has since died at the age of 95 and he is truly missed. Whatever Nan is on, I'd like some please!

Now, I've digressed as usual. The following year we had our honeymoon proper. I had always wanted to visit Italy. Thus, in May of 1998 we did what only the Americans do well; we went on a two-week tour taking in some of the highlights of this beautiful country. We flew to Venice and crumbs, was it cold! Especially when travelling along the canals. We did a tour of the city taking in the wondrous Basilica of St Mark with its surrounding square, tower, restaurants and upmarket shops. I could not get over the unbelievable detail in the architecture. Tiny pieces of mosaic made up the facade of this beautiful church; there were golden horses rising up above the parapets and huge uneven floor slabs inside that really could trip you up as you were gazing in awe at the splendour of it all. I literally had goose bumps. We walked over the Bridge of Sighs to the Palazzo Ducale and crossed the Rialto Bridge too, witnessing all manner of craft including the water taxis and gondolas flowing up and down the waterways.

The next day we travelled by coach through the scenic lands of Tuscany filled with tall, slender cypresses, then across the Alpenine mountains down to Rome via Francis of Assisi's village where we had a short visit and stopover. The marvellous sights and sounds of Rome were truly unforgettable. The Basilica of St Peter together with its associated artwork by Michelangelo and other Baroque and Renaissance artists was beyond superb. Yet I never got to see the Pope. Despite all of my misgivings involving the Catholic faith I would have liked to have heard his address to the people. This was held the following morning when we were due to leave and that was my only regret. The Roman ruins strewn through the city, which the chic Italian people surely didn't take for granted, were overwhelming. The Vatican, Roman Forum, Arch of Titus and Colosseum were just as magnificent as I had imagined them to be. Following an evening meal where waiters flirted outrageously with us ladies and troubadours sang songs in a bid to get our men folk to purchase us a rose, we visited the Trevi fountain where we threw coins in, in the hope our token gesture would follow superstition and enable us to return to Italy one day. I am quickly running out of superlatives to describe this fascinating country that I was fast becoming enamoured with. Suffice it to say that with my equal love of history and architecture, I found many of the antiquities exquisite; and the tantalising glimpse I was getting of these cities that I had read so much about wasn't nearly enough to satisfy my ongoing interest.

Now anyone who knows me well, will know I'm *not* a morning person. Indeed, I may well have mentioned it already! But I was so filled with anticipation and excitement of the day's forthcoming events that 6 am starts seemed no trouble at all. I was up with the lark and raring to go.

From Rome we travelled down to Sorrento, which is located in southern Italy on the edge of scenic jagged coastline. This coastline also features sheer drops to one side of the narrow roads and rising steep terrain to the other. Before we arrived in Sorrento, our coach took us through the busy city of Naples, where the drivers drove like something out of a Charlie Chaplin film. Obviously, health and safety did not form part of an Italian's make up; scooter drivers with no helmets on were riding up the middle of tram lines and cars appeared to be nearly colliding with one another for the sheer hell of it! We witnessed several discarded vehicles with dents in them; abandoned as if they were solely to blame for the misfortune that had occurred. Sitting in the front seat of the coach I was given to letting out the odd scream myself as our coach driver expertly narrowly missed hitting the sides of anyone or anything in his path.

We got to stay for several days in this glorious place where, with new friends we had made on this trip, we decided to organise our own tours of the nearby sights. **Big mistake**! Our first venture took us on the train to the ruins of Pompeii that were excavated in 1748. These ruins were situated not far from the slopes of the volcano Vesuvius. In AD 79 this Mount had erupted burying the town below in 20 feet of pumice and ash. We didn't realise how large an area the town covered but purchasing a guide book we tried to fathom our way around. Our decision was good in the sense we could take our time without a guide urging us on but not so great in learning anything about the history of the site nor seeing everything there was to see. To top it all, having completely lost our sense of direction, we left the town by an exit that was, unbeknown to us on the opposite side to where we had entered. Not realising our mistake, we marched off to the nearby railway station only to find the train we needed would be arriving at our original station, which was by now located several miles away. In the heat of the day we had to trudge around the perimeter of the town in order to make good our error. We were all shattered, although it added to the feeling of adventure somehow, or so we tried to convince ourselves!

David, Arthur and Hazel inspecting remains (of what they're not sure) at Pompeii

Not having learned our lesson, four of us embarked on another trip to the Isle of Capri. This is where I had my first sight of a Bottle Brush plant with stunning red flowers. I am delighted to say I now have one growing in my own garden, together with two slender cypress trees and an olive tree. The focus of our trip to Capri had to be a visit to the famous blue caves situated on the shoreline of the island. What we didn't know was where these caves were, in relation to where we had landed. Undaunted, we set off following the signs. We walked and we walked and we walked. Time was passing by and we soon registered that we needed to find these dam caves soon otherwise we would miss catching the boat back to the mainland. In the end we had to give up and make do with colourful postcards to remind us of what we had missed. Nonetheless, we did get to see Gracie Fields home (not that we were invited in) and we certainly saw lots of the island itself.

It was on this holiday that we became good friends with Hazel and David who originally lived in Surrey but who moved down to the West Country some twelve years ago. Just prior to going to Italy, they suffered one of the worst tragedies any parent should have to go through, their eldest son had died of bone cancer. He was only in his late twenties, a fit and super looking young man who would be the last person you would think of to fall victim to this dreadful disease. We got really close to them on holiday and have remained friends with Hazel and David to this day. Hazel was recently invited to the Queen's garden party as over the years she has helped raised funds for bone cancer research to the tune of £50,000. She even sky-dived out of a plane, admittedly strapped to a young male skydiver, but at the age of 70 plus this was no mean feat.

Whilst staying in Sorrento we took a bus ride down the Amalfi coastline, which is not for the faint-hearted. In the first instance I sat on the front right-hand seat so as not to miss the views. What I didn't realise was that every time we went around a hair pin bend, my seat seemed to swing out over the abyss! The other passengers were not enamoured with my screams of terror thus it was not long before I was encouraged to swap seats to the other side of the bus and peace reigned once more. We went on to Positano where we saw a lovely wedding taking place on the steps of the local church, before calling in at the nearby potteries. The area is well known for growing succulent lemons and the local drink was a liqueur called Lemoncello (that reminds me of a Beatles song, or am I getting my words confused again?). This liqueur is said to be good for indigestion so that's as good an excuse as any to give it a try.

It was then time to begin the second part of our tour, taking in the cities of Florence with a second visit to Rome before stopping off at Pisa. In Florence we witnessed another wedding with the bride and groom both elegant, sat in a horse drawn carriage. I gazed in wonder at yet more beautifully detailed architecture. We visited a grand old manor house with views over the river; and beautiful gardens laid out with Mediterranean plants and other flora that can survive a hot climate. We crossed the Ponte Vecchio bridge built in 1345 that spans the Arno River and pressed our noses against the elegant shop windows displaying exquisite gold jewellery. The queues for the Uffizi Art Gallery that houses some of the most famous paintings in the world were two hours long. As we only had several hours to be in Florence, we ruefully elected to give that spectacle a miss. So, we wandered into local churches, the names of which I have long forgotten, to soak up the atmosphere and admire the riches contained within. I must have lit umpteen candles to honour the dead. There is something so spiritual about these places that I felt close to those no longer here.

On the return journey to Rome we caught the local train into the city and visited more churches with famous tapestries, murals, crypts and history going back centuries. After staying overnight, we went on to the city of Pisa where we saw the famous leaning tower, which has been the subject of much debate as to how best to stabilise it and prevent its total collapse. I've since watched documentaries on TV and seen the engineering genius that has allowed for this work to be undertaken. From a surveyor's point of view, it is quite mind blowing to think that the angle of this ancient tower's lean has been rectified to a relatively safe degree in recent years.

It was all too soon before we had to go back to Venice for our return flights. The plane happened to be late taking off, so our new friends Hazel and David kindly offered to let us stay at their house the night, should we have missed our train home in England. We did manage to catch the train but only because a guard had forgotten it was his night on duty. He had arrived two hours late to man the thing. We could not get over him admitting to such a mistake; he thought it was funny! Then there were maintenance works on the last part of the track so we had to get off the train and catch a coach, which arrived back in Taunton in the early hours of the morning. But nothing could dent what I felt to be, the best and most interesting holiday (and honeymoon) I'd ever experienced. And one with no games of golf in it!

During the late 1990s I was in more of a relaxed and healthy frame of mind and this is when my other hobby of gardening came to the fore again. We had inherited a 100' x 30' rear garden that was chiefly laid to lawn, as was the 60' x

30' frontage. I spent the next 10 years or so digging it up in various stages, so passionate was I about putting in more shrubs, trees and plants. In 2001, I entered a garden competition held by the Taunton Flower Show and gained the highly recommended award in the Best Rear Garden category. I particularly adore herbaceous (not sebaceous!) plants and never get over the wonder of each spring when everything has died down during winter; and then fresh new shoots miraculously pop up as if to say, 'I'm still here'. Whenever I visit a National Trust place, nearby Hestercombe House and gardens or a Royal Horticultural Society's garden I have to bring something home. As we have a more temperate climate in the South West, I have brought back Trachycarpus plants from the Lost Gardens of Heligan as well as various varieties of Cordylines, Lavenders, Camellias and Aeoniums, the latter being a type of succulent plant. I spent hours training 80 small Box bushes to grow into a hedge and this is back breaking work I can tell you. I also grew Box balls here and there because I love to plant topiary due to its continual interest throughout all of the seasons. Last but not least I have an obsession with tubs and baskets. At the last count I had 75 plus filled with all manner of colourful and scented flora.

In the very late 1990s and early 'noughties' we were fortunate to go on several golfing trips to France with our good friends Bob and Joan. We've spent many happy days in the Picardy, Brittany and Normandy regions and stayed in the historical town of Amien, not far from where my gramps was a dispatch rider on the Somme. Aside from playing golf at a spectacular course called La Belle Dunne, we did lots of sightseeing. Amongst the highlights was a visit to Bayeux to see the famous tapestries depicting William the Conqueror's defeat and takeover of Britain. We saw the wonderful church at Rouen, climbed the innumerable steps to reach the old monastery of San Mont Michelle and delighted in the Art Deco Cathedral located on the top of a hill in the town of Liseaux. This latter town is actually twinned with the town of Taunton where we now live. We also rubbed shoulders with the 'well to do' at two famous seaside resorts, Le Touquet and Deauville. It was whilst driving us around Deauville that Bob had a momentary blank about which side of the road he should be on and we drove around an island the wrong way—much to the surprise of an oncoming vehicle. We couldn't resist the delicious baguettes and French pastries, although food in general did seem quite expensive there once the Eurocurrency had been introduced (following the formation of the European Union).

Arthur and I also went on several holidays to the beautiful islands of Menorca and Majorca. Both boasted numerous scenic coves with aqua marine sea, wonderful nature reserves and the interesting respective capital cities and ports of Mahon and Palma. Citadella, an early Roman town, was another atmospheric place not to be missed.

Last but certainly not least, we took the opportunity to return to Italy, this time staying at the Art Deco seaside resort of Viareggio for the week. Apparently, at the turn of the century many of the properties on the sea front were primarily of wooden construction and there was a huge fire that destroyed a good number of them in the 1920s. Hence, the late 1920s and early 1930s architecture of many of the buildings occupying the sea front today.

When we flew in to Pisa we were waiting for the local train and got talking to a couple who we discovered were from Watchet in Somerset of all places. Not only that, they were acquainted with our golfing friends Ros and David who lived there too. What a small world it is. Shortly after this meeting there was one really amusing incident when we realised, we were on the wrong platform. This meant we had to carry our (very heavy) suitcase up a legion of stairs to get to the other side. Arthur was struggling and so, not speaking Italian, I did a pantomime of asking where the lift was to a young man standing nearby. He seemed to be a bit slow in getting the gist of my enquiry and so I bobbed up and down and lifted my arms up and down, shouting Lift, Lift pointing at the suitcase. With that he grabbed the other end of the case and hoisted it up the entire staircase just like Hercules. We were so grateful for his misunderstanding and managed to catch the right train.

Viareggio itself has an extremely long promenade which is great for cyclists, although you do risk life and limb as a pedestrian. The town is only an hour's scenic bus ride away from the Roman town of Lucca. We had such a great day out there walking the length of the Roman walls and taking in all of the historical sights.

I feel so fortunate to have had the opportunity to visit so many fascinating and iconic places and these memories will remain with me forever.

Fitness wise, aside from the ongoing issues with my back, I had a nasty case of Costa Condritus, which is basically a painful rib condition thought, in my case, to be due to attempting more rigorous yoga postures. I also had continuing bouts of pain and sickness that I later discovered meant a fairly serious (and awkward) intolerance to pork and peppers. Whenever I had eaten either of these two things,

I would get a ringing in my ears, go all hot and sweaty, be dreadfully nauseous and sometimes even pass out. Trust me when I say, it is really embarrassing if you are at another person's house when this happens. For several years, Arthur blamed me for drinking too much but I wasn't ill every time I had drunk one wine too many. It was a relief to find out that I could take evasive action and cut these pesky food items out of my diet.

You may be wondering what had happened to my interest in stamps during this period. Well, it hadn't faded by any means and they were still in my possession, just. When I had been made redundant from County Hall, and Arthur and I were facing the possibility of losing our home, I had taken them into the local stamp shop in Taunton to see what they might fetch should I have to sell them. I'm glad to say the owner wasn't in and his elderly assistant asked if she could retain them so the owner could assess them upon his return. Well, being the trusting Scorpio that I am (not) there was no way I was going to leave my years' worth of stamp collecting with a complete stranger. As many were not catalogued at that time, how would I know if any went missing? So, fate took a hand and I kept hold of them—thank the Lord.

Whilst I had been studying and working simultaneously, I didn't have the time or energy for much else to be honest. Then when I got depressed, I didn't have any energy or interest in anything at all. But that's the good thing about a stamp collection, it doesn't go away and you can always come back to it later on when time permits. My dad still worked at Industra and due to his firm having dealings with companies all around the world, he saved all of the stamps that came into his office and passed them on to me. Over a period of twenty years this was a lot of stamps. Yet it would take another particularly difficult period in my life before I got back to immersing myself again in this spirit saving hobby. The events that led up to that, I will go on to describe now.

Chapter Twelve
Challenging Times

1999

British Millennium Series, Soldiers' Tale 19, 26, 44 and 64 pence

Following a relatively stable period during which, at 40 years of age I married for the second time, I also went on to appreciate job satisfaction for about eight years. Arthur and I were more financially secure than we had ever been. Not well off by any stretch of the imagination but we had a good social life, we both belonged to the local golf club and had enjoyed some super short breaks away. We felt so lucky to be living in this part of the country where we were spoilt for choice in where to go for a wonderful day out.

On one of these short breaks, we went to stay in a mobile home at a site in Challaborough, Bigbury. This holiday home was owned by our dear friends Mel & Ros (who lived in the bungalow next door to our former cottage at Lydeard St. Lawrence). The site had far reaching views across the English Channel and included in this vista was Burgh Island. This Island was the location for a famous 1930s hotel built in my favourite Art Deco style. For those of you Agatha Christie fans this is where the author stayed when she wrote one of her earliest best-selling crime novels. In 1998 as a treat for my 48th birthday, the four of us booked a meal in the restaurant of the Burgh Island hotel. And what a treat that was! The way Arthur and I justified the cost of this meal (£200 for the four of us) was the free accommodation for three days away and for the rest of the time, home cooked meals cobbled together in the caravan! It was worth every penny. You could only reach the Island by foot or car when the tide was out; otherwise you were dependent upon this tall tractor-like mobile with huge wheels. This was the mode of transport for getting to and from the Island when the tide was in and the place was cut off; aside from a boat of course. Arriving in our finery we sat and drank cocktails in the lounge surrounded by stunning 1930s furniture and furnishings. Linked to the lounge was a fabulous conservatory with one of the most special multi coloured leaded light circular glass roofs I've ever seen. It was magical. In the restaurant a female singer, dressed of the period, sang songs from the 1930s and following our meal we got up to have a dance. Our friend Ros had a smile that could light up a room and the kindest of hearts. She and Mel were never too busy to make you feel special or give you a hand. And we did have a laugh together. Ros really got on well with Arthur and she became one of his favourite friends.

Mel, Arthur, Ros and I in the lounge of the Burgh Island Hotel

Just prior to our marriage blessing and us selling the cottage we had a bit of a calamity. It had teemed with rain for one whole day and night when I got up in the early hours of the morning to get a Lemsip for my cold. I didn't put the lights on as I didn't wish to wake Arthur up but I seemed to trip over the rug that for some reason wasn't lying flat on the floor. Or so I thought. I switched on a light and to my horror discovered the whole of the ground floor carpet was soaked in over an inch of water. We had had a flood. I immediately woke Arthur up and we endeavoured to get as many items as we could upstairs before trying to bale some of the water out. At around 8 am I was in floods of tears and decided I would go to work because I couldn't deal with sorting out the mess. To make matters worse we had sold the cottage subject to contract to a lady who came from Snowdonia and her survey was due any time! With no hesitation, round came Mel and Ros to our rescue. They kindly helped Arthur to rip up carpets and move furniture out etc. It was a nightmare I do not wish to repeat. Yet, due to a couple of dehumidifiers running constantly for a week and the lower internal front wall being re-plastered, the damp didn't seem too bad. I knew however the Surveyor's damp meter would be off the 'Richter' scale in terms of a high reading. It was likely we would lose our sale. Unbelievably, this was not to be. The dear lady who was purchasing our cottage claimed her cottage in Snowdonia flooded once a year. So, this once in a lifetime flood caused (we discovered later) by an external pipe blockage was not to her a big deal! We agreed to drop the price and phew, the sale went ahead.

Sadly, we had lost Bubbly Boy to an illness soon after we moved to Taunton. As a consequence, we adopted two (ungrateful) tabby cat sisters from the Cat's Protection League called Whisky and Brandy. And no, I didn't name them! They took years getting used to us and us to them. Their former owner who had spoilt them rotten chose to keep hold of a boyfriend instead of these two cats. Apparently, he had given her an ultimatum, it was them or him—and she chose him—stupid woman! This decision on her part led to their constant bewilderment as to why they were now living with us rather than her.

Tragically, we also lost two good friends at very young ages. Rachel in her early 50s, who had returned to America in 1998 suddenly developed cancer; and unfortunately, it spread. She and Mervyn did regain contact with us during this difficult time as I think they realised how deep our friendship had once been. Rachel died only two years later. Then Ros our dear friend of homemade wine fame, died from an epileptic fit during an afternoon nap. It was a massive blow to us all, not least her husband Mel. We really miss them both.

British Millennium Series, Christmas Stamps 19, 26, 44 and 64 pence

On 31st December 1999, we experienced a New Year's Eve going into the new millennium like no other. The celebrations going on around us were something to behold. But we didn't end up celebrating it ourselves because Arthur was quite ill. He was in agony with nerve ending shooting pains that were travelling from the back of his head to the front. It was scary to see, as he could get little relief. He saw several doctors over the Christmas and New Year period. Either they didn't give him the right treatment or when they did, forgot to explain that he could take the epilepsy tablets he'd been prescribed together with the painkillers. We were hugely relieved when he recovered a couple of weeks into the New Year but he has been plagued with further episodes of this type of pain ever since.

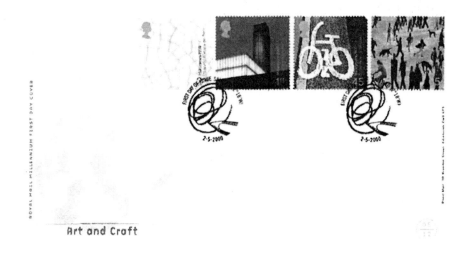

Art and Craft

British Millennium series, Art & Craft 2nd class, 1st class 45 and 65 pence

In 2001, it was Arthur's 65th birthday. His son Timmy rang me to ask if I minded if his father went on a golfing trip with him as a treat. I had never been asked if I minded before, usually they just took off when they fancied it, so I was a bit bemused. Magnanimously I said, 'Oh, how super, are you thinking of taking your Dad away for a weekend?'

'No' said Timmy.

Then I said thinking a bit further afield, 'A few days in Spain perhaps?'

'No' said Timmy. Then he thought he ought to spare me any more guesses so he said, 'I was thinking of taking Dad to South Africa (slight pause) for two weeks.'

'South Africa!' I shouted out, nearly ruining the surprise of it all. Now, how this came about was that Timmy, who worked for what was then The Royal Military College of Science, had become friendly with one of the lecturers. He and his father were going over to South Africa, partly for work reasons but mainly for golf. They suggested that Timmy and his father make up a four.

Initially I was happy for them both to be going on this fabulous holiday together. However, as the time of Arthur's surprise trip got nearer, I will admit to feeling somewhat left out, especially when Timmy presented his father with his plane tickets. Arthur couldn't contain his excitement at going away. He was obviously not going to miss me at all it appeared. So, I swallowed my disappointment and did my best to be pleased for him. But when they told me their plans, I was genuinely concerned about them going off alone in a rental car driving up the garden route. My yoga teacher at the time, Trish, who came from Cape Town was taken aback to hear they were not going with a guide. She stressed to me that some areas were unsafe and that they really should take care. Feeling anxious following her reaction I learnt to text by phone so I could keep in touch with Arthur during his time abroad. However, it was Timmy who made the first contact between us and I was so relieved to hear from him. This relief was short lived. After two days in Cape town and four days into the garden route trip no one got in touch with me or replied to my texts to say where they were. I was worried sick and imagined them captured or murdered by maligned black people who were avenging whatever action the whites had taken against them.

During the 1990s South Africa was in the midst of political turmoil and civil unrest. Since Nelson Mandela's release from prison on Robben Island, and the subsequent end of apartheid, the situation over there remained volatile. There were factions, including one led by Winnie Mandela (Nelson Mandela's wife) who were not happy to form a new government with the white people who remained in power. Many thousands of black people existed in townships (many of them shanty towns) and poverty and crime were rife. Meanwhile many of the white people lived in gated and guarded communities. Due to these circumstances, I felt my concerns for Arthur and Timmy's safety were justified. A couple of days later Timmy sent me a text and when I indicated how worried I was, I was told I was overreacting.

Timmy, Arthur and friends with caddies on holiday in South Africa

Another week went by and I missed Arthur very much. Despite the fact I had gone up to Wiltshire to spend a couple of nights with my friend Mary (to attend her son's wedding), it felt like he was away forever! Home he came and I was so pleased to see him. But Arthur went on and on about how wonderful the holiday had been, how gorgeous the scenery was, how amazing the golf courses were and what tremendous fun they had all had. Not once did he say he would have liked me to have seen the place, and his gift of a cheap golf shirt and two bags of herbs (yes, really) purchased last minute at the airport did little to make me feel any better. I stupidly asked him if he had missed me at all and he replied, of course he hadn't—well there's nothing like being honest. I began to feel rankled. Because of my off-handedness, Arthur felt I had taken away some of his pleasure, whereas I felt he had been thoughtless, tactless and selfish. But this was Arthur we were talking about. He had never been dependent upon me to feel good about himself, it just came naturally. My upset reaction caused a big rift between us. I think I realised at this point that, although I believe he loves me to the extent he could love anyone, it wasn't the all-encompassing love I think I was craving. I certainly didn't feel cherished. They say you can sometimes be lonelier in a relationship than if you are on your own. After this episode I definitely experienced that feeling.

Reflecting upon things now though, I can appreciate the two sides to this story. Some of you may even be thinking I was the selfish one spoiling Arthur's precious memories by my behaviour. Being truthful about it, I've realised I'm not much cop at unconditional love. Part of me wonders whether I was envious of his ability to enjoy good times without me. Was this my mum's and Nanna's inherited trait of jealousy coming to the fore? Even in the words I've chosen I get a sense of the bitterness I felt and that is pretty sad. I'm sure Timmy would be horrified to learn of the repercussions from his generous gift.

Later in the year I organised a 65th birthday party with surprise guests, which we held in the garden in August. Yet despite all my efforts Arthur remained distanced from me. It was his way of punishing me for upsetting him.

Our dear neighbours Nan and Les had baked and iced this wonderful cake for Arthur's birthday. He was thrilled with it and delighted to see some of his old work friends from Western Trust, so the party wasn't a total disaster.

We were due to go to Bournemouth for four days on our annual break away together with a view to celebrating our 6th wedding anniversary on the 12th September. In reality neither of us was looking forward to it and our resentment towards one another grew.

The day prior to this trip many people around the world witnessed something that will never be forgotten by those who saw it. And that was the terrorist attack by two planes on the World Trade Centre's Twin Towers in New York, that killed around 3,000 people in all. A third hi-jacked plane was brought down in

Pennsylvania by brave passengers who fought the terrorists, and a fourth plane crashed into the Pentagon. The first attacks happened between 8.30 am and 9.30 am USA time on 11th September and the event would be forever after known as 9/11. Arthur's friend George had been watching his television that morning when a newsflash came on showing hugely distressing scenes. He rang us up saying we should put on our television, which we did and then we actually witnessed the second plane crashing into the adjoining Twin Tower.

We stared in disbelief. Initially we thought it was a hoax as it was like watching a disaster movie. It has to rate as one of the most shocking and dreadful things to happen in my lifetime. Following both crashes both Twin Towers collapsed killing even more people including those brave firemen who had tried to get up inside the sky scrapers to rescue folk.

I think it is worth trying to explain to you (hopefully as simply and clearly as I am able to), as to how the world had gotten to the point of these abominable terrorist acts being committed. Initially, the Russians whose country bordered Afghanistan had for many years been fighting different Tribal factions with little success. The terrain and topography of Afghanistan meant any invading army would be at a disadvantage because the tribesmen could hide in the mountainous regions for months at a time. Especially when the weather was at its worse. Within the many different religious factions in the Middle East there were two groups of Muslims at odds with one another, namely the Sunni faction and the Shiite faction. I believe the main difference in their beliefs came down to their individual interpretation of the religious book known as The Koran and who the Prophet Mohammed was descended from.

Osman Bin Laden was an educated and wealthy young man from Saudi Arabia. He and his family had made their monies from the construction industry. He took his wealth and began to use it to follow his ideologies forming a terrorist group known as Al Qaeda. Many impressionable young men from Afghanistan, Iraq and the Middle East joined his cause, that basically was to rid the world of (as they saw it) the West's debauched ways of carrying on. Our drinking and promiscuity, including the way women were allowed to dress, all of these things were seen as evil by these fanatical sects. Since then another rival group called ISIS or Islamic State has been formed.

Meanwhile, Tony Blair, the Labour Prime Minister who had taken office in the early 1990s formed an alliance with George Bush, President of the United States in order to try and deal with these groups and their disruptive influences.

During the 1990s Blair accused Saddam Hussein and the government of Iraq of holding 'weapons of mass destruction'. Years later it was discovered that there was no substance to these accusations but Britain and the United States invaded Iraq on this basis. Our troops were sent out there to fight along with the American soldiers resulting in a huge number of dreadful casualties. On occasion men were kidnapped by these terrorist groups and subjected to public be-headings. Sharia law was extremely oppressive for its own civilians let alone invading armies. Women would be stoned to death for infidelity, limbs cut off for stealing and little mercy was shown for captured soldiers. I will never forget reading *'The Kite Runner'*. This book highlighted the sad divisions of two friends growing up on different sides of this civil war. There was (and still is) the impact on innocent civilians whose lives were (and still are) overtaken by marauding warriors; and changed forever by unspeakable atrocities.

After several years of fighting, Saddam Hussein was captured. He was discovered hiding in a drain and put on trial. He was later hung for his crimes against humanity, including those towards his own people. Little thought was given to what would happen to Iraq once so called 'victory' and the withdrawal of troops had taken place. There was a void in government. Then even more in-fighting began as various groups tried to take control. This was a huge mistake on the part of the coalition. So, the unrest and instability has continued to spread within the Middle East affecting currently Yemen and Syria where untold casualties are occurring and refugees are leaving in their thousands. For those left behind it must be hell on earth.

Osman Bin Laden claimed responsibility for the 9/11 attacks and was eventually killed by American troops who discovered his whereabouts. His body was buried in a secret grave so that he could not become a martyr for his cause. The world as we knew it would never be the same again. Terrorist attacks continue to occur in different parts of Europe to this day, three of which I will write of later. I have recently learnt that Bin Laden left some 29 million dollars in his will to continue the fight for Jihad.

For me, what occurred on the 11th September, put any of our personal differences in perspective. I suppose I thought with all of this tragedy going on, we would get ourselves back on track yet Arthur didn't quite see it like that. Things didn't improve when we got to Bournemouth. Finally, I said we may as well go home if we were not going to make the best of it. Something must have struck a chord with him because Arthur then began to be more civil towards me.

We went to the pictures to see Captain Morelle's Mandolin, which we both enjoyed enormously. We sort of healed our rift but I finally acknowledged that part of me was clinging on to an illusion of how I wanted our relationship to be, rather than how it actually was in real life.

I still loved the bones of the man but I had to toughen up. I kept busy at work, got my therapy and relaxation from yoga, golf and gardening in my spare time and Arthur played golf as much as he had always done. We had lots of friends around for meals and on the surface life was good.

By now Arthur was getting that bit older. I celebrated my 47th birthday and he celebrated his 67th birthday. He was still astute and mentally young in his outlook but his contentment level became somewhat lower than mine. During the winter months he was quite happy to watch all manner of sport on the telly and, if I'm totally honest, I was beginning to get restless and ever so slightly bored again. Work-wise, Arthur's short-term contracts at the Valuation Office had come to an end when he reached 60. To his credit he got a job reading gas and electric meters to supplement our income until he retired with back issues when he was 63 years of age. Hence for four years he had stayed at home and become my house husband, so to speak. He thoroughly enjoyed mooching around having the house to himself all day.

Things were changing for me at the council and departments were amalgamating left, right and centre. Staff were leaving and not being replaced. I got frustrated when visiting folks on the waiting list not being able to give them any hope of a move. Following the introduction of the 'Right to Buy' legislation, homes were being purchased by tenants at quite a rate. The only new properties being built were by Housing Associations. No new investment was being made by the councils to replace existing stock.

It was then that Arthur's friend Ray, who worked at a central government agency suggested I apply for a job being advertised there. The role involved valuing commercial and residential properties for taxation purposes, e.g. Capital Gains Tax and Inheritance Tax, and also valuing council properties which were the subject of an appeal under the aforementioned 'Right to Buy' legislation.

The only drawback was, that although I was to be based in an office in Taunton, the areas of properties I had to cover were in South London, primarily the districts of Lambeth and Southwark. I did occasionally get to value the odd property north of the river in Kensington and Clapton (of all places). This provided an interesting change. In 2003 South London had huge redevelopment potential and property and land values were shooting up at a rate of knots. The redundant docks and derelict warehouses, leftover from the heady days of the East India company, were transformed into 'Des Res' (desirable residence) apartments with views across the river, Central London and beyond. All manner of property was being redeveloped into a mix of retail and office premises as the Victorian era of industry was replaced by commerce.

Once a fortnight I would go up to London for either two or three days in the week to undertake inspections, gather evidence and property details from our rating records, and negotiate with other agents who were acting on behalf of their clients. The rest of the time I would be doing research and working on my valuations, in addition to speaking with agents and taxpayers themselves on the phone.

I'll never forget going up to London for my first day at work, with Ray for company. I was completely out of my comfort zone. Although I was grateful to have this opportunity to finally undertake the job, I had studied for so long to do, at nearly 50 years of age, I was no longer as confident as perhaps I was when I was younger.

I was so nervous but Dennis, my new team leader turned out to be a really nice guy. Everyone I met at the Lambeth office seemed to have worked there for years. But no formal training had been put into place. Despite the fact that I had revised taxation law and the various valuation methods I had no idea of how to use their computer systems. Everything seemed very daunting indeed. In fact, during my first day there, having had no real induction or training (I was just handed a pile of files and expected to get on with it), I told Ray I thought I had done the wrong thing in accepting the job.

Therefore, Ray took it upon himself to show me how things were done. Now this sounds really helpful but trust me it wasn't! To explain; Ray himself is one of the most kind-hearted chaps you could wish to meet. But he is super intelligent, has little patience (just like my father!) and had been working at this same place since he left university. Without actually explaining anything to me he grabs a file and calls up some details of (I later found out) comparable evidence on the computer. Then in a loud voice he asked me, looking at the screen, 'Now what does that particular figure suggest to you?' Well I hadn't a clue what he was on about and to make matters worse we now had the attention of one entire floor of the Lambeth office's staff. I was going redder and redder, hoping for the same floor to open and swallow me up, before quietly admitting that I didn't understand what he was getting at. He seemed to forget that I was not familiar with the screens or systems that he so obviously took for granted; and his lack of patience was not the best quality for training anyone.

He also struggled to look people in the eye when talking to them. If I ever mentioned anything of a medical or emotional nature, he immediately called a halt to the conversation; as if he couldn't deal with it. Whenever I asked him for a second opinion about a valuation I was working on, he would say something like, 'Well, you've got the evidence and arguments, just go with it,' which wasn't particularly insightful. In the end I rarely asked him for advice any more. I explained my predicament to Dennis, our team leader, who I used to see once a fortnight. He said Ray used to speak to him like he was daft too. Dennis said he had to occasionally remind Ray that not anyone was as quick at getting the gist of things as he was.

Thankfully, after about four weeks of struggling on, I was sent on a week's induction and training course, up to Derbyshire of all places, and this was great. I was able to meet and talk to other new members of staff. When we compared notes, we found we were all somewhat floundering. I was pleasantly surprised that I knew quite a bit about Landlord and Tenant law and answered a question relating to 'Propriety Estoppel' that no-one else knew anything about. This raised a few eyebrows and I gleamed a bit of respect from the others from that moment onwards. It was nice to know that I wasn't quite as dumb as I'd been made to feel in previous weeks!

And once I got over the fear of being overwhelmed, I thrived on going up to London to see my new friends in Lambeth and going out on inspections, learning all I could about my new area. I rarely took the tube as it didn't give you a sense of how one district leads into another. I nearly always went by bus, apart from travelling to the Lambeth office first thing in the morning. I found Brixton and Peckham particularly fascinating due to the colourful local markets and all of the different cultures living cheek by jowl. I could never get over the many spices and varieties of vegetables being sold and bananas so overripe they were almost black! The buzz of being in London brought back memories of my childhood and teenage years where upon I had been a townie used to city life in Nottingham and Derby. The streets of London rebuilt in Wren's time were so wide. All of the sights from the various bridges along the river could hold my attention indefinitely. I even braved going on the London Eye, a giant ferris wheel located on the embankment opposite the Houses of Parliament. I remember looking upwards and backwards as our 'pod' swung over the top of the wheel. My stomach literally did a flip. I gingerly made my way to the middle of the 'pod' and clung on for dear life to the slatted seat, along with two other cowardly individuals. The views were tremendous and I would dearly love to go on it again, even though I have no head for heights. When I went for my first interview for this job, Arthur and I had also visited Westminster Cathedral but the few hours we had to spend there did not do it justice.

I could never get over the scale of the place. I had my trusty London A-Z and usually tried to cover eight inspections in a day, which was rather optimistic. I soon got used to the idea that half an inch on this map was a very long walk! And I walked miles getting from one property to another. Yet it did give me 'a feel' for the various districts and how the properties could change in status from one end of a road to the other. Taking in the whole boroughs of Lambeth and Southwark, I travelled as far south as Dulwich (Maggie Thatcher's constituency at one time) Norwood, Streatham and Wimbledon; as far north of the river as Kensington, Clapton and Finsbury; and as far east as Rotherhithe covering many redeveloped wharfs along the way. I do recall at the end of one long exhausting day I ran for a bus with Morden on it and it wasn't until we got to Wimbledon that I realised I had got on a bus going in the wrong direction. I didn't get back to my hotel until nearly 8 o'clock that evening. I was so tired I couldn't do anything but lie on the bed with aching feet and throbbing legs.

It was in Dulwich that I met a really nice agent in one of the local offices there. He was not your typical city agent and quite a gentleman. He did offer to take me out to the theatre but I refused as I didn't wish to get into any entanglements with another man. I always found city agents viewed me with some amusement, as though I was a country girl with not a lot of nous. However, armed with much evidence I let them continue with this thinking until I had lulled them into a false sense of security, and then I would play my ace card.

I visited numerous blocks of flats in connection with 'Right to Buy' appeals and couldn't get over the high values, which the sold ones that were let out, were fetching. Some visits were a bit unnerving because you'd knock on the door and who ever opened it possibly didn't speak English and wouldn't, or couldn't, identify themselves as the actual tenant. Then you had to step over the various bodies sleeping on the floors (or wherever else they could find a space) and it was slightly intimidating to say the least.

I met some really nice characters too. During one particularly cold winter I had a tight bobble hat on underneath my sheep-skin lined, trilby-styled hat. Well, this bubbly young black girl couldn't stop smiling when she opened the door to let me in. When I came face to face with a mirror in the property, I could see the reason why. My trilby hat had risen upwards revealing the bobble hat underneath. I looked like I was doing an impression of Boy George. We did have a laugh about it together.

Once, when I was looking at shops in Whitechapel Road and taking notes for comparable evidence, I was challenged by a local market stall holder as to what did I think I was doing? I explained I worked for a government agency and showed him my pass and he left me alone. Then I realised I was being followed along the length of the road. When I had finished my inspections and moved on, he appeared to lose interest but it made me wonder what it was that this man was so concerned about.

Another time, admittedly with a *mild* hangover, I set about inspecting a flat above some shops in Clapham. Having borrowed the keys from the agent two floors below, I left these and my bag on the occupier's coffee table and proceeded to go through what I thought was a door to a roof terrace. As the door slammed shut behind me, I realised I was in fact entering a fire exit with no way back into the flat. So, I wedged the fire door open at ground floor level and got the agent to come back up the fire escape with me. I was highly relieved when he managed to break back into the flat. That was the last time I ever had one too many to drink the night before any inspections.

In the evenings I went out with two new girlfriends I had made in the Lambeth office, Gillian and Hilary. We would have a meal and a couple of wines and generally soak up the hectic atmosphere of night time London. We visited Convent Garden and the theatre and it was great to feel so alive again. I think Arthur, through my absence, began to appreciate me a little more. Upon my return he would collect me from the station to return home to a readymade Marks and Spencer's meal for two.

One night, Ray, Hilary and I went out for a meal together. Foolishly, Ray was drinking the same number of pints of lager that Hilary was drinking. But he was 'out of his league' I'm afraid because Hilary could take her drink a whole lot better than Ray could! Ray and I were staying at the same hotel and the next morning he turned up for breakfast looking the worse for wear. It transpires that in the early hours of the morning Ray had decided he needed the loo, but rather than opening the bathroom door, disoriented, he opened the door to the corridor instead. The door shut behind him and there he was, locked out of the bedroom with only his boxer shorts on to cover his modesty. Well, I started to laugh but that wasn't the end of it. In desperation, he went down in the lift to try and get a spare key card from the reception. As the doors of the lift opened, he was met by the rather astonished stares of the folks having drinks in the lobby!

In a panic Ray went back up in the lift and managed to locate a telephone on one of the floors. He got through to reception and requested he be let back into his room. By the time he had gotten to the end of this story, I was in stitches and I was laughing about it for the rest of the day. A more unlikely chap you could not imagine this sort of thing happening to, and this is what made the whole episode funnier, I think. To his credit, Ray did see the funny side of it eventually!

On another occasion, I was going to attend an office darts and quiz night but as I boarded the bus to get to the venue, I realised that I was haemorrhaging rather badly from down below: It was far in excess of a normal period and I had to return to my hotel room. Well, the bleeding wouldn't stop and reception were going to call for an ambulance but I didn't want to be taken into a hospital in Central London. After all, who would visit me? So, using up all the towels the hotel provided me with I got through the night and came straight home the next morning. It was after a clinic appointment that I discovered that I had got polyps in a place it's best not to have them. I explained to the consultant that I was the main breadwinner and couldn't afford to take time off work. Thank goodness I was operated on as an urgent case. Then in September 2004, Arthur was diagnosed with advanced prostate cancer. He was now 68 years of age and we were both shocked at this news. His consultant advised Arthur to undergo a radical Prostectomy that carried some risks and side effects but would be the best way to get rid of this awful disease. I asked if I could work four days a week, rather than five, as I knew I would need to support him through this traumatic time. This request was granted and in January 2005, Arthur had the operation and began his road to recovery. We later discovered following a scan on the removed prostate that if he had chosen not to have the procedure, the cancer would have spread. So, despite one disappointing consequence, we were both highly relieved he had made this decision.

The year prior to Arthur's diagnosis, another event happened that would have quite an effect on my life. I began training a young man from the Lambeth office who had joined us with a view to dealing with 'Right to Buy' appeals. One morning he was complaining about his salary of £33,000. This figure was around £5,000 per annum more than I was on! In addition, he had no investment valuation experience whatsoever and therefore was unable to value commercial premises as I was doing. I was gob smacked, to say the least. I began making discreet enquiries as to how much some of my fellow colleagues were on. I discovered that all of the men were on a higher salary than any of the women. It appeared that when any women had been taken on, they had all commenced work at the bottom of the salary scale, whereas the men started at a higher level; thus, the gap widened.

I couldn't come to terms with this injustice. So began my fight with the government's solicitors. Every spare moment of the next one and half years of my life was given up to undertaking research on the appropriate legislation, writing letters and sending off questionnaires. Building up a case took huge quantities of time and without the support of the union, it was tough. The reason the union's solicitor deemed my case could not be supported was because of a fairly recent agreement made between this central government agency and the union. This stated that pay relating to women would go up gradually so that over a period of several years, they should eventually catch up with what men were being paid. I personally could not see how this would work in practice, as men would still get annual pay increases. And why should I wait some five years to be put on par with my male counterparts.

The government's solicitors did nothing to assist me easily. It was like pulling teeth trying to get data from them under The Freedom for Information Act. I persisted and persisted and it took over everything, even putting a strain on Arthur and I in private. I would get frustrated and although Arthur backed me, he thought I would never see a positive outcome. I applied to go to Industrial Tribunal in the summer of 2005. It wasn't until the beginning of the week prior to the hearing that the government's solicitors caved in. They decided they would try to settle the matter out of court. My union representative then became involved with these negotiations. I was put on a more equal footing with my male counterparts, with back pay to when I had first begun proceedings. I was also given a small amount of compensation for the 'lost' year and half.

After all that effort, part of me wanted to go to tribunal to bring the matter out into the open. Yet I was warned that if I did not accept what was deemed to be a reasonable offer then the tribunal would not look favourably upon me. I had to sign a confidentiality agreement that stated I would not divulge to anyone the details of the settlement reached. It's little wonder that pay between men and women remains unequal to this day (in 2018). I shall be forever grateful to those Ford Dagenham lady workers (yes, sewing machinists everyone) who challenged the government in the late 1960s to recognise they were semi-skilled workers, not unskilled. As such they argued they were entitled to be paid the same as their male counterparts. Their actions led to the introduction of the 1970 Equal Pay Act. Regrettably equal pay is still not readily implemented by firms and companies today.

Ironically enough the union asked if they could use my paperwork, obviously blanking out my private details, to train new members of staff in presenting their arguments at tribunal. I suppose I must have impressed someone in the way I presented my own case.

In July 2005, I went up to London as usual to undertake some inspections. For once I wasn't looking forward to the trip because it was the week following the 7/7 terrorist bombings. This was also, unbeknown to me at the time, the week prior to the 21/7 terrorist bombings. Following the horrendous attacks on two tubes and the bus in Tavistock Square on July 7th, I nervously caught the tube on the Northern Line to our Lambeth office. Suddenly, it stopped unexpectedly in a tunnel between two stations. You could have cut the atmosphere with a knife. Everyone began looking around them to see if there may be a clue as to quite what was happening. The tension was palpable and although this infrequent stoppage lasted for only a few minutes it did shake me and, I'm sure, most of my fellow passengers up.

Meanwhile, our friends Mary and Daniel moved to the west country. Initially they were going to live in Cornwall but found the most popular places were too expensive and the less popular ones were pretty out of the way and bleak. So, they settled in a small village outside of Taunton and we saw a great deal of them. Mary joined our golf club, which was great and almost like old times when we played together at Marlborough.

Arthur and I had never truly been sure of Daniel though. If I'm being honest, he seemed a bit of a 'know it all', although this may have been due to a lack of confidence. He often said he'd done things and then we'd find out later this wasn't quite true. So that was a bit strange. And then he developed depression. Unknown to him or us, he suffered from episodes of bi-polar. Several times Mary rang me to say he had put a rope up in the garage and was threatening to hang himself. To start with this really worried us but, thank God, initially nothing ever became of these threats. I must admit to getting angry with him in the end as this was having a devastating effect on my friend Mary. We tried to support them as best we could; yet it was difficult at times. They would come over for supper and he would just be lost in his own world. He finally saw someone about his health issues and was put on a form of medication. It didn't have the desired effect. Then Daniel got it into his head that all would be well if he moved back to a village where he could be near to his family. So, they returned to Wiltshire some five years after moving down here. I was sorry to see my friend Mary leave and hoped all would be well for them both.

And then in the autumn of that year I contracted Lyme Disease. We are fortunate to have deer on our golf course but unfortunate for some of them to be bothered by tics who carry this form of disease. I had 'spent a penny' in some long grass at the far side of the 14th tee. I didn't realise that a tic had jumped out of the aforementioned grass and attached itself to my nether regions.

I never felt a thing but later that day when I was in the bath looking down at my lower tummy, I saw what looked to be a spot of congealed blood. Thinking I had caught myself on a bramble I burst the bubble of blood. Upon closer inspection I saw what appeared to be a big blown up body on a small head with pincers. I screamed out loud at the unexpected surprise of retrieving this creature from my body. Arthur (as usual) ignored the rumpus I was making.

It was just my bad luck that this discovery was made a week before I was due to go on a fortnight's leave. I was undertaking a housing survey that meant I remained in the Taunton office all that week but I don't know to this day how I managed to keep on working. I had awful headaches, my joints ached and I felt quite ill. I thought, blimey, I must be getting stressed, such was the pressure on me completing the survey before my holiday.

That first weekend Arthur and I, and our friends Janet and Phil, were going to a wedding in Wales and staying overnight. Gosh, did I feel poorly later that evening and night. By morning a bull's eye rash appeared to cover the lower portion of my abdomen. Arthur took me home immediately and on Janet's advice on Monday morning I went to the doctors. My doctor seemed quite excited by this development and was 99% sure I had Lyme Disease, which I had never even heard of. He even took a photograph of the rash so somewhere out there my nether regions feature in a medical journal. Bloods were taken, but as he suspected, there was no evidence of any anti-bodies showing up during the initial 4-week period. However, four weeks later following a second blood test, they did show up. As a result of contracting this disease, I spent the entire two weeks leave feeling as though I had been hit with a sledgehammer. I was then signed off work for a further week. Apparently, the symptoms are as bad as having a dose of flu' and if that's the case I'm glad I've never had flu. What I didn't realise at the time was how serious this could have been had I not received the necessary strong antibiotics to deal with the problem. There had been a delay ten days prior to my treatment so I hoped there would be no adverse effects due to that.

In October of that year I went for a routine mammogram and was relieved to get a letter to say nothing untoward had been found. The previous year I had had two cysts aspirated to ensure they were nothing onerous. They were deemed to be oil cysts so no further action was required.

Then work began to get stressful. My targets were getting harder to achieve because I was being given more and more development properties to deal with. Often, I had no full details of the extent of the demise, whether it be exact boundaries or number of floors; or details of existing interests e g leases or sub leases; or the exact planning permissions for existing use. Any easier cases dried up and I was left isolated in the Taunton office as Ray was given a secondment to the Treasury for a period of time. My team manager, Dennis who was based in Lambeth took forever to return my calls. If I had anything contentious to discuss I was left for days not being able to come to a firm conclusion. This abandonment really took its toll and one day back came my 'fight or flight' response. I sat in my office picking up one file after another, not knowing which case to deal with first. My heart was going ten to the dozen and I felt physically sick. I was feeling really tired too and I'm not sure it was anything to do with not getting enough sleep. I just felt everything was too much effort to deal with. Looking back at the previous two years' events, then I am not surprised I was unable to cope. And yes, I felt overwhelmed.

I thought I ought to go and visit my doctor to get myself checked out. And the minute he asked me how I was, I began to cry and I couldn't stop. He kept asking me different questions and registered that all my answers involved my job. So, he signed me off work for a month with stress and in actual fact I was relieved. I needed some time out.

My team manager Dennis came to Taunton to visit me whilst I was off sick. We went for a coffee to talk about how things had got to this sorry state. I don't think he realised what little support he had given me and I think he felt bad about it. He said upon my return to work he would be spending a week in Taunton going through my cases with me and reducing my workload. At one time I had a huge number of cases registered in my name. Although my targets were lowered to reflect the fact, I was currently working a four-day week, taxpayers and agents were given my name upon registration. This meant that I was often fielding calls trying to explain that I would not be getting to them for several months, which understandably did not go down very well. I had no administrative support to take messages and typed all of my correspondence myself because it was quicker to do that, then send tapes off for other folks to deal with in Lambeth. I don't think Dennis could believe that the bubbly confident person who had been part of his team was this timid quiet person sitting in front of him.

But before I returned to work, I made another discovery that was to change the course of my life yet again.

Chapter Thirteen
Traumatic Times

2006

British 1st Class Stamp from The Ice Age Animal Series

I was sat in the bath washing my top half, as you do, when I noticed a large firm swelling in my left breast. I thought it was odd but I had only recently been reassured by a mammogram that all was well. I even wondered whether I was being a bit paranoid in mentioning it to the doctor when I was next due to see him.

We had recently had a new doctor join the practice who was wonderful, unlike our old doctor who was rather scary. Hence, I did tell him of my recent findings. He examined me and decided that to be on the safe side, the Breast Care Clinic should take a look. I got an appointment within a couple of weeks. After a further examination it was decided to take a biopsy. The doctor there was fairly confident it was nothing to worry about; it was most likely a benign cyst. So, the following week Arthur and I went to the hospital for the results not feeling at all perturbed. Along came the consultant together with a lady nurse to tell me that my lump was cancerous and classed as Grade three because it was growing rapidly. And I would need an operation early in the new year. The date I received this surreal information was 13th December, 2006. It came as quite a shock and it did not occur to me to question the results of the recent mammogram that had indicated all was well. Yet the weirdest thing was, I can remember feeling glad that I would get some more time off work! How sad is that? To be told you possibly have a life-threatening condition and be relieved in some way about it. I think that says a lot about the state of my mind then, seeing this diagnosis as some form of escape.

Now, it is strange when you get news like this because you don't take it in initially. Then when you have to break the news to people you care about; you end up trying to reassure them that you are all right about it—in order to make them feel better! When the news had sunk in a bit, I started to wonder how this swelling could have been missed on my mammogram. So, I rang the hospital and asked to speak with the radiographer. She told me that what they had found on the X-ray was deemed to be three oil cysts, when in actual fact they were three tumours that had grown rapidly in the space of eight weeks to form one large tumour. She went on to say my cancer must be of a rarer type because with any Oestrogen type cancer the tumours are of an unusual shape, whereas my tumours were perfectly round. It seems the bottom line was, that I had had a history of oil cysts and due to funding shortages, the department had stopped aspirating them as a matter of course. If I hadn't been referred to the hospital by my GP, or indeed, if I had remained reassured by my mammogram results, then I would not be relating this story to you now. (I've recently learnt there are nine different types of breast cancer. Mine was of the Triple Negative variety).

I returned to work until the time of my operation and Dennis was true to his word. He visited Taunton to go through my files with me. Following the operation to remove the tumour in January and a period of recovery, I was to begin a gruelling round of six months of chemotherapy. At that time there was no specific drug available which would deter my type of cancer. Then I would go on to have radiotherapy.

The Catholic conscience side of me began to wonder whether Arthur and I were being made to pay for our sins and earlier adultery, so I never got around to thinking, why me? My friends and most of my family were all marvellous and positive but the news of my illness did hit my mum and dad badly. I didn't tell them how aggressive the cancer was but I think they guessed, due to the extent of my treatment regime, that things were not good.

My critical illness policy even paid out, and it began to dawn on me that my condition must be serious. By that time, breast cancer had become so common that often a policy would no longer pay out as the odds for survival were increasing; thanks to all the research and new drugs coming onto the market. It appeared this wasn't so with the rarer type of breast cancer that I had had the misfortune to get. Survival rates were low, especially in the first two years, although I did learn later on that if you got through the first two years then your chances of surviving for longer increased. And so, with my insurance pay-out we were able to pay off our existing mortgage and that was a huge benefit. Every cloud has a silver lining, as they say. When I came around from my operation my amazing consultant had been able to perform only a partial mastectomy and retain a good deal of my left breast, albeit much of it is now scar tissue. He went on to say if the cancer returned then a full mastectomy would be required.

And then began the most awful period in my treatment. I knew that I was being given two of the most potent intravenous chemotherapy drugs going. My hair fell out after the first session. I had been warned this would happen, so in trying to make the transition an easier one, my dear friend and hairdresser Ken cut my hair really short all over for free, bless him! It was rather a severe look I have to say but not as bad as when clumps of my remaining hair fell out unevenly all over the bath. This loss hit me harder than losing part of my breast funnily enough and I sobbed relentlessly afterwards. I did, however, choose a chic blond wig with short hair, a style that I hadn't been brave enough to try before. I decided that was the look I was going for when my hair eventually grew back.

I ballooned in weight because I was put on a strong course of steroids in a bid to keep my strength up. These made me really constipated and it was painful to try and go to the loo. In between all of this I felt as sick as a dog. The way I felt initially came in waves of good and bad. Straight after the early sessions I'd not feel too weak but then I would go downhill whereby doing anything at all was a struggle. Once my system had dipped then my blood count seemed to climb again ready for another blood test and another session. Early on during the process Arthur and I did manage a short trip to Dunbar in Scotland to stay with our friends Judy and Patrick. Judy had suffered with cancer a couple of years prior to me when she lived in Taunton. Thankfully she did not need to have the intravenous chemotherapy as there were oral drugs available to treat her more hormonal type of breast cancer. That break did me good because I was with friends who understood what I was going through. I could just go off to bed if I needed to any time during the day.

Following my third session I was in the garden trying to trim a bush for some reason. All of a sudden, I didn't seem to have the strength to open and close the shears. It felt as though I was doing everything in slow motion, it was most weird. I went in doors to answer the phone and it was the nurse from the hospital who said my blood cell count was extremely low and I really should be admitted to Ward 9. She asked me to take my temperature but I didn't have a thermometer. I said I thought I would be all right at home. She couldn't believe that I had been out in the garden trying to do stuff and I was to let the clinic know if my condition worsened. I was advised not to be in anyone's company in case they had germs, which would further compromise my already weakened immune system.

A few weeks later I recall my friend Mary ringing up to say she was bringing her new granddaughter around to see me, thinking of-course that this dear little baby would be a way of cheering me up. I said I really didn't think that was a good idea as I was not feeling at all well, yet still she came. Mary's son came along too and I think he was shocked at how ill I looked. I'm relieved to say they didn't stay long. I'm also guessing my bald look didn't help either! You also lose your eyebrows and your eyelashes through the therapy and that I certainly hadn't taken on board until I realised, they too had disappeared. By the time of my fifth session, my face and mouth were covered in ulcers and I looked as though I had gone several rounds with Mike Tyson. I felt so weak and ill I couldn't get out of bed and I certainly didn't wish to see anyone. I refused point blank to have the final session, even at a reduced dose. When I saw my consultant, feebly weeping, she said I had done really well as some people didn't get as far as I had on this particular strength and type of treatment.

Unsurprisingly, two things kept me occupied during this period. One, was completing jig saw puzzles (my mum had a penchant for doing these too) and the other was cataloguing all of those sets of stamps I'd kept for years in a shoe box. Despite the continuing feelings of nausea, especially when my head was bent low over my various albums, it gave me a great focus and satisfaction to get them all sorted out and mounted neatly in order. The only remaining mystery was that I seemed to have mislaid my British Guinea auction 'lot' purchased back in the 1970s. I couldn't for the life of me think where they could be and wrongly, as it turned out, blamed the little old lady assistant in the Taunton stamp shop for possibly holding onto them!

Then I had a couple of months reprieve because I had to gain back some strength in order to commence the radiotherapy treatment. During this period, I had rashly tried to organise a charity fund raiser, not realising how ill I was going to feel during the latter part of my chemotherapy.

Photograph included by kind permission of the County Gazette June 2007

Some of our wonderful friends and I, presenting the cheque to Eric from SURE

Thankfully, due to the wonderful support of all of our friends, we managed to raise £1,535 from a Cream Tea Party, an amazing raffle and some fantastic donations. The monies went to a Charity called SURE (Somerset Unit for Radiotherapy Equipment) because we didn't have such a clinic in Taunton's Musgrove Park Hospital.

Whenever anyone in the Taunton area required radiotherapy, they had to attend another hospital. Either Bristol hospital where parking was a nightmare and that was if you had some form of transport, or as I discovered, I could elect to go to Exeter hospital instead.

All of our dear friends from the golf club and beyond rallied round and took turns to take me there for daily sessions over a period of four weeks in all. I recall one journey when my friends Tottie and John kindly took me down to Exeter. John had bought a new Satellite Navigation system for his car. Whilst I was having a dose of radiotherapy, he managed to set it up for the return journey home. Out of the hospital we drove but instead of directing him to go left, this stern woman's voice said, 'Turn right, turn right!' This John elected to do and up the road we went towards a set of traffic lights. Then a new instruction was issued, 'Turn right, turn right!' Well, the lights were on green and the closer we got to this junction, the more urgent and more persistent became the command, 'Turn right, turn right, turn right!' So, John obeyed and turned right straight into the path of an oncoming vehicle! We were extremely fortunate that the driver of this vehicle was a Learner driver in a car with dual controls. The instructor jammed on the breaks thus narrowly avoiding a collision. I tell you, there's no end to the excitement in my life, wanted or otherwise!

Now the radiotherapy treatment did make you tired and your skin sore but other than that it wasn't too bad. Little did I know what would happen next. Unbeknown to me the radiotherapy had split my skin below my breast and an infection had got into it. I subsequently found out that this was MRSA and it was decided I must have caught it when I was undergoing chemotherapy. I did report the area being sore to the nurse at the Breast Care Centre but unfortunately, she didn't bother to take a swab. As a result, I began to feel really poorly again. I couldn't seem to get warm at all and shivered constantly. My GP thought I must be suffering from an infection and prescribed me with penicillin. Then my body began to swell up, even my head, and this did cause me some wry amusement amid all my woes. When I looked in the mirror, I was the splitting image of my brother Paul, who has a round face, blue eyes and no hair! My skin also became blotchy. I rang the out of hours number who advised me to go to the GP based at the local hospital. Well, this doctor thought I was allergic to something and prescribed me with anti-histamines. The next day I was feeling even worse and went back to see my own GP. He doubled the dose of penicillin saying I really didn't look well at all. By this time, I knew something was very wrong so I rang the nurse in the chemotherapy unit. She said I must ring my GP and tell him she thought I should be admitted to hospital immediately. My GP fortunately did this and Arthur took me to A & E with the required documentation.

I still didn't know how serious things were but I did in fact have septicaemia plus I was having an allergic reaction to the penicillin I'd taken. My body was now going into anaphylactic shock. So, doubling the dose of penicillin wouldn't have been helpful to me at all! I'd also developed a dry cough and my urine output fell to a low level. I was put into a shower in an isolation ward and washed all over with anti MRSA soap. Despite my shivering for some reason they had to wait until my temperature rose to a certain level before administering intravenous antibiotics. I was so fortunate to receive the care I did in Ward 9. Two gay men looked after me and nothing was too much trouble. One went in search of ice-cold milk from a machine as my throat was so dry. They were absolute angels the pair of them. I spent a week in hospital and was grateful that the septicaemia had been recognised so I could be treated accordingly. Once the medication took effect, my yoga tutor Trish visited me and went through a meditation exercise to try to help me relax and get some sleep.

On the way home from hospital I dropped off my discharge letter at the doctor's surgery. My GP rang me up within minutes of us getting through the front door. He said he was so sorry to read about how ill I had been and how he had got it 'so wrong' Well, I thought a lot of him for admitting that he had misdiagnosed me. I responded by saying it couldn't be easy doing his job and, after all, he had referred me to the hospital with my initial swelling so the cancer had been spotted early enough to treat. I shall be forever grateful to him for that.

All of these shenanigans took up much of 2007. We had booked a holiday in Italy when I was initially diagnosed as something for us both to look forward to and as a goal for me to get well for. We cut it a bit fine though because I came out of hospital following the latest episode and two weeks later boarded a plane for the Italian Lakes. I did struggle somewhat as my body was full of swellings and my joints would seize up if I was in any one position for any length of time. Yet to feel the warmth of the sun on my face did me the world of good. We crossed Lake Garda several times to visit various local villages but the highlight for me was a coach trip to the Dolomites. The driver we had was fearless and the way he drove us up the mountains around the hairpin bends was something else. I even got on the cable car that took you to the top of the peaks, admittedly clinging to a rail crouched on the floor, but I did it! And we have the photos to prove it.

On top of the world- the Dolomites

We met a super gay couple from Bournemouth and another fun couple who lived in Torquay. The only thing I felt self-conscious about was not wearing my wig. I had taken it with me and worn it when we went down for our first evening meal. The snag was it was so hot and itchy. The next evening I decided to do without—and this raised a few eyebrows. I think some folks may have thought Arthur had got himself a different woman! My hair had begun to grow back but instead of a mousy brown colour it was dark brown, just like my sister Kim's hair colour. In addition, it was growing out in tight ringlet curls all close to my head. I could have given Shirley Temple a run for her money. One of the gay guys who was sat at the next table said he thought I'd been out to the hairdressers and gotten myself a whole new look. I shan't ever know if he was telling the truth but I was thankful for his tactful and nonchalant approach. This holiday was the best tonic ever and well worth the donation we made in the Trevi fountain on a prior visit to Italy.

And then reality set in. Upon my return I had to visit the doctors to continue to be signed off. He did give me some time to get over the initial effects of the treatments and sepsis etc. However, Human Resources began making contact with me in a bid to know when I would be getting back to work. Most of the time I had little energy and still experienced pains in various joints and parts of my body. And then my back started to play up again. I knew I could not face a return to working twelve-hour days in London and all that that entailed. I agreed to meet with a manager from Human Resources to discuss rehabilitation. I thought they would give me a position based in Taunton with the idea I would be covering property in the locality as well. This they refused to do, saying I would spend several months being office based in Taunton but I would still be expected to cover the London regions. How they expected this to work I really don't know. I was not at all happy with the idea that I would be valuing properties without even inspecting them.

Now at that time my place of work was asking for voluntary redundancies so initially I thought that would be an option for me. I spoke with my union representative and she said I really ought to be eligible for early retirement on sick grounds. At that time, I paid a higher level of pension rate. This meant (apparently) that all I had to prove was that I wasn't capable of going back to the job as I had known it before. Honestly, I knew this to be the case. When I consider what my body and mind had been put through during the past three years, in terms of physical illness and the additional stress and anxiety I'd been subjected to over my claim for unequal pay, then I realised I was burnt out. My energy levels were at zero.

But despite being assured by the union representative that I had a case to be considered, then began *another* fight for this right to be recognised. My doctor and more importantly, my consultant both agreed that going back to London to work was not feasible and would be detrimental to my health. These expert opinions were not sufficient for the powers that be and I had to spend another year worrying about what was going to happen next.

During this period Arthur was not at his most supportive. He initially felt I ought to go back to work! However, much I tried to tell him that I didn't feel capable of doing this he didn't seem to hear me. Now this may come as no surprise to those of you who know us well but Arthur's hearing has been a bone of contention throughout our relationship. As with many men (if my friends are to be believed) when he couldn't be bothered to listen to me, he would nod and pretend he understood something; only for me to discover later on he hadn't heard a word.

It was some twenty years after we got together before I realised, he really did have a problem with his hearing. He began to turn the television up so loud it was deafening. Eventually I said he would have to get his hearing tested otherwise I would be applying for a divorce. We would also have conversations that went something like this; I'd say, 'Have you seen the cat?' He'd say, 'We don't need a new mat,' I'd say 'I never said that,' and he'd say, 'I'm not getting fat.' And on it went. You can imagine my frustration.

As I was at my wit's end trying to extract myself from my current job, and with Arthur not understanding how exhausted I continually felt, I got really low again. I remember one day I was thinking of all the times that I had supported him, through thick and thin if you like and I started to weep. And then this weeping turned into a sort of animal like howl. I was so hurt that Arthur could just leave the house for another game of golf, not being able to deal with any emotional outbursts. If ever I cried, which wasn't that often, it sent him running for the hills—literally (our golf course is located on the Blackdowns).

Thankfully, the doctor referred me for some counselling and that was one of the most insightful experiences of my life. My counsellor was a lady with great empathy. She made me see that I wasn't being selfish in trying to achieve what I wanted to do in life, for a change. She summarised the situation like this; as a youngster, I had helped my family, I had done everything my parents had ever asked me to do; I had been employed continually for 39 years, I'd financially and emotionally supported Arthur through all of his difficult experiences; and now was my time. And (most importantly) I didn't need to feel guilty about it.

This gave me the strength to write a letter to Arthur saying that if he wasn't prepared to support me in my decision to give up work then there wasn't a future for us. I think this came as a bit of a shock to him. He finally realised how serious I was about not returning to work in London.

I finally won the right to early retirement on ill health grounds. Arthur and I began a new chapter in life, in what I hoped would finally be a harmonious time together.

Chapter Fourteen
Painful Years

2009

British 1st Class Stamp – Royal Navy Military Uniforms

The relief I felt when I had achieved my latest victory (if you can call it that) was tinged with ongoing exhaustion and various ailments that I believe to be the culmination of having survived the depression, cancer, chemotherapy, sepsis and Lyme Disease. Now for someone who didn't wish for this book to be all about me, me, me, I am not doing too badly at featuring most of the time during this particular period. I realise I chose to write a memoir in part (so this latest observation is a slight contradiction in terms) but it has all been a bit melancholy of late. Suffice it to say that without the unfailing love and support of amazing family and incredible friends this difficult patch would have been a lot harder to bear.

The uplifting part is that when life becomes challenging all manner of good things seem to come out of it. You may not spot it at the time but one day you look back and realise, flipping heck, if so and so hadn't have happened, such and such may not have done. There is not a day that doesn't go by when I don't thank God that I am still here. I am very content with my lot. Even when I continue to experience the odd disappointment, I say to myself, just think, you can walk down the garden and enjoy nature in all its glory. Or (after I got a lot fitter) go and smack a ball around our fantastic golf course appreciating spectacular views. Or I can spend time listening to a meditation tape contemplating my naval. Or read a good book. Or get my stamps out and mull over them for an hour or two or three. One of my favourite pastimes is to purchase a £2.50p bag of stamps from the local stamp shop and sort through them hoping to achieve 'a find' amongst the basically rough and ready samples (sad but true).

As I had retired on ill health grounds, I was able to benefit from my small private pension from May 2009. Although we had experienced a big drop in income, because we had paid our mortgage off, we were able to manage financially. We didn't need loads of money. We had been fortunate to enjoy some fabulous holidays abroad in the past. Providing we had sufficient funds to re-join the golf club each year, pay all our bills and have a few days annual break away then we were happy.

From my pension I elected to take a lump sum of £30,000 in order to finance much needed improvements to our house. Part of the rear wall only had a single skin and our floor standing gas boiler was more than thirty years old. The kitchen was dated and all of the windows needed renewing. The conservatory was dilapidated, and the roof required a complete overhaul. As a consequence, all of these defects meant the house lost a lot of heat and energy. So, work began on making improvements. We were very lucky to find talented workmen to undertake the renovations and we were thrilled with the outcome.

This was also the year that I witnessed the first black American become President of the United States. Barack Obama was inaugurated as the 44th President in 2009 and he served in office until 2017. This truly was an impressive achievement, especially in terms of the fight for equal rights. Obama was such an articulate speaker. He put me in mind of another great black campaigner for racial equality, Martin Luther King. King 'had a dream' for all black people, that one day they would have the same rights as white people. Tragically he was assassinated in Memphis in 1969 before he could see any of his dream realised.

Closer to home, in 2010, things started to go downhill for my dear mum and dad. Around the turn of the Millennium they had decided to move from their 4-bedroom house in Hemingford Grey to a bungalow, to cater for Mum's mobility issues and Dad's breathlessness. Unfortunately, although their house had gone up considerably in value (by then Dad had purchased it with a mortgage under the Right to Buy scheme) due to high land values, there weren't that many bungalows in the village. And those that were, were way out of Mum and Dads' price range. Hence, they had to move away from Cambridge and closer to Peterborough where values were relatively lower. They purchased a brand new two-bedroom bungalow on the edge of the Fens in the historical village of Thorney. They had a lovely little garden and for ten years life was good to them. They spent most days going on off on jaunts and discovering all the stately homes, historical towns and cathedrals within 100-mile radius. Then they'd head home, have a snooze, and then watch a film or two on the telly.

But then Mum's sight began to worsen. To give some background to this, in 1996, Mum was taken severely ill and rushed in to hospital where the doctors fought to save her life. She had in fact become an insulin diabetic overnight after collapsing and suffering the opposite of a Hypoglycaemia attack. Her sugar levels had gone through the roof and her sight was badly affected. Despite seeing the village doctor on a number of occasions complaining of a constant thirst and tiredness, he hadn't recognised these most basic of symptoms. I was taken aback when I saw Mum shortly after her return home. From a young looking 60-year-old woman she had aged overnight. To her credit she did deal with the diagnosis of this disease extremely well and, fortunately, she had some respite from ill health until 2009 when matters became rather more serious.

Mum began to suffer with depression again; this time it was due to her deteriorating sight. I spent several hours on the phone each week talking to her about it and trying to get her to visit the doctor but she refused. Whether this was because she had a fear of admitting to depression following her electric shock treatment, I am not sure but she was definitely a frightened lady. Then she got Labyrinthitis, which is a truly horrible illness as the whole ceiling spins around; it is easy to lose your balance and you feel dreadfully nauseous. The paramedics were called out more than once to treat her and Dad continued doing his best to cope. Then her sugar levels started to get wildly out of control, or so it appeared. We found out much later that the blood testing machine she was using had gone awry. It was registering that her sugar levels were fairly normal when they were anything but, and she was at great risk of hypo's. Her diabetic nurse Diane had retired and, regrettably, no one replaced her. This was a great loss to Mum I know. Tony, myself, Kim and Paul all tried to help Mum and Dad but our parents stubbornly refused any assistance saying they could deal with things. They didn't even want me to go and stay with them and I found that very hurtful. Mum said she couldn't deal with visitors. I reiterated that I was her daughter not a visitor;

all to no avail. In the end I did manage to persuade Mum to visit a Psychiatrist for the elderly. I was relieved to find he was a man with great empathy and Mum did accept his prescribed medication.

Then something else occurred that sent Mum's health spiralling even further downwards. In addition to Glaucoma, she had developed Macular disease in both eyes. Due to her worsening sight her brain began to visualise things that weren't there. Mum was seeing images of babies faces coming towards her and all types of zig-zag and peculiar patterns floating around in front of her. I think she thought she was going mad with hallucinations. Eventually, she was diagnosed with Charles Bonney syndrome.

Mum and Dad had always been fiercely independent. They kept quiet about how they were no longer able to cope. They certainly did not want Social Services to become involved. It was really frustrating trying to give them any help. Dad was trying to care for Mum with no assistance from anyone. We did not realise how bad things were until it was too late. His health began to suffer too and he collapsed with low blood pressure and nearly died (again) in 2010. I stayed with mum for a time trying to get the bungalow up square as it had become quite neglected. I was up at 6 am (yes, really!) cleaning, washing and ironing and trying to encourage Mum to eat any meal I cooked for her, which was an uphill struggle. I tried to persuade her to go to the doctors but she adamantly refused. Meanwhile Dad did make a full recovery. Sadly, Mum had a severe stroke within weeks of him coming home. She lost her speech, her ability to understand us and her mobility. It was like her mind was trapped inside of her body.

Mum went into a Nursing Home in July of that year for what we all thought was a temporary stay. She never regained her speech, nor mobility, and refused to eat and drink properly. Dad couldn't bear to see her like this and stopped visiting her altogether. I went up once a month to see her and left broken hearted each time. I felt so guilty that I hadn't responded quicker or taken more notice of her cries for help, except in my defence, she was impossible to do anything for. Then a nurse discovered a lump in Mum's breast and she was diagnosed with breast cancer; a slow growing hormonal type. The subsequent visits to the hospital obviously added to her fears. As we were unable to communicate with her and explain her diagnosis properly, she became more and more withdrawn.

My sister Kim and her partner Bryan were angels during this period. Despite Kim working full time, they visited Mum twice a week at least. Kim spent hours trying to encourage her to eat a little, stroking her face and hands. Bryan was amazing with Mum and she responded to him in a way she wouldn't respond to us. I felt this was a small miracle and hoped she knew how helpless we all felt.

Describing the last months of her life is really difficult for me. The only consolation I have is that I spent the last three days prior to her death with her. Even though she was barely conscious I chatted away to her about old times. I tried to tell her how much we all owed her, how grateful I was for everything she had done for us in the past; and how sorry I was that I hadn't been able to ease her suffering. Tragically, one year on from being admitted to hospital following her stroke, Mum died in the Nursing Home on 6th July, 2011. She is missed so much by us all.

I remain close to her in spirit, especially when I am in the garden and can imagine her delight in all of the wonderful sights and sounds. We shared a love of the birds singing or having a shower in the bird bath, the frogs suddenly hopping out of the undergrowth making you jump, the scents of the lavender and honeysuckle with the bees and butterflies getting drunk on the nectar, and the various colours, hues and textures of the flora, grasses, shrubs and trees, that any artist might struggle to recreate. Amongst all of the lovely plants she gave me, there is a beautiful Magnolia Susan tree growing in our back garden that flowers each and every Spring.

Now whilst all of the early dilemmas were going on with my parents, I had in November 2010 been asked if I would consider becoming the Ladies' Captain at the golf club. This involved a year acting as Ladies' Vice Captain, a term beginning in March 2011, and then a year spent as Ladies' captain from March 2012 to March 2013. Initially I felt perhaps I ought to refuse because Mum and Dad may need me; but as they sort of made it clear they didn't, I thought it would be a way of taking my mind off my concerns in regard to them both. I did explain to the committee that if needed by either Mum or Dad I would be away in an instant and I may not always be available to undertake all of the duties expected of me.

As the ladies' section was desperate (no other silly sod would do it) these conditions were agreed upon. Just as well really, because as already described Mum never recovered and died during the year of my vice-captaincy. I would be lying if I didn't say her death was a relief in the end. We realised she had given up and it was mental torture seeing her constant anguish. Organising the diary for my captaincy year was therapeutic in a way as it gave me something else to focus on, other than the overwhelming grief I was feeling.

In a weak moment, I was also rashly talked into doing a sponsored disco dance wearing a ridiculous costume, by Marlene, the current ladies' captain, for her nominated charity. The outfit I borrowed was kind of Hawaiian themed with a grass skirt, and a cropped top. The top had two pink hands, a left hand and a right hand, strategically placed on top of each respective boob. A flashing light inserted into my belly button completed the picture. Needless to say, I swallowed a few wines to get me up on that dance floor. But instead of making my sultry and upbeat entrance to Billy Joel's 'Uptown Girl' (as I'd requested) The Jackson Fives' Rockin' Robbin' came on. Now if you've ever tried to dance to this tune you have a better sense of rhythm than me. Think of a demented chicken and you will get the general idea. Somehow, I managed to stay the course, dancing for four hours nonstop. Unfortunately, towards the end I got rather carried away and, to my constant regret now, began shaking my head from side to side in true Tina Turner style. The following day I experienced a bout of strange buzzing noises in my left ear. Mind you, Arthur accidentally shutting my head in the car boot that same day may not have helped. From that day to this I've suffered with Tinnitus. The moral of this story is don't pretend to be 'Simply the Best' whilst flinging yourself around the dance floor. The dancing challenge is the only bright spot I can recall in the whole year to tell you the truth. I think my memory must have been trying to wipe out some of the distressing images I had of Mum as she shrank away to nothing before my very eyes.

In addition to the terrible strain of wondering whether the next phone call would signal another downturn in my Mum's health, back in January 2011, I received a phone call from my dear friend Mary. She told me that Daniel, her husband, had had yet another disturbing episode and was threatening to end his life again. Despite the optimism with which they had returned to Wiltshire in the hope that Daniel would be happier there, this hope wasn't realised. The Mental Health services team in charge of his case did not seem to be getting to the crux of his problems.

Now, to put this latest threat into context, if you recall, Daniel had on a number of occasions within the past three years said he was going to end his life. Each time Mary had rung me in a panic feeling at the end of her tether. She often didn't know what to do for the best. He had never attempted to do the deed and we had no reason to think this time would be any different. I asked her where Daniel was. She said she wasn't sure, but she thought he had gone up to the shed, which was perched half way up their very steep rear garden. It was about 6.30

pm and pitch-black out, so I suggested she contact Daniel's brother who lived close by and get him to come over immediately in the hope he would be able to deal with the situation. Mary agreed to do this and said she would ring me back later on that evening. Well time went on and as it got to about 9.30 pm, I began to wonder if things were all right between the two of them. Generally following one of these episodes there would be a row at the very least.

I rang her number and for a moment didn't recognise who was answering the phone straight away. Then I realised it was Mary's sister. I was naturally surprised at this and I asked to speak to Mary. She said I couldn't speak with her because Daniel had taken his own life earlier on that evening. God, I was stunned. I went cold all over and couldn't take in what she was saying. I muttered something about giving my love to Mary and put the phone down visibly shaking. It was awful to think that anyone would feel that low and desperate they were unable to carry on. Arthur fetched me a large brandy.

I tried to keep in touch with Mary but this sad loss happened around the time I was driving up and down the motorways to and from Cambridgeshire in a bid to support Mum and Dad. Whenever I tried to contact her, she seemed strangely remote. I was initially hurt that she didn't appear to want my help. Then I finally accepted she must be in unbelievable despair herself. At Daniel's funeral she kept herself surrounded by her family and hardly spoke to us. I did have one odd telephone call with her a couple of months later when she was going over what had happened that fateful night. Gradually it dawned on me that she may have felt I was in some way to blame for Daniel's death. Now you may think this is ridiculous but in that same telephone call, I had mentioned my concern over not advising her to go and check on Daniel immediately when she first rang me. I wondered whether she felt there had been an unnecessary delay until his brother came around and they went up the garden to find him together. I will never know for certain. What I do know is that she didn't contact me again until the September after I had lost my Mum in the July. She wrote me a letter saying she had had counselling and felt more at peace with herself and wanted us to resume our friendship again. Regrettably, this letter left me feeling somewhat indifferent. I too had struggled through the past year, watching my own mother waste away. I felt Mary's lack of faith in me as a friend was not warranted. I could not see a way of us getting back together on to an even footing. And I wrote and as tactfully as I could, told her so. Perhaps I did feel some guilt over Daniel's death.

What I do know is that no-one, other than Arthur and I, could have been more supportive to them both, when they lived in Somerset.

So, life went on with me trying to keep busy and deal with my own personal grief as best I could. Dad's reaction to Mum's loss was strange. It was almost as though in the year that Mum had been ensconced in the Nursing Home, he had accepted her demise then. We now believe he was depressed because he took up gambling and got involved in all sorts of schemes and scams. I used to go up and stay with him for a couple of days every other month and he got more and more eccentric. He would wake me up at 5 am in the morning thinking this was funny. Trust me, anyone who knows what I am like first thing in the morning will know I did not find this funny. I would try to change his sheets and do some housework for him but all he wanted was for me to keep him company. We went out on little trips together and out for lunch, yet he was still very fussy about what he would and wouldn't eat, often complaining that something was wrong with the meal. He became obsessed with taking vitamin and supplement pills. Unbeknown to my sister Kim and I they were coming through the post thick and fast, chiefly from abroad. When he died, we found sacks full of unopened packets and jars of the blessed things. This was in addition to huge quantities being lined up on any available work surface in the kitchen.

None the less, I am so glad that I spent this time with Dad. I managed to persuade him to tell me his life story and I found out things about him that I never knew before. What his experiences were like during his National Service in Germany following the Second World War. He was in the RAF and at one time guarded the German/Russian border. He had witnessed men and women being shot by the Russians as they tried to escape across this border and this obviously had a profound effect upon him. When he returned to RAF Cranwell in England, Dad was given the opportunity to learn to become a pilot. He passed all of the preliminary tests with flying colours (no change there then!). Following this he went up in a Gloucester Meteor Mark 7 with a trained pilot who completed various manoeuvres to see if Dad could withstand the different G forces involved. However, in order to be trained as a pilot, Dad had to sign up with the RAF for nine years. By now he was nearing the end of his engineering studies and Apprenticeship at the Royal Ordnance Factory. With some regret he decided he would return to complete his final exams and become an engineer instead. It was during these chats together when he related to me how he had suffered as a child, losing contact with both his mother due to her illness, and not long after, when he was separated from his father too. It was also then when he told me how his father had been requisitioned by the government as an engineer to explore mine fields for oil in Nottinghamshire. His father had left home in order to do so. Hence why Dad, as mentioned earlier, was later brought up by his rather strict Victorian grandmother. He said the reason he had remained with my Mum during the worst of her mental health problems was because he didn't want us children not to have parents whilst we were young. I got rather upset over this admission because it didn't match with my vision of a passionate but volatile love that Mum and Dad had for one another. The idea that they had only stayed together for the sake of us children didn't fit with this image at all.

Together we mulled over my appreciation of collecting stamps and he generously gave me gifts of presentation packs for my birthday and Christmas presents. He saved all of the envelopes he was now receiving from around the world (due to all the supplement pills) but instead of postage stamps, these were printed editions of stamps. I don't get quite the same thrill as I do with actual postage stamps though; somehow, they don't seem authentic. I tried to get Dad involved in the local community but he had always been a bit of a loner. He and Mum seemed so wrapped up in one another there didn't seem to be room for anyone else. I tried to get him help with a private operation that was being pioneered for people with emphysema whereby the damaged parts of the lungs were 'sectioned off' so to speak. We drove up to Leeds to see the Consultant but before he was properly assessed, Dad had a bad fall in the garden and broke his shoulder.

During this period, I had begun my tenure as Ladies' Captain at the Golf Club. I was very fortunate to share my captaincy year with the Club Captain Neil Grout who was such a nice chap, with infectious enthusiasm about everything and so easy to talk to. He knew I was dealing with lots of personal stuff and had a lot of empathy. Also, I didn't have a vice-captain until the Autumn of my year. Thankfully a former ladies' captain, Shirley came to my rescue. All that aside, our Captain's 'Drive In' was huge fun. I dressed up as Mini Mouse in order to raise extra funds for our charity (folks had to guess who I would be dressed up as beforehand). I wished to be remembered indefinitely so I practised having an air shot. Strangely, this is really hard to do on purpose! Thanks to a large brandy I hit the best drive I've ever hit off the first tee and as a result sank into obscurity! And Neil did what came naturally to a good golfer with a low handicap—he hit a huge drive down the fairway over the crest of the hill.

This was a hectic time for me as I was on call 24/7. I had emails flying in and decisions to make on a daily basis about all manner of things. Just my luck we endured the wettest summer for over one hundred years in 2012. It rained and it rained and it rained. Competitions and matches were continually being postponed and then we still had to play them in dire conditions. Greens were saturated and no relief could be found. I, and our ladies' Club Champion, had also been chosen to represent Taunton & Pickeridge Golf Club in the Somerset County Centenary Plate competition. And that is one of the things I am most proud of doing during my captaincy year, apart from our charity fund raising achievements for the local hospital. My partner Fi (short for Fiona) and I won the Centenary Plate. We both had no expectations of how we would do beforehand. It was a Foursomes knock-out competition, which meant you had to play alternate shots. She was the most accurate player I've ever had the pleasure and privilege of playing with, her handicap being two no less. My putting that year was red hot, if I say so myself, I practised and practised it because you really could floor the opposition if you kept sinking the putts. I played off a handicap of 24 at the time so my shots came in useful too. We played on lots of different courses throughout the County with the final being held at Enmore Golf Club in the Autumn of 2012. Fi, who is now 33 years of age going on 18, now holds the distinction of winning Taunton & Pickeridge's ladies' club championship for the past eight years! Young Emily won the Nett Salver at her first attempt!

2012

Fi on the left with the Ladies Club Championship Trophy, me, and young Emily with the Salver

Another highlight from this year was Britain hosting the 2012 Olympics in London. The opening and closing ceremonies were spectacular and made one feel extremely proud to be British. Even the Queen was featured (allegedly) being lowered into the Arena by James Bond from a helicopter! Our athletes achieved tremendous success, each one seeming to inspire the next. One particular day became known as Golden Saturday with gold medals being won by Mo Farrah, Jessica Enniss and Greg Rutherford within hours of one another. In total our British team won 19 individual gold medals with a further 29 team gold medals in sports as diverse as rowing, cycling, equestrian, athletics, boxing, taekwondo, shooting and last but not least, Andy Murray in tennis. The whole country was gripped with Olympic fever! The Paralympics were hosted next and further outstanding performances were witnessed. No less than 31 individual gold medals were won, together with 10 team gold medals. If that isn't a testimony to overcoming adversity, I don't know what is. This was the year the nation took swimmer Ellie Simmonds to their hearts. Her smile and bubbly personality when she won both her gold medals lit up the entire pool! Two special editions of stamps to celebrate these great sports men and women were issued soon after. I was fortunate (via a friend) to get hold of the first edition featuring the Olympic champions but my acquisition didn't include the second edition featuring the Paralympic champions and that *is* a source of regret.

2012 was also the year of our Queen Elizabeth's 60th Jubilee. Many Royal visits and ceremonies were organised in celebration of this special anniversary. In one of our ladies' annual golf matches we held a match between a team of ladies representing the Olympians versus a team of ladies representing the Royals. The prize for originality (and daftness) was awarded to Gill who was dressed, and played a round of golf, as the Olympic torch! She was a sight to behold.

Our ladies' section went on to raise even more funds for my nominated charity, Taunton hospital's League of Friends thanks to the generosity of Theresa. She kindly hosted a tennis and bridge day with wine and lunch included, the food all being prepared and supplied by our super lady members. Tennis and bridge are not my strong suits (forgive the pun!) but I made short work of the food and wine tasting.

One of the most dreaded things for me about being ladies' captain was all of the speeches you had to make. At each and every event something apt was required. As you may recall, I was (and still remain) terrified of getting up to speak in front of people. Somehow it seemed worse doing it in front of my peers at our Golf Club. I lost a lot of weight that year chiefly due to the large amount of time I spent sitting on the loo before each presentation!

Meanwhile Dad was released from hospital with a haematoma in his left arm. We now all think he had convinced the medical staff he could cope because all he wanted to do was get back home. I cannot imagine it being the doctor's decision to discharge him with this abnormal condition. I know he was worried about his two cats, despite Kim and a neighbour taking care of them. He did agree that Social Services could call on him daily but he refused outright the offer of Meals on Wheels saying he would not 'eat that muck'. He was so stubborn and even refused to go and stay with my brother and his wife, Paul and Theresa for a while. Then he had another fall which burst open this huge swelling in his left arm. He also injured his right elbow too. This was the beginning of the end for my poor Dad. An infection set in and Kim got him readmitted to hospital. It was at the weekend so instead of the surgeons operating on him immediately the duty doctor put him in a geriatric ward where he got very sick indeed. On Monday he was taken to theatre and his wounds on both elbows were scrapped out to the bone itself. He was then transferred to the trauma ward and this was where I was to spend many days over the next few months. I went up and stayed with my sister Kim so I could be with Dad during the week days, when my siblings were working. I would go home for the weekend but blimey it was exhausting. I witnessed him in great pain as the doctors fitted some type of drainage pumps onto his elbows that should have got rid of the infection which was poisoning his body.

We had periods of hope and then Dad began to hallucinate. I asked the nurse what was causing this and she felt it could be attributed to the morphine he was on. He didn't improve and then it was recognised he had a massive water infection. Dad only weighed about seven stones at the best of times and he was wasting away in front of me too. To see the parents you love having to suffer like this, is an excruciating and unforgettable experience. These images still haunt me. Writing this account has brought much of it back but this was part of what was happening to me and my family so I feel it appropriate to include it. Finally, Dad's fight for life came to an end. It still didn't register with me that he wasn't going to get better. I genuinely believe that he died due to the hospital's failure to act straight away when he had been readmitted. And that's allowing for the assumption that it was possibly Dad's request to go home with the haematoma in the first place. He should have had an emergency operation; of that I am certain. Whether it would have saved his life, of that we will never know. Whatever the failures of the system, I realise any further investigation won't bring him back. I miss him dreadfully; he was the most unselfish Dad ever. I can still feel the hurt and pain vividly, nearly seven years later. My hero of a Dad died on 4th October, 2013 and my one regret is that I didn't do more to help him.

Understandably, Christmas 2013 was not a time for celebration. Arthur and I spent it for once on our own. In previous years we had invited our friends Marion and Stewart for Christmas Day, Stewart being our old neighbour from Lydeard St Lawrence. But sadly, he too had died in March of that year. I felt I needed time to grieve for my Dad, and I was still grieving for the loss of my Mum, who died two years earlier. Following a good brisk walk Christmas day morning we had our smoked salmon, followed by duck etc and I drank the best part of a bottle of Prosecco and half a bottle of white wine. In the afternoon I put on a Compact Disc of the latest '*Les Miserables*' film and cried buckets when it got to the part where the young girl's father dies at the end. I ended up with a chronic headache and went to bed at 9.30 pm glad that I didn't have to pretend to be happy that it was Christmas any more.

We cautiously welcomed in the New Year hoping against hope 2014 would be a much better one than the previous three years. Now this is worrying. I'm trying to recall what happened in 2014 and it must have been an unremarkable year in many ways because I can't think of anything out of the ordinary happening, nor thank goodness anything desperately sad happening. Ah, something has come back to me.

This was the year that my dear Auntie Marge kindly treated Arthur and I to a super week away in Guernsey. She came down to see us for her annual visit, only this time she came in August rather than September. Following a couple of days here in Somerset to find her feet, we all flew from Exeter airport in a bone shaker of an aircraft. This particular model had twin turbines on the front and rattled rather alarmingly when we came in to land at Jersey en route and then took off again. The plus side was that we were only in the air for some 20 minutes at a time. I even got a bit blasé about take-off and landing following this experience.

We didn't get off to a great start because the airline wouldn't take our luggage using some unreasonable excuse saying the conveyor belt had broken down. We were promised it would be flown over the next day and delivered to our hotel (the luggage that is, not the conveyor belt). Then the transfer taxi was nowhere to be seen at Guernsey airport, so we had to hire another one and pay out for that. Then when we checked in to our lovely hotel overlooking the ocean, our room didn't have the bath we had requested. So, all in all it was a bit frustrating trying to remedy the situation. Arthur and I moved rooms the next morning but we all had to go into this posh dining room in our travel clothes the first evening because of course we had nothing else to wear.

Despite these small irritations, we had the most wonderful time. Aunt Marge is my Dad's older sister and she and I get on very well together. She is the most independent person I know. From the outset she didn't want us to feel that we had to spend every minute with her, which was really thoughtful. We sampled the best cuisine and both rooms had sea views with balconies outside. The weather wasn't 'wall to wall' sunshine but it wasn't cold either.

One morning we set off to catch the bus for a tour of the island. It was spotting with rain and my aunt Marge should have been in the boy scouts because she was prepared for every eventuality. Out came this white 'pack a mac' that ballooned into the largest item of clothing you've ever seen. Aunt Marge is only 4 foot 6 inches tall and this raincoat looked like a tent when she finally became ensconced in it. Arthur looked down at her and said, 'Blimey Marge, you look like something out of 'Silent Witness!'' She has a great sense of humour and we were laughing about this for the rest of the trip.

Another day we went to visit the underground caverns where the Germans held fuel storage tanks and set up workings when they occupied the island during the Second World War. We read about how difficult it was for the local people who had to follow stringent rules and regulations, or risk being imprisoned or even worse shot. It was here that I found, to my surprise, loads of stamps on sale. They appeared to be collections that the generous folks of Guernsey had donated to the local charities. I was in my element and spent a good part of my spending money on some great First Day Covers.

We even managed to visit the small island of Sark. This was a feat in itself because the only downside in trying to do stuff with my aunt Marge is that she takes forever to get going in the morning (remind you of anyone?). We had to be at the port to catch the boat by 11 am but we had a bus ride first of all to get to the port, so extracting Aunt Marge from her room in time to begin the trip took some doing. It was wonderful at Sark and like stepping back in time as there were no motorcars at all. Everyone went by foot or horse and cart. We had a trip around the island and it was so pretty. Then on the way back to Guernsey, the sea got a bit choppy and it was hilarious because everyone who sat near the bow of the boat kept getting soaked. Everyone was laughing about it in the end. All too soon it was time to return home to Somerset.

By the time Aunt Marge visited us the following year, I was well into researching my family history and had got back as far as the early 1600s in the Barrable line; the mid-1800s in the Jones line (yes my great grandmother's maiden name Jones is really difficult to accurately trace back), the early 1700s in the Elvidge line (my nanna's maiden name, although another family member had made much headway with this already); and the early 1800s in the Cook line (my gramps' family name).

Then to my huge excitement, I discovered a link from the Barrable line that led to the aristocratic Arundell family that eventually took me back to Michael

De Trerise in the early 1300s. I even discovered my Normandy roots! Hence, when Aunt Marge next came to stay we went to visit our ancestral home, namely Trerice Manor, near Bude in Cornwall. Before we got there, I was all for claiming our inheritance. But upon our arrival workmen were renovating the intricate plasterwork on the ceilings and donations were needed to the tune of £250,000. So, I thought I would hold my horses and wait until the works were completed before making any further overtures. Here is the brief(!) version of my family's link on my father's side to the Arundell family in Cornwall.

Chapter Fifteen
Sir John IV's Story

C1495

British 78 pence Stamp – The Tudor Rose

Whilst researching my family history, I was fortunate to meet up with historian Diane Green who works as a volunteer at the local Museum in Holsworthy. If you recall, this is the small town in Devon where my 2nd Great Grandfather Henry Pethick Barrable of illegitimacy fame was born in 1854.

Diane kindly helped me trace through Parish records the Barrable lineage back to my 8th Great Grandfather, William Barriball who was baptised in 1671 in the small Cornish village of Alternon. He married a lady called Mary Vosper on 18th April, 1705, when she was 5 months pregnant. Sadly, this child also called William, died when he was 1 day old. Despite the 'shotgun' wedding they were married for 30 years and raised eight children together including my 7th Great Grandfather, unsurprisingly another William Barriball who was baptised in 1727. William and Mary, my 8th Great Grandparents died at the ages of 64 years and 80 years respectively. I can't help noticing how, in general, the women often outlived the men by quite a number of years, so there's hope for me yet! I'm guessing that the tradition of naming the first-born child after its parents is probably linked to the Royal tradition of doing much the same thing.

Now, Mary's 2nd Great Grandfather was Daniel Vosper and he is my 11th Great Grandfather. Daniel married into the Dinham family which would have been spelt Dynham, the letter I being a 'y' in those days. He and Judith Dinham got married on 1st November, 1621 in Saltash, Cornwall and one of their children who was also named Joseph (Vosper) was born in North Tamerton in 1624. He was my 10th Great Grandfather too, in that particular family lineage, in case you're losing count!

Judith Dinham's father was called Oliver Dinham (or Dynham) this being my 12th Great Grandfather. And it is he who married Miss Mary Arundell of Trerice (a daughter in the noble family of Arundells) in 1589. As a result, Miss Mary Arundell is my 12th Great Grandmother. Sadly, records seem to suggest that her husband, Oliver Dinham only lived until he was 28 years of age, the cause of his death I have yet to discover.

Mary's grandfather was John of Trerice otherwise known as Jack of Tilbury Arundell West Sherriff. *Now comes the exciting bit!* And possibly why I am so enamoured with the Tudor period in history. According to historical records Sir John Arundell IV (John of Trerice/Jack of Tilbury), this being my 14th Great Grandfather was knighted at the Battle of Spurs in 1513, and was twice Sheriff of Cornwall, 'esquire of the body' to *Henry VIII* no less! Sir John was only in his late teens or early twenties in 1513 so that was some achievement.

This same account records that Sir John was vice-admiral of the west under both Henry VII and Henry VIII. In 1520, Henry VIII entrusted him with the preparations for the reception of the Emperor at Canterbury. In 1523 Sir John captured, after a long sea battle, a notorious Scotch pirate Duncan Campbell who had for some time 'scourged our coasts'. The Duke of Norfolk later wrote requesting Sir John bring his prisoner to the King's presence and thanking (sic) him in the King's name for his valiant courage. In 1544, Henry VIII wrote requesting Sir John's attendance in the wars against a French king (at this time Francis I was on the throne) and in 1553, when he was Sheriff of Cornwall, Queen Mary wrote requiring that he 'should see the Prince of Spain most honourably entertained if he fortuned to land in Cornwall'.

Sir John Arundell IV is thought to have been born c1495 (although it may have been slightly earlier) and died in 1561. He is buried at Stratton Church in Cornwall where there is a monument built to his memory. He came from the Protestant side of the family, hence his relative longevity.

It is interesting to note that the Catholic side of the Arundell family in Cornwall, who were related through my 15th Great Grandmother Jane Grenville, did not get off so likely. Thomas Arundell was executed during Edward IV's reign in 1552. At this time folks with religious leanings towards Catholicism were still paying a heavy price for Henry VIII's break with Rome, due to his divorce from Catherine of Aragon and subsequent marriage to Anne Boleyn.

A further connection with myself and Henry VIII relates to my 13th Great Aunt Juliana Arundell who was the sister of Miss Mary Arundell. Juliana Arundell married Richard Carew who was a great philosopher at the king's court.

Sir John IV's son John V, my 13th Great Grandfather, was the man responsible for the rebuilding of Trerice Manor much as you see it today, minus a whole wing of the property, which fell down due to neglect in more recent years. The Manor is now cared for by the National Trust and this mainly Charitable institution is doing a grand job of it.

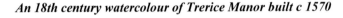

An 18th century watercolour of Trerice Manor built c 1570

Image included by kind permission of the National Trust

Juliana Erisey, my 14th great grandmother (not to be confused with my great aunt Juliana above) was the second wife of Sir John IV (or Jack of Tilbury) and her granddaughter was Miss Mary Arundell, the lineage from whom my family and I are descended. Now the Erisey coat of arms can be found in Mullion Parish church located on The Lizard in Cornwall, although I have yet to see it. We have dear friends, Simon and Margaret, who live in Mullion and we have visited them many times in the past but mainly before I gleamed all of this fascinating information.

The Arundells of Cornwall are one of the few Cornish families of Norman origin. Now the other odd thing that strikes me, is that I have such an affinity for the French language, and the *fleur de lys* pattern which has featured in curtains and ornamental plasterwork in my own home. By coincidence the *fleur de lys* forms part of the Coat of Arms of this amazing (there, I've said it) family. With acknowledgement to author Jo Wood's Arundell family tree I have printed off a copy of part of the lineage in the hope it is slightly easier to understand than the written version above.

The Barrable family link to the Arundells of Trerice

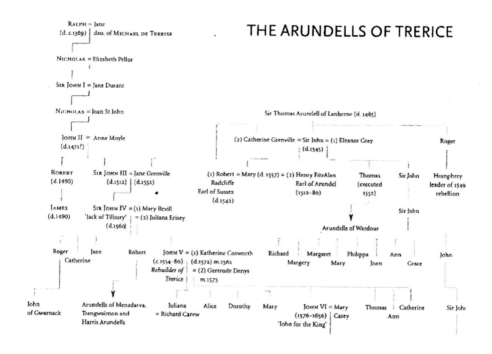

Mary Arundell my 12th Gt Grandmother, daughter of Sir John Arundell V & Katherine Cosworth marries Oliver Dinham (Dynham) in 1589

Daniel Vosper my 11th Gt Grandfather marries their daughter Judith Dinham in Saltash in 1621

Joseph Vosper my 10th Gt Grandfather marries Mary Frane in North Tamerton in 1649

Joseph Vosper my 9th Gt Grandfather marries Mary Prest in 1679

Mary Vosper my 8th Gt Grandmother marries **William Barrable** in North Petherwin in 1705

I think it most peculiar that I have returned to live in the South West of England, near to the place where my 2nd Great Grandfather Henry Pethick Barrable set out on his own journey from Holsworthy in North Devon to travel as far north as Newcastle. Then his descendants moved down to Old Ollerton, in Lincolnshire where my dad was born. He moved to Nottingham where I began life. And now I have ended up back in Somerset close to my original family roots for all the reasons already described.

Barrable is a Cornish name. Although the spelling is varied, this is because the people undertaking the census may not have had great writing skills. Often many ordinary folks were illiterate as they were unable to attend school. In my 4th Great Grandfather's family, Richard Barrable is the only sibling to spell his name as just written. In the census and Parish records there are four variations for Thomas Barriball, his father, as follows: Bewriball, Barable, Berible, and correctly for him, Barriball. In old Celtic language Bar a Bel means 'top of the mine' which leads me to believe that my earliest ancestors may have been involved in tin mining at some point. I aim to return to Altarnon (now known as Altarnun) in the near future in the hope of discovering more. It's put a whole new light on watching 'Poldark' of a Sunday evening I can tell you!

There is one thing I regret enormously. My father always believed he came from 'good stock' as he put it. He would have been just as excited as I am to learn of this early family history but sadly, he died before I learnt of this rich and interesting past. I hope he is up there watching.

Below I have drawn up the Barrable family lineage going back to Christopher Barriball who was born in 1597 and for whom I am so grateful to have a copy of his Last Will and Testament.

Barrable family linege

Christopher Barriball born Alternon (1597–1662) marries Alice (1599–1666)

Nevill Barriball born Altarnon (1620–1683) marries Ann (1620–date unknown)

Hezekiah Barriball (1648–1714) marries Jane (1647–1700)

William Barriball baptised Altarnon (1671–1735) marries **Mary Vosper** (1685–1765)

William Barriball baptised North Petherwin (1727–1801) marries Mary (dates unknown)

Thomas Barriball baptised Treneglos (1750–1832) marries Sarah Downing (1750–1826)

Thomas Barriball born Werrington (1774–1855) marries Grace Parsons (1775–1860)

Richard Barrable born Luffincott (1799–1879) marries Grace Harris (c1799–1878)

Ann Barrable baptised Holsworthy (1835–1913) bears son of Henry Pethick (c1816–1892)

Henry Pethick Barrable baptised Holsworthy (1854–**1929**) marries Ellen Turner (1853–1939)

William Henry Barrable born Birmingham (1877–1943) marries Emma Jones (1874–1958)

William Henry Barrable born Aston (1901–1980) marries Lilian Maud Makin (1905–1991)

Ronald William Barrable born Old Ollerton **(1929**–2013) marries Ann Cook (1935–2011)

Chapter Sixteen
More Recent Times

2014

British 1ˢᵗ class Stamp – Centenary of the Start of the First World War

Without waxing lyrical too much I've realised I've forgotten to let you know about one of the most inspirational gardens that Arthur and I are fortunate to have on our doorstep. Hestercombe House is less than 4 miles away and was, up until 1872, originally the home of the Warre family. The formal Grade I listed gardens located to the south side of the property were created by two extremely talented people, namely the architect and landscaper Edwin Lutyens and the famous horticulturist Gertrude Jekyell. They worked in tandem on many gardens from the year 1889. In 1904 the pair were commissioned by the Portman family to create the formal gardens that are in existence to this day. The hard landscaping is superb and leads the eye through various stone features to the Vale of Taunton and Blackdown Hills beyond. The sunken parterre surrounded by retaining stone walls and stone steps leading up from each corner was actually dug out by hand; as were the two rills laid out in symmetrical fashion to each side of the parterre. This was a massive excavation project and we have viewed the photographs that prove it! Obviously, the planting is not original but thankfully the detailed drawings and designs by Gertrude Jekyell are retained on the premises. Subsequent head gardeners have faithfully replicated her whimsical cottage garden style of informal planting within Edwin Lutyens formal framework. Included are many of the different species and varieties of plants with spectacular colours that Gertrude Jekyell would have used.

This year marks the 175th anniversary since the day this famous plants-women was born. Her trademark style of planting has been left on some 400 or so other gardens. Arthur and I feel privileged to be members at Hestercombe. Over the years, when either of us has been going through a bit of bad patch (forgive the pun) health wise, we find these gardens very therapeutic. Due to masses of succession planting there are carpets of pure white snowdrops in January, hillsides covered with yellow daffodils in February/March, followed by swathes of bluebells in the woodland walk come late April/May time. A couple of years ago nature got confused as we had seen an exceptionally mild winter here in the west country. The daffodils came out before the snowdrops! According to Monty Don, the well-known TV gardener/presenter, snowdrops require a cold snap in order to burst into action. No matter what time of the year you visit Hestercombe you will always find something fascinating to delight the senses. And the plant shop always contains something to drool over. If you ever come to Somerset it really is a 'must see'.

I believe it was around this time that I received a second most generous gift of stamps, this time from our good friend Phil. He had been left a box full of albums of first day covers by his late father. Rather than sell them, egged on no doubt by his equally generous wife (my dear friend Janet) he brought them over to our house and handed them over to me! I was so gob smacked I nearly fainted. But once I got over the shock I was really touched by his marvellous gesture. I still see myself as custodian of his father's collection and am chuffed to be able to mull over the 'covers' especially those from the late 1990s through to the early Millennium years. In my view these British stamps have to be amongst the most varied and interesting issues to celebrate this once in a lifetime milestone.

It was in 2014 that I experienced a rather scary road accident. I was driving home alone one mid summer's evening from a super day out with my dear friend Juliet at Clevedon Golf Club. It was about 7 pm, traffic was light and the sun was still shining. As I attempted to turn left onto the slip road leading to the M5 southbound carriageway, a guy cut me up on the inside lane and drove straight into the side of my car. I had put my left-hand indicator on prior to the previous junction and done everything correctly. Funnily enough, as he was accelerating really fast to the side of me, I did glance to check that he too was proceeding onto the motorway. In that split second I realised I had little choice but to keep to the right-hand lane of the slip road. Then at the last moment I registered he wasn't even driving on to the motorway. So, I spun the wheel hard to the right but not in time to avoid his car hitting my car on the front left side wing. He pulled up sharply in front of me and jumped out of his car. I felt a moment of panic. He was a tall lean but muscular chap with a shaven head. As he ran menacingly towards me another car drew up. I breathed a sigh of relief and thought thank goodness, I have an independent witness. *Wrong!* This second chap was his mate. The police later told me this other chap was seen on camera having a race with the guy whose car had hit me. It turned out they were both Polish and they tried to say the whole incident was my fault. They refused to give me any details or documentation. Then when I threatened to call the police, they turned tail and fled the scene.

Luckily, I caught sight of the registration number of the car which had collided with my own and was able to give this to the police who a short while later came to my rescue. It was discovered that both cars had no insurance, tax or MOT, nor did the offending driver hold a British driving licence. Later that evening the police found one of the cars and impounded it but there was no trace of the other car or driver; both had gone to ground. The policeman who had taken my statement informed me several days afterwards that the tall Polish guy was wanted by the Polish Authorities and was awaiting extradition from this country in connection with an unrelated crime. What a lot of grief this all caused me. Because my insurance company deemed the motorway junction was a roundabout, they said any claim would be on a 'knock for knock' basis. I tried to explain it hadn't been my fault and that the person responsible shouldn't even have been driving the vehicle. But to no avail. We would have to pay £400 excess towards the cost of repairs and our insurance premiums subsequently went up. I got to learn about the Uninsured Driver's Fund and decided to write to the Ombudsman about my case. This all took a further six months. Then early in January 2015, I had a call from the insurance company to say that my claim should have been settled by the Uninsured Driver's Fund because it wasn't my fault that this guy had since been deported back to Poland. Our £400 excess was refunded in full and the increase in premiums was retracted. This was a big relief! What bothers me somewhat is that I am able to cobble together a letter stating my case but what about someone who is vulnerable or less educated, unable to do this? If I had not appealed the insurance company's decision, I would have lost out altogether. There is much injustice in this life.

It was also around this time that Arthur begun to experience some falls and accidents. Two of these occurred when he was out and about. Once he fell off the elevated 16th tee on the golf course and shortly after he fell backwards through the greenhouse door shattering the glass. God only knows how he didn't cut himself to ribbons in this incident but thankfully he was relatively all right. He was mainly badly shaken and bruised. Then during his sleep one night he leapt up and swung his fist into the bedside cabinet cutting and bruising his knuckles. There's a modicum of relief on my part that he didn't turn and swing his fist in my direction!

The worst incident was when he leapt, still asleep, out of bed and landed on the floor on all fours. Unfortunately, on the way down he hit his head on the handles of a new bedside cabinet and was bleeding rather profusely. The bang of him landing on the bedroom floor woke me up instantly. I got up really quickly not knowing what had happened. I put the light on and Arthur was still kneeling at the side of the bed somewhat dazed. Well, I saw the blood and nearly passed out. He asked me to get him a flannel from the bathroom but I felt so faint I had to get down on to the floor myself. You're possibly getting the drift that I am not the best person to have around in the event of an emergency! I managed to pull myself together and get him a clean flannel to dab his wound but he would not let me ring for any help.

A few weeks later I read an article in the paper that gave the various symptoms of Parkinson's disease and Arthur was experiencing three of them. He had the tremor in his right hand, so much so that he couldn't hold a full cup of tea without spilling it, he had severe constipation and he had begun to 'live out' his dreams and nightmares. He finally went to the doctors. I suggested he took the article with him to ask the doctor whether Parkinson's disease might be his problem.

Our dear doctor agreed it was Parkinson's, yet he was unable to give him any medication until the diagnosis had been confirmed by the relevant consultant. So, a referral was made but when Arthur rang up for an appointment, he was told there weren't any appointments for the foreseeable future; he would have to contact the hospital in three months' time. I was so worried about his falls we decided to pay to see a consultant privately just so he could be prescribed the correct medication. His appointment came through in December 2014 and the relevant tablets were issued. He now doesn't shake so much and we get some relief from his night time forays. Arthur does suffer from pain in his lower limbs and gets restless legs in bed but at present his condition is not deteriorating too quickly.

I did try getting him to do some yoga warm up moves, which the consultant felt would be a good idea but Arthur's commitment to undertaking this daily task did not last long. At home his love of his I Pad comes first nowadays and he watches every sport going. However, since being referred to some Parkinson's Balance & Strength classes at the gym he is now a Gym Bunny! He has a personal trainer and yes, it's a younger woman, and yes, she has blond hair. Despite being a bit strict Arthur is really grateful for her help and guidance.

Meanwhile, every other year I continue to go on my weekend yoga retreat to Exeter University whilst I am still able to. The grounds are beautiful and planted with lots of majestic trees. It is an oasis of calm in a busy city and so peaceful. I come back feeling a new woman. These past few years I have also been away for a couple of nights on several ladies' golfing trips. Once to Meon Valley Golf and Country Club in Hampshire, one visit each to St Mellion and The Vale Golf and Spa Resort in South Wales, and lastly to Bryn Meadows earlier this year. I jokingly call these trips my respite. Though being serious for a moment I do realise some respite may become a necessity at some point in the future.

I have to confess to being a great Graham Norton fan and aside from him keeping me company on the Radio during my trips up and down the motorways I always find time to watch his TV show on a Friday evening. What I adore most about him is his infectious giggle. When he begins to say something funny, he often laughs himself at what he is saying. And then I'm laughing at him laughing, regardless of whether I find the subject funny or not. Now I have a Red Chair story that I would love to be able to relate live on TV but the problem is I laugh so much in the telling of the story that no one can understand what I'm trying to say. Then of course there would be the nerves beforehand to handle and whether I would be capable of uttering a word live on TV, so I have decided to write it down and that way hopefully the message will come across.

If you have been paying attention you will recall that I was once ladies' captain of our esteemed golf club, Taunton & Pickeridge. One morning when visiting our local upmarket store, I was in the food isles surreptitiously chewing some gum, which I often do as I obsess a bit about having fresh breath. I turned around and bumped into a rather 'well to do' lady who is a member of our golf club. She greeted me enthusiastically and I tried to acknowledge her without her realising I was chewing some gum. At the time I was getting over a really bad cough and cold when all of sudden I began to cough badly. Naturally, I turned away from her and thank goodness I did because out of my mouth flew the chewing gum straight into a box of loose red onions. I was mortified and torn between retrieving the offending lump and trying to pretend it hadn't happened. Then with little notice down the gum sank to the depths of the box waiting for some unsuspecting shopper to find it. I'm relieved to say the lady from the golf club left in a hurry due to the coughing fit and didn't witness a thing (as far as I know!).

And then in June 2015, I succumbed to a mystery illness. Before going out to Margaret and Rogers' cream tea party Arthur and I were trying to get the front lawn cut between us. Usually this entails Arthur using the lawn mower and me hanging on to the electrical wiring so he doesn't run over it. Well, we were in a bit of a rush. Whilst he was emptying the mower I, armed with my secateurs, reached over to deadhead a rose; and pierced my left breast on the thorns of a Pyracantha bush that was planted in front of it. Gosh, it made me jump backwards. I shrieked out as I was only wearing a thin tee shirt. I never thought any more of it but rushed inside to have a bath. When I took off my clothes a squashed ear-wig fell out of my bra on to the floor. I decided the ear-wig must have fallen off the tree we were jointly mowing beneath but didn't have time to inspect it further.

During that night I woke up in a hot sweat with severe chest pains, so bad that I couldn't get my breath. Arthur woke up to ask what was the matter and I tried to tell him the pain was bad. I got out of bed and my forehead was all clammy, then I got back in again and all Arthur kept saying was, how is the pain now? Blimey, if it had been a heart attack, I'd have been dead by the time he felt the need for any action. After a few minutes it subsided, we settled down again and I eventually went back to sleep. The next morning, I felt rough. Then I noticed that underneath my left breast I had the most peculiar rash. That afternoon I was so tired and my ribs began to ache so I went back to bed. The next day the rash had spread so I rang the doctors. When I mentioned the chest pain, I got an appointment that same day and an examination and echo-cardiogram followed.

Then I was referred to Musgrove Park hospital for various tests. My doctor was not at all sure about the rash and initially thought it may have been the start of shingles. But the rash itself wasn't painful, it was nerve ending type pains shooting all over my body that weren't pleasant. Meanwhile, I was sent to the Cardiology department for various tests and the Breast Care Centre to ensure I didn't have any form of cancer returning. I was convinced that I may have some sort of infection from the Pyracantha bush itself as they can transmit fungal type infections from the soil in their thorns. I actually felt it may have been Rose Gardener's disease but my doctor wasn't convinced. She said she would refer me to the Dermatology department but that meant a long wait. As I felt really poorly with very little energy, we decided yet again to pay for a private consultation.

Following an examination, the Dermatology Consultant initially told me straight off I had morphea. I asked him what that was and he described such and such. Then when I dressed and he asked me further questions about my medical history, he changed his mind and said, 'Well, this must be part of your existing problem, sclerosis of the skin.' Now, this is an auto-immune condition that I had developed recently in my nether regions. I was seeing a different consultant about this disease. The thing is, that up until that point he had been adamant about the morphea diagnosis. I didn't feel particularly convinced that this latter diagnosis was correct. Eventually, I did have a further appointment with the dermatologist at the hospital and a biopsy was performed. After much too-ing and fro-ing during a period of about nine months, a diagnosis of Koebnerisation was reached. It was felt that the thorn going into my breast had caused my immune system to react similarly to how it did when I originally had Lyme Disease. In fact, this had shown up in more recent blood tests not long after the rash first appeared but my doctor just felt that it was maybe antibodies leftover from the original infection. There is no cure for either disease. By now I was visiting my therapist for Cranio-sacral treatment and this has helped get me back to reasonably good health. I missed playing golf for the remainder of that summer and our garden was neglected big time.

Machin definitive issued to celebrate our Queen becoming the longest serving British Monarch

We were again relieved to see in another New Year. Our extraordinary Queen was also celebrating her 90th birthday in this particular year. I say birthday, she actually has two birthdays. Now for someone like me who loves celebrating their birthday I feel this is a tad greedy, although I guess it's no good being royalty if you don't command the odd privilege. Despite this I feel that the Queen must be one of the most dignified ladies ever. In the past, even in the face of adversity, Queen Elizabeth has managed to appear serene and unruffled by various tumultuous events; a number of which were closer to home than she could possibly have wished for. You've probably guessed I'm a bit of a royalist but with my pedigree what can you expect! Suffice it to say, I admire her very much.

In May 2016, our dear friends, James and Margaret, organised for us all to go to Nice for four nights. It really was a special break. We had a wonderful time thanks to them and their kind generosity in showing us all the best bits they had discovered from a previous trip. One day we went to Monaco on the train; and another day we went to the medieval village of Eze set high up in the hills overlooking the sea.

At Eze there are fabulous gardens with all manner of cacti and succulents growing out of the rocks. This holiday was a true tonic for Arthur and 1. We were able to fully relax and unwind. It was a treat to be so well looked after. On two of the days we insisted that our friends have some time to themselves to do their own thing.

Arthur and I were content to wander around Nice admiring the Art Deco quarter and sculptures in the local park; and sit on the sea front sunning ourselves. The 7 kilometre walk along the front is known as La Promenade des Anglais because the English aristocracy used to spend their winters in Nice. The walkway was funded in part by the Holy Trinity Anglican church who arranged for the local poor to work on its construction. Two weeks after we arrived home, the local French people were celebrating Bastille Day in Nice when a terrorist drove a huge articulated lorry along this same promenade swerving into the crowds. Eighty-six people were killed and four hundred and fifty people were injured. It was difficult to reconcile our lovely holiday memories with such horror.

Margaret and James (Sean Connery lookalike) at Eze

Arthur and I had been away previously with James and Margaret in 2013 on another short trip to Bruges. At a vastly reduced rate we all enjoyed a three-day cruise on one of Cunard's latest ships, the Queen Elizabeth. This experience felt like the height of luxury to me; and I have graced a few upmarket places in my time. This superb ship was decked out (sorry, another pun) in true Art Deco style! I think the architecture of many Art Deco buildings is inspired by the clean lines of the upper decks of a ship. There was chrome work and coloured glass work in abundance, the attention to detail unrelenting. The food was sublime but the vast quantities of it seemed slightly obscene. I tried not to think of the starving masses as I heartily tucked in. I now know I couldn't be on board a ship any longer than three days unless I had access to a second suitcase with larger sized clothes in it. No wonder folks who go on cruises get so fat! One night at dinner, two elderly ladies joined our table. They were convinced that James was Sean Connery. Apparently, this mistaken identity occurs quite often with him. Nonetheless, James was quite flattered and posed for photos with them both. On their return home, the ladies concerned intended to show their husbands what they had both been missing!

Our visit to Bruges was one not to miss; and climbing the spiral steps in the famous historical clock tower, all 200 plus of them, went some way to burning off those extra calories.

Then in May of last year (2017) we received the most devastating news. The police visited us at home because for some reason our land line was down. In disbelief we listened to a community officer telling us that Arthur's youngest son had taken his own life. We were shocked to the core. Everything suddenly seemed surreal. This was a huge thing for Arthur to be taking on board especially at 81 years of age.

Sadly, he had already lost his eldest son Stephen a couple of years prior; and now to lose Jonathan too, who was only 46 years of age and a gentle giant of a man seemed mightily unfair. If Timmy takes after his father, Jonathan definitely takes after his mother. Unfortunately, Jonathan had suffered with depression for the past twenty years. If this tragedy had occurred at the outset, I feel sure it would not have been so unexpected; but who knows. I am grateful for the fact that Arthur visited Jonathan a few weeks beforehand and they had spent a happy day together. I had spoken to Jonathan on the phone for longer than usual, only a fortnight earlier as it happens. He sounded so calm and we had a laugh together about something. Arthur and I are both still concerned for his mother, as he had gone back home to live; and she alone had got him through the worst of his fears during those years. Naturally it hit his brother terribly hard too.

Arthur and Jonathan in happier times

The most comforting thing we all did was to visit Stoke beach, a place that the family had gone to when the boys were young. It was the most beautiful sunny autumnal afternoon there, with them all recounting happier times. I felt honoured to be included in this day.

Now life is slowing down for Arthur and he is no longer able to walk too far. But he can still play golf providing he has a buggy. I am hopeful he will get at least one more summer this year to enjoy his lifelong passion.

As far as my health goes, I managed to do a backward flip off the work surface at the end of July 2018. Had it been captured on You Tube I'm sure it would have had a million hits so sensational was the fall. Not renowned for my patience, I had tried to heave myself up onto the work surface via a chair (instead of getting the steps from the garage) in order to read our electric meter. It was at this point that I hit my head on the meter cupboard door. The surprise of this knock meant I began to fall back down. In order to save myself I managed to step on to the edge of the chair, which then shot off at speed whilst I fell backwards onto the quarry tiled floor below. Anyone will tell you that a quarry tiled floor is an unforgiving thing; crocks get smashed to smithereens on it. The weirdest thing was, the fall itself happened in slow motion. I actually had time to think, is this what it must be like to fall from a great height? I realised it was essential to keep my head up but my left arm bounced off the cupboard door handles. I used my right arm (of twice broken wrist fame) to try and save myself. I then lay there for several seconds before screaming out loud. Luckily, I found

217

I could move. A visit to A & E followed early on Sunday morning and x-rays were taken of my left shoulder and right wrist, that had swelled up out of all proportion. I was truly shaken up though and, yes, you've guessed it, more Cranio-sacral treatment was required.

Another period off golf ensued but this time it was only for about five weeks. Then in mid-September off we went to stay again with our dear friends, Simon and Margaret in Cornwall. I had been invited to play in Margaret's ladies' captain's day at Mullion golf club. Arthur went off with Simon for the day. We had a super couple of days with them and on the way home visited Trerice Manor, as Arthur had never seen my ancestral home. We also called in to the village of Alternon, which, as previously related, is where my 11th Great Grandfather Christopher Barriball was born in 1597. According to local parish records he was a yeoman and benefactor to the poor in this picturesque village. There is a pretty river running through the village with a medieval bridge leading across it to the largest church in Cornwall. The church is so large in fact that the wedding ceremony in the TV series of Doc Martin was recently filmed inside it. Christopher Barriball's Last Will and Testament dated 1640 shows that he left a considerable amount of money to Alternon church for the poor and sums of £40 together with sheep and lands to his wife, Alice. Both his sons benefited with the sum of £20 each and his grandsons (including my 9th Great Grandfather Neville) were left a further £20 each. These are fairly substantial sums of money for the times and I'm guessing this is why William Barriball was able to marry in to the local nobility. Arthur and I only stopped off for about an hour as time was getting on. I really need to return there to soak up the atmosphere and investigate my Barrable lineage more thoroughly next time.

Following this trip, and after my fall, it was decided we may need to consider having new smart meters installed. In order for the engineer to gain access to the gas meter under the stairs, I set about clearing out all of the old brief cases and small suitcases that had been put in there on a temporary basis, some *20 years* earlier. What a job! I can't recall the last time I had cleaned this cupboard out properly. I decided that maybe the time was right to get rid of these brief cases, one of which Arthur had bought me when I first passed all my exams. Upon opening this particular case, I was astonished to find the bag containing the Auction Lot of envelopes with British Guinea stamps on that I had purchased some *40 years* earlier. In addition, there was another huge bag of all the stamps that my dear dad had diligently cut off and saved for me from his time at Industra.

I was *so* excited to have another cache of stamps to go through, I could hardly wait. I forced myself to finish the job in hand. A couple of days later I went up to my hobby room to study my finds in more detail.

And that's when it happened. I was sorting through the envelopes with mainly British Guinea stamps on looking with interest at the various addresses, when the hairs suddenly rose on the back of my neck. I got goose bumps too! The majority of the letters were addressed to Mr Edward C Luard of La Bonne Intention on the East Coast, Demerara; but a couple of them bore South London addresses. One was in St Julian's Farm Road and the other was in Idmiston Road, both addresses being in Norwood, South London.

I couldn't believe it. I had actually been to both of these properties whilst working for the central government agency. I'm positive I inspected them for reasons I am not at liberty to say. I remember the addresses so vividly because the 'head case' was a holding outside of my area. I was asked to value and provide reports on these two properties because South London was my patch. I didn't receive any fees for doing this work and with targets ruling my life at that time every case counted. To say I was miffed would be an understatement.

What an amazing coincidence though. If you recall, forty years earlier when married to my first husband in the late 1970s, I had been to an auction held in Wiltshire and purchased this lot of stamps still stuck on to their original envelopes. Now I was examining this bundle again, only to find I had visited the homes that once belonged to, or were occupied by the Luard family in the course of my work some twenty-five years later.

And then to my immense delight I found a letter, dated 31st October, 1898, inside one of the envelopes. It was addressed to Edward C Luard in British Guinea from a lady called Marjory Wilson living in Argyll House, Crieff, Scotland. Marjory and her family had been former neighbours of Mr Luard. The letter describes how a Mr Morrison had helped her brother Tom gain employment on the Plantation Ogle, where Mr Luard was apparently in charge. She tells of how grateful the family are for his kind benevolence and forethought to Tom and other young men who set out from Scotland in the late 1890s on the S S Torgorm to work in Demerara. She mentions how the Wilson family business of Wood Merchants had been dissolved by their uncle since their father's death and there was little other employment for young Tom to find at home. I think this is a wonderful testament to Mr Luard's good character. I have since found out that Edward Chaucy Luard was also a philatelist. How uncanny is that! I'm given to understand that he discovered the first known pair of 2 cent British Guiana cotton reels and these stamps now reside in the Royal Collection. King George V was an avid stamp collector too and it is his collection that has been passed down through the generations. How marvellous is it that my appreciation and hobby of collecting stamps has provided me with the strangest of coincidences; and a link and a glimpse into the lives of other intrepid families in days gone by. It remains a mystery as to whom Katherine Luard is (she is also an addressee on one of the envelops in my bundle), but I'm guessing she could be either Edward's wife, his mother or sister. It would be nice to find out how she fits into the jigsaw. Nonetheless, what pleasure this Auction Lot of stamps and family's story have given me.

Chapter Seventeen
Reflections

2017

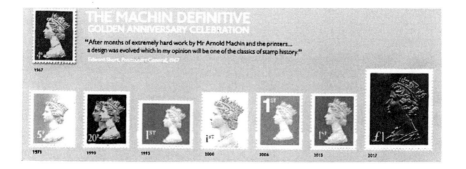

British Stamps – Machin Definitives from 1967 To 2017

I've always dreamed of owning a Penny Black so I was delighted when a local Auction house advertised it was offering at least 40 of these iconic stamps in their next collectors' sale. I figured if there were that many available, surely, I could come home with one of them. Off I went to the viewing morning and I was in seventh heaven. Not only were there masses of British stamps but also, many different European ones too, including three astonishingly good German albums. The latter featured the unbelievable story of the rise of The Third Reich with mint examples included, all incredibly well mounted and documented.

The Penny Blacks themselves had estimates from £40-£70 for each individual one rising to £120 for a pair. The single ones in better condition actually fetched £120 – £150 so the estimates were rather low. Possibly a 'sprat to catch a mackerel' as they say.

Anyhow, after drooling over various documents and considering the condition of several specimens and many albums, I made various notes on the catalogue and attended the auction later that week. I was up early with excitement and this state of mind nearly finished me off- literally. The Auction House was a converted modern church and it contained a metal spiral staircase up to the galleried seating area above. This mezzanine style upper floor was covered in grey plastic tiles. What I didn't realise was there were several steps going down to the front of the balcony area. I missed my footing and half fell down a step or two only just managing to save myself from going over the railings to the rostrum below! Gosh, it did give me a fright. At that point I felt I had to calm down and witness what the initial lots were going for before getting involved in any bidding. The purchaser had to pay a 22 and ½% commission so I needed to remember that before getting too carried away.

2015

175th *anniversary of The Penny Black & Tuppenny Blue postage stamps*

I missed out early on one of the Penny Blacks and then the last Penny Black, that I thought to be in the best condition, came up. The bidding had gone up to £130 and it was my turn to agree to this princely sum. Well, I panicked a bit trying to work out frantically what an extra 22 and ½ % would bring the price up to, and sweating profusely I shook my head from side to side to indicate the price was unacceptable to me. However, in not obtaining this iconic stamp I did manage a successful bid for the last stamp lot, an 1840s Tuppenny Blue instead. The auctioneer who had watched me sigh and peruse over nearly all of the stamp lots actually said, 'Thank Goodness for that!' as he brought the hammer down. I had successfully bid £65 for a stamp with three good borders and spent the princely sum of £80.22 pence including commission to bring it home. Despite my earlier disappointment I was delighted with my purchase.

Last year, following the loss of my dear dad back in 2013, I was going through some of the more recently printed stamps he had put by for me, when I came across a letter from Stanley Gibbons, congratulating him on his recent purchase of (you'll never guess) a Penny Black! Well, this was news to me; heavens knows what happened to it because he never let on, he had bought one. I wondered if he had intended to surprise me with it one day. As it's never been found I shall never know if that was the case. So there remains another mystery.

A couple of months ago I had yet another opportunity to purchase a Penny Black, this time at an auction being held in North Devon. After a couple of hours viewing on a prior afternoon I arrived in good time for the start of proceedings. The room was fairly packed and the only seats left vacant were in the central area. Hence, yours truly sits down, a couple of seats in from the middle isle, and tries to look as though she is an old hand at all of this. Shortly afterwards a well-built chap asked to get past me to take a seat at one end. Why he couldn't just have sat on one of the two empty seats to my left was beyond me. Especially as there was little room between the rows to let anyone pass. Once the auction got into full swing, he made his bid and then wanted to leave. He mutters something to me, pushes himself across the front of my seated frame and the next minute loses his balance and ends up falling on top of me. Aside from the fact he weighed rather heavy he had smacked me across the face in trying to save himself. I was caught between feeling horrified and embarrassed as we had the attention of the entire room by this time. He hauls himself up gruffly asking me if I'm al' right? To which I replied, 'yes' through gritted teeth as I just wanted him to disappear. Unfortunately, I had been sat on a chair with no support to my lower back and his weight landing in such an awkward fashion really did hurt me. I decided to go home early and left with not so much as a look in, in my quest to bid for a Penny Black. Thwarted again!

The following week I was relating all of this to my friend Jane from our yoga group. She said she too had been to see this very same auctioneer with a view to selling her stamp collection and was not at all impressed with his attitude. This led her to make the decision to leave her stamp collection to charity instead. Now Jane owned a precious Penny Black and I have her to thank for me finally getting my mitts on one. She kindly let me buy this iconic stamp for a very reasonable sum, together with other stamps I didn't have in my own collection. What a serendipitous quirk of fate that was. It was nearly worth the injury!

The other thing I've always wondered about is; do schoolchildren collect stamps nowadays? It can be a fairly solitary occupation but it doesn't have to be. I can't somehow see how having an all singing all dancing phone or I-pad can be of much help in this fascinating hobby. Just looking at a picture of a stamp on line is nothing like getting up close and personal with the real thing, or having a rummage through a cheap bag of mixed stamps. Who knows what you may come across? Other than special edition covers, often issued for no other purpose than to be put in an album in the hope they may one day increase in value, the actual everyday postage stamp appears to be in demise. More and more envelopes are being franked with an amount of postage stated on them. How boring is that? Not only are people not writing in pen and ink to one another as much, emails have taken over from letters. This, in my view, is a real shame. Quite frankly, I believe with all the weird 'text' words and abbreviations sent via phones in today's world, the use of our English language may now be at risk. I really hope that youngsters will be left stamp collections in their ancestors' wills so they too can gain an insight into this thought-provoking and interesting hobby.

All that aside, in looking back over my life time I have been so fortunate in much of what I have been able to experience and achieve. At times it has been a struggle. But if you don't experience real sadness how do you measure true happiness? When something bad happens then more often than not, some good appears to come out of it.

I do have some major regrets though, one being the hurt and anguish I caused Arthur's ex-wife and his two boys also. She said recently she has forgiven me for what I did. I'm not sure I've forgiven myself yet. Another regret is the hurt I caused Stirling, my first husband. I only hope he has found the happiness he deserves. I wish I didn't have to live with a Catholic conscience; those nuns and priests do have a lot to answer for.

Indeed, the Catholic faith as a whole has a lot to answer for. The abuse and shameful acts committed by members of the clergy towards innocent children and young people in particular is despicable. The cover up by those held in esteemed high office is equally dreadful. In Ireland, as recently as the 1970s, young unmarried mothers were taken in to the 'care' of the church. Their babies were forcibly removed from them and put up for adoption. These young girls were then kept locked up and made to work for the church as some form of penance. It is hard to believe that society as a whole went along with it.

I am truly saddened by the wars and atrocities undertaken in the name of any particular religion. If only people could find some tolerance towards one another. One of the most mind-numbing things I've ever seen on recent Newsreels was of the destruction of a World Heritage Site in Syria by ISIS. They deliberately blew up or smashed down early temples containing tombs and frescos some 2000 years old. As if trying to obliterate the past and re-write history.

Another poignant reminder of relentless persecution was highlighted in the Holocaust Exhibition I visited a number of years ago now. This was held at the Imperial War Museum in Lambeth. There, on display were endless glass cases just filled with shoes. Shoes that at one time carried the Jewish people from the Ghettos to The Concentration Camps to the Death Chambers during the Second World War. And of course I could go on. But the seemingly endless destruction of humanity during even my own lifetime is too massive to list here.

When I think of how my gramps Cook lost his teenage years to the horrors of the Great War, and his brother and all of those thousands of young men who gave their lives so completely that we might live in a better world, it really could make you feel desolate. But any hopes for world peace today seem completely forlorn. We must never forget the sacrifice those young men made, together with those lives lost in all other senseless wars since; and hope it will one day not have been in vain.

My dear friend Janet, who by the way, shares the surname of Cook by marriage (how spooky is that?) visited the War Graves around the battlefields of Ypres with her brother and uncle earlier this year. And guess what, she located my Great Uncle Fred's beautifully manicured grave! And took a photograph too. The poignant inscription on his headstone reads as follows: 'Until the day break and the shadows flee away'. When she revealed what she had done, it was such an emotional moment for me. I am now nearing the end of my book and the date is 11th November, 2018, which is the 100th anniversary of the armistice of the Great War and also the centenary of the Royal Air Force, formally known as the Royal Flying Corp. This weekend, and over the past four years, I have witnessed the most moving of commemorations and heard tales of remarkable heroism of those who died and incredible fortitude from those left behind.

I have seen unbelievable changes in technology; not all for the good mind. From computers of huge proportions that took up whole rooms to a microchip invented so small it's hard to envisage how it operates at all. I don't personally carry a mobile phone as I don't wish to become a slave to its relentless interruptions. I am grateful for my laptop though. I acknowledge the usefulness of emails even though I don't generally use them as a constant way of keeping in touch. But I admit I couldn't have written my book in long hand. I may be able to print and draw well but my long hand is rather a scrawl.

Since man landed on the Moon back in 1969, shuttle flights have intermittently gone on voyages of discovery in space. In 1981 seven million people around the world saw the doomed Space Shuttle Challenger explode and become a fireball in the sky killing all six Astronauts and a teacher on board. The disaster shook the American nation and all those who saw it live on television. All space flights were grounded for some time. Who could forget the extraordinary courage of all of these early explorers?

As a woman I have seen immense changes in attitudes towards our gender over the years. Having been the subject of inequality in the work place I feel there are still huge strides to be made. There can be little progress made with ongoing secrecy and unaccountability. I am proud to come from a long line of strong women on both sides of my family, none ever ready to shirk their responsibilities. I don't regret not 'taking on' the head of Property Services. Karma has a strange way of working out and he has since had his comeuppance.

With all of the difficulties I have experienced during my relatively short life (at the time of writing I'm now 62 going on 63), I will always be glad to have had the support and love of the most wonderful family and friends. Arthur's friends Mike S, Bill, James, Ed and Mike C and their dear wives deserve a special mention as they have been a tower of strength to us both. No favours have been too much trouble for them and they have always been there to lend a hand. There are too many other dear friends to cite individually. I would hate to do any one of them the injustice of missing them out.

Early last year my dear friend Judy died of bone cancer following a six-year battle against this awful disease for which there is no cure. She had originally overcome breast cancer some two years earlier than me. I really believe that stress has a part to play. Three friends who also succumbed to cancer, worked in stressful environments too and have had no children. I genuinely hope I haven't frightened anyone to death with my own personal experience of intravenous chemotherapy. There have been huge strides made in the development of treatments for all types of breast cancer. Usually, Triple Negative type breast cancer is more commonly associated with African-American and Hispanic women. Asian and white women are less likely to fall victim to it. This leads me to wonder whether I may have a few exotic genes within me. The great news is that I am a survivor of over ten years now. I won't pretend that subconsciously the thought of its return isn't there at all. But what is the use of having a life if you don't make the best of it?

Speaking of family: my four brothers all have families of their own now. Both children and grandchildren punctuate their busy lives. Anthony, or Tony, my eldest brother married to Trish has two gorgeous girls. One daughter is a talented pianist (just like her great grandmother whom we never knew) and the other daughter sadly has Williams Syndrome. This disease is caused by a deficiency in the blood and it means she will remain 'forever young' in her mind. She now lives nearby to her parents with huge support and care. I am extremely proud of Tony. From the introverted child with dyslexia, often getting into bother, he completed his education later on in life too. Before retirement he was a union representative attending Tribunal to defend a worker's rights. He actually went to a congress held in Belfast, Northern Ireland and gave a speech in front of thousands of delegates. That I am in awe of. Tony features regularly in the Derby Telegraph for his frequent Marathon wins and holds the distinction of beating Lord Sebastian Coe's time in the London Marathon one year. He and his wife Trish are both tennis mad and fitter in their mid-60s than I have ever been. Tony is currently trying to break into films as he claims to have an interesting face with long hair like his hero Borg, the famous tennis player. He is going to feature as an extra in the next TV series of Victoria. So, watch this space!

Paul, my brother one down from me, is the spitting image of our great uncle Baden when he was younger. He is married to Theresa and they have three beautiful girls too. Two of the daughters have children of their own now. One niece is a creative hairdresser and the other works in insurance. Their eldest daughter was formerly a model and 'The Face of 97'. In her heyday she was the 'mystery redhead' seen out on the town (years ago now) with Jamie Theakston. Paul takes after our dad and his two grandfathers with his quick engineering brain. What he can't fix, build or make good is nobody's business.

Peter, my brother two down from me is so laid back he's horizontal. He has such a loving nature and is married to Gail who is a keen photographer. They have two children, one boy and one girl both good-looking individuals. I'd like to say all of these nieces and nephews get there looks from me but unfortunately,

I'd be fibbing! My nephew is a talented artist who will soon be holding an Art Exhibition in South London in conjunction with other artists too. My niece is married and worked as a florist before becoming a stay at home Mum with two children of her own. Peter is currently struggling with some health issues and is constantly in my thoughts.

I've never really spent much time with Ian, my youngest brother. When he was a little boy I looked after him but he was only 9 years old when I left home at the age of 19. After various relationships he has finally settled down with a younger woman called Catherine who already has two children of her own. Ian has adopted these two lovely young people and now has a son of his own. He also has the most adorable young lady as his eldest daughter by his first wife.

Kim, my 'baby' sister lives with her chap Bryan who is somewhat older than herself. She is academically bright and works as an accountant in Cambridgeshire. Kim is full of fun and she is very sporty too. Oddly enough, like me, she never had any children either. I'm supposing her career got in the way. She and I are very close and keep in touch regularly.

At the last count, I have at least seven nieces and two nephews plus one adopted niece and one adopted nephew, together with nine great nieces and great nephews. Blimey, that makes me feel old! The Barrable line can only continue through my two nephews and they both have no children to date. I do hope that situation changes one day.

I feel that because I have had some interesting medical problems, maybe I should donate my body to science. I do have a vested interest in this, in that I am terrified I may not be dead when the coffin lid finally comes down. I would eventually like a coffin made with willow grown on the Somerset Levels. I thought if my body was stored and used for medical research initially then I would definitely be dead by the time I am to be buried or cremated. I hope folks will have a huge party to celebrate my life with plenty of Prosecco to go around. Should I go before Arthur I expect him to erect a 'Mrs What If' sign as my epitaph. Inheriting Dad's perfectionism and Mum's anxiety is not a useful combination.

I also hope I find the strength to care for Arthur in his later years. There have been times when I could have cheerfully got in the car and driven off leaving him forever. I'm sure Arthur has felt the same way too at times. Despite all we have gone through together, I don't regret for one minute sharing the majority of my life with him. We have known such sadness and such joy together. When I was ill with cancer a friend gave me a plaque that bears the words 'Life is not measured by the number of breaths we take, but by the moments that take our breath away'. How true that is.

NAMESTE

Epilogue

Since the completion of my Memoir Arthur has, unfortunately, suffered a series of mini strokes and undergone emergency surgery to clear his carotid artery. This has hit us both quite badly. Thankfully he is slowly recovering but he now recognises his limitations and sadly playing golf may now be out of his reach. For me, life as a full-time carer edges ever closer but I know things could have been so much worse. We realise how fortunate we are to have the care and expertise of the staff at Musgrove Park Hospital on our doorstep. They have saved both of our lives on more than one occasion. We cannot thank each and every individual enough. Timmy has been a huge support to his dad. Also, many of our friends have come to our rescue yet again. Each of Arthur's golfing buddies have cajoled, assisted and taken Arthur out into the real world again. Thank you all from the bottom of our hearts.

On a brighter note, for Christmas, Arthur and I treated ourselves to a DNA genealogy test. And the results are in! My genes show that 91% of me is originally from England, Wales and North-western Europe. The latter area takes in Northern France, Belgium and the Netherlands. 3% of me is from the whole of France and guess what, the tip of Spain and the tip of Italy is included too! I feel this small Hispanic link gives a possible explanation as to why I succumbed to the Triple Negative form of cancer. My French and Italian genes must explain why I have such an affinity for both countries, notwithstanding my known ancestral ties. In addition, I've learned that I have 3% DNA from Sweden and 2% from Norway plus 1% from Ireland and Scotland. So, there must be some Viking and Celtic blood in me too. What an interesting mixture! Arthur also has 91% of his DNA linked to England, Wales and a much larger area of North-western Europe taking in the Netherlands, Belgium and a greater area of France. He also has 11% of his genes from Ireland and Scotland. I felt he must have some Nordic ties too due to his Dupetryns disease (this causes his fingers to curl inwards on each of his hands). But although Sweden or any of the Nordic countries are not specifically mentioned in his results, he may still have some of their genes. Because the Vikings raided much larger areas of the world than many people realise. They invaded not only huge parts of Europe but explored many parts of Asia and Russia too, which I find incredible. Apparently, they encountered more than 50 cultures overall and colonised huge swathes of land. Many of you will have heard of the raid at Lindisfarne, in northern England but perhaps not so many folks will have heard of the earlier Viking attack at Portland in 789 A.D. I have only recently learnt of the reasons for their excursions. In Scandinavia in 536 A.D. there were at least two volcanic eruptions that lowered the Summer temperatures for several years and this extended cold and darkness brought death and ruin to its people. With as much as 75% of villages succumbing to both starvation and fighting, no wonder they set out to find pastures new.

And finally, I've recently joined the Back to 60 campaign and the WASPI campaign. As a woman born in the mid-1950s, three years prior to my 60th birthday, I was sent a letter telling me that my pension age had been raised to 65. The following year I received another letter stating my pension age had now been raised to 66. This news came as a blow to me financially because I had relied somewhat on receiving my state pension at the age of 60. Despite the fact I have worked and paid into the system for 39 years continuously I, and others are being subjected to a change in legislation that occurred in the 1990s. No government department has ever notified me before about these changes, which surely cannot be fair. I understand now that the government's actions are the subject of a judicial review as they are deemed to be outside of its jurisdiction. From memory this is called Ultra Vires but I may be showing off now! I sometimes feel like I've been battling against one form of injustice or another for most of my life. Oh, well, at least this time I am not alone. You may yet see me marching up and down outside parliament with a placard. Wish me luck!

Whilst my book has been in production the pandemic of a coronavirus disease known as COVID-19 has shaken the nations of the world. In particular, there have been over 60,000 deaths to date in Great Britain alone and thousands more will endure long term health problems, if they have been fortunate enough to survive the infection. In this country, we were in complete lock down since the end of March and this state of affairs lasted for 100 days. One could only go out for food shopping or prescription collection and anyone over the age of 70 was forbidden to go out at all. The scariest aspect of this disease is that you can have it and not present with any symptoms. Hence, you could well be passing it on without knowing it.

Arthur and I have had a dreadful time of it because he was rushed into hospital with chest pains in the early hours of one Friday morning at the end of May. Later that day I was told he had a possible blockage in his system which required further investigation but worse still, he had tested positive for COVID-19.

I honestly thought he was going to die. In fact, the next morning, having been told Bed 28 was empty, I thought he had died. I began sobbing relentlessly, until I had a job to breathe, at which point the nurse came back on the phone to tell me Arthur had been moved to the 'COVID' ward. It was at this point that I went in to isolation myself, waiting for the disease to strike me down. Our friends rallied around again. Nearly a fortnight later, the evening news came on the television, and a hospital spokesperson stated that 78 people who had been admitted to Musgrove Park hospital at the end of May had all been given false positive results and were now testing negative. In other words, they didn't have the coronavirus in the first place. But they were still put into a COVID ward. Arthur was one of these folks, yet, I had to contact the hospital to verify this information. Instead of feeling elated that he did not have the disease, I felt like all of the energy had been sucked out of my body. This may have been due to the stress of thinking Arthur may well not survive this ordeal. At 84 years of age, with underlying health conditions, he was in the extremely high-risk category.

He was a changed man when he did come home, very frail and thin, stooped, frightened and agitated, and in lots of pain with his arthritic knee. He cannot recall anything of his time in hospital during the first week and a half, which concerns me somewhat.

I am now a full-time carer and it was certainly a baptism of fire in the first few weeks. I am adjusting to this way of life now and Arthur is immensely grateful for everything that I do for him.

Which has to be a first!

Seriously though, time together is precious now as it may well be in limited supply. Life seems surreal somehow and I don't think we will take anything for granted ever again. One of the good things to come out of this period, is that the presence of nature has begun to shine again. The skies seem so blue and clear. During lock down there were no cars on the roads or motorways, and no planes flying overhead. The birds and animals were out in full force and the blossom seemed more prolific than ever before.

Folks also had time for one another again and neighbours did kind deeds. There were many unselfish acts undertaken. Not to mention, of-course, the huge bravery of our front line workers, including all of the NHS staff, the checkout operators in the supermarkets, the delivery drivers ensuring the shelves were stocked with food, the post men and women who continued to bring our mail, the refuse collectors who still took away our rubbish, and the public transport drivers who ensured that vital workers could still get to work, and countless others going about their business without much thought of what their daily sacrifice may entail.

Thank you, one and all.